Inside the World's Largest Legal Employer:

Careers and Compensation with U.S. Federal Agencies

John Okray

Lawyerup Press LLC
P.O. Box 156148
Fort Worth, TX 76155
Fax: (888) 672-2833
editor@lawyeruppress.com
www.lawyeruppress.com

Library of Congress Control Number: 2010917722

ISBN-13: 978-0-9829658-1-8

Cover Photo of the Apex Building (Federal Trade Commission headquarters in Washington D.C.) by Carol M. Highsmith. LC-HS543-197 (Library of Congress).

Dedication

To the attorneys working in U.S. Federal agencies

Inside the World's Largest Legal Employer:

Careers and Compensation with U.S. Federal Agencies

© 2010 Lawyerup Press

Table of Contents

About the Author

John Okray serves as Assistant General Counsel of a financial services firm. He received his BA in political science from the University of Massachusetts Boston, a JD from Suffolk University Law School, an MBA from the Suffolk University Sawyer School of Management, and an LLM in taxation from Boston University School of Law. He has served on various public service and non-profit boards and is active in organized bar activities.

Also by John Okray

U.S. Federal Courts: Attorney Admission Requirements

Disclaimer

The information provided in this book is meant to provide a general overview of legal careers with U.S. Federal agencies. This book is not an official government publication and it is possible that it contains typographical or substantive errors. The information in this book is not legal advice or government policy and readers should not rely on the information provided in this book for any reason. Lawyerup Press LLC is not engaged in rendering legal advice. This publication was not prepared by persons licensed to practice law in all jurisdictions mentioned. Individuals seeking employment with any particular agency should always check the requirements directly with that agency prior to applying.

Paintings and Photos

Photos or artwork in this book are not subject to copyright protection, however, credit has been provided.

Agency Descriptions

Many of the descriptions of Federal agencies have been adapted from U.S. Federal Government publications or websites, such as the U.S. Government Manual. Works of the United States Federal Government are in the public domain under Title 17, Chapter 1, Section 105 of the US Code.

Employment and Compensation Data

Specific employment data cited in this book is derived from public data maintained by the U.S. Office of Personnel Management (OPM) in the Central Personnel Data File (CPDF). As noted by the OPM, accuracy of CPDF data is affected by omissions, duplications, invalid data and miscoded data. Additionally, given the voluminous amount of data, it is possible that there could be errors in the analysis or reporting of information in this book. The CPDF does not include certain agencies within the executive branch and data from the judicial branch has not been included. The Department of Defense figures include only civilian attorneys. Unless a 2010 date is specifically indicated, data from September 2009 is used. State judge salary data is from the National Center for State Courts.

Improving Future Editions:

The author intends to write periodic editions of this book. Therefore, any feedback would be greatly appreciated. Comments and suggestions may be submitted to the publisher:

Lawyerup Press LLC
P.O. Box 156148
Fort Worth, TX 76155
Fax: (888) 672-2833
editor@lawyeruppress.com
www.lawyeruppress.com

Preface

Within the U.S. Government, Federal agencies employ tens of thousands of legal professionals, including general attorneys, patent attorneys, administrative law judges and law clerks. This book covers over 35,000 jobs across approximately one hundred entities including all Cabinet level agencies and large, medium and small independent agencies.

The primary purpose for writing this book is to provide a straightforward guide for attorneys, judges and law students who may be interested in employment in U.S. Federal agencies. The book will answer questions, such as:

- How many attorneys, judges and law clerks are employed within each agency?
- What do these agencies do and what roles and responsibilities do attorneys have?
- What are the specific attorney compensation levels within each agency?
- Where can I find information on agency-specific law clerk, new attorney and experienced attorney hiring programs?
- In what States, territories or foreign countries are agency attorneys located?
- Where can I find attorney employment statistics for each agency – male/female, minority employment, etc.?

Across the spectrum of agencies and departments there is an incredible amount of diversity of legal careers. Attorneys of almost all disciples work on legal topics including but not limited to civil rights, labor and employment, ethics, elections, criminal law, environmental conservation and protection, natural resources, foreign affairs, international trade, national security, military, agriculture, education, contracts, taxation, transportation, banking, finance, securities, communications, intellectual property, science and technology, health, housing and consumer safety.

While some agencies have only a few attorneys, several employ thousands. The compensation of attorneys can also vary widely and the highest salaries are not necessarily at the largest agencies. For example, some might be surprised to know the salary of the General Counsel of the National Credit Union Administration is considerably higher than the Chief Justice of the Supreme Court of the United States. Some law clerk salaries can be quite impressive as well, even exceeding $100,000 at the Securities and Exchange Commission.

Inside the World's Largest Legal Employer: Careers and Compensation with U.S. Federal Agencies and future editions will provide not only a snapshot in time, but also a historical record of the makeup and compensation of attorneys in U.S. Federal agencies.

John Okray

Position Descriptions

The following are the general descriptions for the legal positions in each Federal agency.

Administrative Law Judge ("ALJ"): ALJs serve as independent impartial triers of fact in formal proceedings requiring a decision on the record after the opportunity for a hearing. In general, ALJs prepare for and preside at formal proceedings. ALJs rule on preliminary motions, conduct pre-hearing conferences, issue subpoenas, conduct hearings (which may include written and/or oral testimony and cross-examination), review briefs, and prepare and issue decisions, along with written findings of fact and conclusions of law. Cases may involve Federal laws and regulations in such areas as admiralty, advertising, antitrust, banking, communications, energy, environmental protection, food and drugs, health and safety, housing, immigration, interstate commerce, international trade, labor management relations, securities and commodities markets, social security disability and other benefits claims, and transportation. An applicant must meet both the licensure and experience requirements and pass the Office of Personnel Management administrative law judge competitive examination to qualify for an ALJ position.

Applicants must be licensed and authorized to practice law under the laws of a State, the District of Columbia, the Commonwealth of Puerto Rico, or any territorial court established under the United States Constitution throughout the selection process, including any period on the standing register of eligibles.

Applicants must have a full seven years of experience as a licensed attorney preparing for, participating in, and/or reviewing formal hearings or trials involving litigation and/or administrative law at the Federal, State or local level. Qualifying litigation experience involves cases in which a complaint was filed with a court, or a charging document (e.g., indictment or information) was issued by a court, a grand jury, or appropriate military authority. Qualifying administrative law experience involves cases in which a formal procedure was initiated by a governmental administrative body. Experience involving cases with no formal hearing procedure and uncontested cases involving misdemeanors, probate, domestic relations, or tort matters is not qualifying.

General Attorney: Professional legal positions involved in preparing cases for trial and/or the trial of cases before a court or an administrative body or persons having quasi-judicial power; rendering legal advice and services with respect to questions, regulations, practices, or other matters falling within the purview of a Federal Government agency (this may include conducting investigations to obtain evidentiary data); preparing interpretative and administrative orders, rules, or regulations to give effect to the provisions of governing statutes or other requirements of law; drafting, negotiating, or examining contracts or other legal documents required by the agency's activities; drafting, preparing formal comments, or otherwise making substantive recommendations with respect to proposed legislation; editing and preparing for publication statutes enacted by Congress, opinions or discussions of a court, commission, or board; drafting and reviewing decisions for consideration and adoption by agency officials. Included also are positions, not covered by the Administrative Procedure Act, involved in hearing cases arising under contracts or under the regulations of a Federal Government agency when such regulations have the effect of law, and rendering decisions or making recommendations for disposition of such cases. Work as a general attorney requires admission to the bar.

Patent Attorney: These are positions involved with performing professional legal, scientific, and technical work concerning patents including rendering opinions on validity and infringement of patents, negotiation of patent licenses, settlement of patent claims, negotiation of patent clauses in contracts, providing professional legal advice to contracting officers and other procurement personnel on patent matters, and the preparation and/or presentation of briefs and arguments before the Patent Office or before the Federal Courts. Patent attorneys may be involved with performing similar professional legal functions regarding trademark. Patent attorneys require training equivalent to that represented by graduation (with a degree in one of the scientific or engineering disciplines) from an accredited college or university, in addition to a degree from a recognized law school and admission to the bar.

Law Clerk: Law clerks are generally trainees performing professional legal work requiring graduation from a recognized law school or equivalent experience, pending admission to the bar.

Hearing and Appeals: Positions that involve the adjudication of cases that typically include the conduct of formal or informal hearings that accord appropriate due process, arising under statute or under the regulations of a Federal agency when the hearings are not subject to the Administrative Procedure Act; or involve the conduct of appellate reviews of prior decisions. The work requires the ability to review and evaluate investigative reports and case records, conduct hearings in an orderly and impartial manner, determine credibility of witnesses, sift and evaluate evidence, analyze complex issues, apply agency rules and regulations and court decisions, prepare clear and concise statements of fact, and exercise sound judgment in arriving at decisions. Some positions require application of a substantive knowledge of agency policies, programs, and requirements in fields such as personnel management or environmental protection. While licensed attorneys would be well suited for these positions, there is <u>no license or bar admission requirement</u> to hold a position in the "Hearings and Appeals" category. Hearing and Appeals positions are not included in the agency employment figures shown in this book except where tables state they are included.

Definitions

The following are general definitions for terms used.

► The ► symbol designates a website for an agency's hiring program for attorneys and/or law clerks.

Ethnicity and Race:
- Hispanic or Latino: A person of Cuban, Mexican, Puerto Rican, South or Central American, or other Spanish culture or origin, regardless of race.
- American Indian or Alaska Native: A person having origins in any of the original peoples of North and South America, including Central America, and who maintains tribal affiliation or community attachment.
- Asian: A person having origins in any of the original peoples of the Far East, Southeast Asia, or the Indian subcontinent including, for example, Cambodia, China, India, Japan, Korea, Malaysia, Pakistan, the Philippine Islands, Thailand, and Vietnam.
- Black or African American: A person having origins in any of the black racial groups of Africa.
- Native Hawaiian or Other Pacific Islander: A person having origins in any of the original peoples of Hawaii, Guam, Samoa, or other Pacific Islands.
- White: A person having origins in any of the original peoples of Europe, the Middle East, or North Africa.

Length of Service: The number of years of Federal civilian employment, creditable military service, and other service made creditable by specific legislation.

Location: The official duty station of the attorney.

Salary: An attorney's annualized rate of pay. An attorney's actual earnings may be more or less than the annualized rate because of factors such as overtime, shift differentials, less than full time work, or leave without pay.

Comparison: U.S. Federal Court Judges

To provide a comparison between the Federal agencies listed in this book and the Federal judicial branch, below are the 2010 salaries of justices and judges in the Federal judiciary. While the salaries of judges in the Federal judiciary are on average higher, there are certain attorney positions within Federal agencies that have higher salaries than even the Chief Justice of the Supreme Court of the United States.

Federal Court Judges	2010 Salary
Chief Justice of the Supreme Court	$223,500
Associate Justice of the Supreme Court	$213,900
Circuit Judge (Court of Appeals, Courts of Military Appeals)	$184,500
District Judge (District Courts, Court of Federal Claims, Court of International Trade, U.S. Tax Court)	$174,000
Bankruptcy Judge	$160,080
Magistrate Judge	$160,080

Historical Federal Justice/Judge Salaries

Position	2010	2009	2008	2007	2006	2005	2004	2003	2002	2001
Chief Justice	223.5	217.4	217.4	212.1	212.1	208.1	203	198.6	192.6	186.3
Assoc. Justices	213.9	208.1	208.1	203	203	199.2	194.3	190.1	184.4	178.3
US Ct. Appeals	184.5	179.5	179.5	175.1	175.1	171.8	167.6	164	159.1	153.9
US Dist. Court	174	169.3	169.3	165.2	165.2	162.1	158.1	154.7	150	145.1

(Salary in $ thousands)

Comparison: State Judges

To show a comparison between the Federal agencies listed in this book and State judicial officials, below are salaries of certain State justices, judges and officials. Unlike Federal judges, salaries among State judges vary widely.

Title	Mean	Median	Range
Chief, Highest State Court	$155,230	$151,328	$115,390 - $228,856
Associate Justice, Highest State Court	$151,142	$145,984	$112,530 - $218,237
Judge, Intermediate Appellate Courts	$146,401	$138,750	$105,050 - $204,599
Judge, General Jurisdiction Trial Court	$136,052	$132,150	$104,170 - $178,789
State Court Administrators	$134,089	$127,026	$76,500 - $211,272

Source (both tables): National Center for State Courts

Chief Justices of State Courts of Last Resort

U.S. State	Salary	U.S. State	Salary	Territory[1]	Salary
Alabama	$181,127	Montana	$107,404	Dist. of Colum.	$185,000
Alaska	$180,048	Nebraska	$135,881	Amer. Samoa	$125,000
Arizona	$160,000	Nevada	$170,000	Guam	$166,000
Arkansas	$151,049	New Hampshire	$151,477	N. Mariana Isl	$130,000
California	$228,856	New Jersey	$192,795	Puerto Rico	$125,000
Colorado	$142,708	New Mexico	$125,691	Virgin Islands	$186,000
Connecticut	$175,645	New York	$156,000		
Delaware	$194,750	North Carolina	$140,932		
Florida	$161,200	North Dakota	$121,513		
Georgia	$167,210	Ohio	$150,850		
Hawaii	$164,976	Oklahoma	$147,000		
Idaho	$121,006	Oregon	$125,556		
Illinois	$196,322	Pennsylvania	$191,876		
Indiana	$151,328	Rhode Island	$167,644		
Iowa	$170,850	South Carolina	$144,029		
Kansas	$139,310	South Dakota	$120,173		
Kentucky	$139,164	Tennessee	$164,292		
Louisiana	$143,815	Texas	$152,500		
Maine	$138,294	Utah	$147,350		
Maryland	$181,352	Vermont	$135,421		
Massachusetts	$151,239	Virginia	$178,043		
Michigan	$164,610	Washington	$164,221		
Minnesota	$160,579	West Virginia	$121,000		
Mississippi	$115,390	Wisconsin	$149,556		
Missouri	$139,534	Wyoming	$126,500		

[1] Salary data for certain territories is outdated: American Samoa (5/26/2006), Northern Mariana Islands (2/26/1993), and Puerto Rico (8/22/2003).

All U.S. Agency Data
(General Attorneys, Patent Attorneys, Administrative Law Judges, Law Clerks)

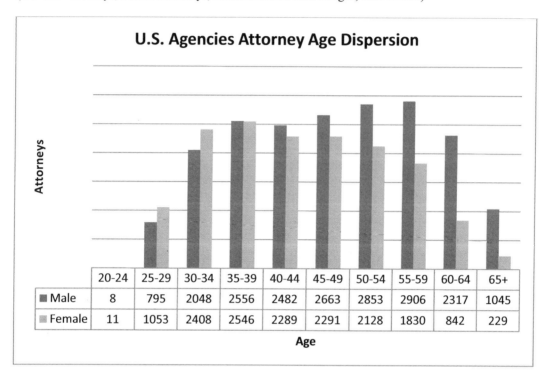

U.S. Agencies Attorney Age Dispersion

	20-24	25-29	30-34	35-39	40-44	45-49	50-54	55-59	60-64	65+
Male	8	795	2048	2556	2482	2663	2853	2906	2317	1045
Female	11	1053	2408	2546	2289	2291	2128	1830	842	229

Age

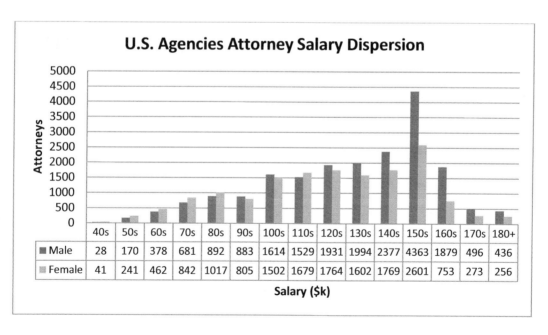

U.S. Agencies Attorney Salary Dispersion

	40s	50s	60s	70s	80s	90s	100s	110s	120s	130s	140s	150s	160s	170s	180+
Male	28	170	378	681	892	883	1614	1529	1931	1994	2377	4363	1879	496	436
Female	41	241	462	842	1017	805	1502	1679	1764	1602	1769	2601	753	273	256

Salary ($k)

U.S. Agency Attorney Salaries by Age Group (#)									
$180+	0	0	2	52	99	142	158	142	75	22
170s	0	0	9	77	84	106	163	169	115	46
160s	0	0	27	130	163	239	365	574	645	**489**
150s	0	2	123	508	**852**	**1242**	**1461**	**1508**	**977**	291
140s	0	2	119	505	711	885	791	663	354	116
130s	1	6	246	634	587	597	589	523	321	92
120s	0	23	518	651	640	612	498	427	243	83
110s	0	32	457	**845**	633	448	358	238	151	46
100s	0	195	**902**	697	409	279	254	207	136	37
90s	1	106	494	327	209	162	151	137	69	32
80s	0	381	710	323	160	109	103	70	39	14
70s	3	**515**	503	211	108	74	51	39	16	3
60s	2	343	240	90	79	33	21	22	9	1
50s	**7**	201	95	41	30	15	8	9	5	0
40s	4	40	9	3	3	7	1	1	0	1
Age->	**20-24**	**25-29**	**30-34**	**35-39**	**40-44**	**45-49**	**50-54**	**55-59**	**60-64**	**65+**

U.S. Agency Attorney Salaries by Age Group (%)									
$180+	0.00%	0.00%	0.01%	0.15%	0.28%	0.40%	0.45%	0.40%	0.21%	0.06%
170s	0.00%	0.00%	0.03%	0.22%	0.24%	0.30%	0.46%	0.48%	0.33%	0.13%
160s	0.00%	0.00%	0.08%	0.37%	0.46%	0.68%	1.04%	1.63%	1.83%	**1.39%**
150s	0.00%	0.01%	0.35%	1.44%	**2.42%**	**3.52%**	**4.14%**	**4.28%**	**2.77%**	0.83%
140s	0.00%	0.01%	0.34%	1.43%	2.02%	2.51%	2.24%	1.88%	1.00%	0.33%
130s	0.00%	0.02%	0.70%	1.80%	1.66%	1.69%	1.67%	1.48%	0.91%	0.26%
120s	0.00%	0.07%	1.47%	1.85%	1.82%	1.74%	1.41%	1.21%	0.69%	0.24%
110s	0.00%	0.09%	1.30%	**2.40%**	1.80%	1.27%	1.02%	0.68%	0.43%	0.13%
100s	0.00%	0.55%	**2.56%**	1.98%	1.16%	0.79%	0.72%	0.59%	0.39%	0.10%
90s	0.00%	0.30%	1.40%	0.93%	0.59%	0.46%	0.43%	0.39%	0.20%	0.09%
80s	0.00%	1.08%	2.01%	0.92%	0.45%	0.31%	0.29%	0.20%	0.11%	0.04%
70s	0.01%	**1.46%**	1.43%	0.60%	0.31%	0.21%	0.14%	0.11%	0.05%	0.01%
60s	0.01%	0.97%	0.68%	0.26%	0.22%	0.09%	0.06%	0.06%	0.03%	0.00%
50s	**0.02%**	0.57%	0.27%	0.12%	0.09%	0.04%	0.02%	0.03%	0.01%	0.00%
40s	0.01%	0.11%	0.03%	0.01%	0.01%	0.02%	0.00%	0.00%	0.00%	0.00%
Age->	**20-24**	**25-29**	**30-34**	**35-39**	**40-44**	**45-49**	**50-54**	**55-59**	**60-64**	**65+**

U.S. Agency Attorneys - United States Location Dispersion

U.S. Location	Attorneys	Percent	U.S. Location	Attorneys	Percent
Alabama	365	0.99%	Nebraska	90	0.24%
Alaska	87	0.24%	Nevada	106	0.29%
American Samoa	1	0.00%	New Hampshire	55	0.15%
Arizona	371	1.00%	New Jersey	426	1.15%
Arkansas	121	0.33%	New Mexico	203	0.55%
California	2,714	7.35%	New York	1,822	4.93%
Colorado	580	1.57%	North Carolina	323	0.87%
Connecticut	167	0.45%	North Dakota	33	0.09%
Delaware	39	0.11%	Northern Mariana Is.	4	0.01%
Dist. of Columbia	**13,088**	**35.45%**	Ohio	670	1.81%
Florida	1,190	3.22%	Oklahoma	236	0.64%
Georgia	935	2.53%	Oregon	245	0.66%
Guam	15	0.04%	Pennsylvania	1004	2.72%
Hawaii	118	0.32%	Puerto Rico	134	0.36%
Idaho	54	0.15%	Rhode Island	57	0.15%
Illinois	1,215	3.29%	South Carolina	181	0.49%
Indiana	240	0.65%	South Dakota	44	0.12%
Iowa	88	0.24%	Tennessee	380	1.03%
Kansas	163	0.44%	Texas	1,880	5.09%
Kentucky	230	0.62%	Utah	181	0.49%
Louisiana	330	0.89%	Vermont	38	0.10%
Maine	52	0.14%	Virgin Islands (US)	17	0.05%
Maryland	1,047	2.84%	Virginia	2,705	7.33%
Massachusetts	604	1.64%	Washington	526	1.42%
Michigan	425	1.15%	West Virginia	146	0.40%
Minnesota	185	0.50%	Wisconsin	159	0.43%
Mississippi	179	0.48%	Wyoming	27	0.07%
Missouri	478	1.29%	Suppressed/NA	88	0.24%
Montana	63	0.17%			

* (Percent of attorneys in the U.S.)

U.S. Agency Attorneys - Outside the United States Location Dispersion

Location	Attorneys	Percent	Location	Attorneys	Percent
Afghanistan	9	3.80%	Korea, Republic of	11	4.64%
Albania	2	0.84%	Kuwait	4	1.69%
Azerbaijan	1	0.42%	Kyrgyzstan	1	0.42%
Angola	1	0.42%	Liberia	1	0.42%
Armenia	1	0.42%	Mexico	3	1.27%
Argentina	1	0.42%	Marshall Islands	1	0.42%
Bahrain	1	0.42%	Moldova	1	0.42%
Bangladesh	1	0.42%	Montenegro	1	0.42%
Belgium	5	2.11%	Mozambique	1	0.42%
Benin	1	0.42%	Netherlands	1	0.42%
Bolivia	1	0.42%	Nigeria	1	0.42%
Bosnia	1	0.42%	Pakistan	2	0.84%
Brazil	1	0.42%	Peru	1	0.42%
Bulgaria	2	0.84%	Philippines	1	0.42%
Canada	2	0.84%	Qatar	1	0.42%
China	1	0.42%	Romania	1	0.42%
Colombia	5	2.11%	Russia	3	1.27%
Dominican Rep	1	0.42%	Saudi Arabia	1	0.42%
Egypt	4	1.69%	Senegal	1	0.42%
El Salvador	3	1.27%	Serbia	1	0.42%
France	1	0.42%	Singapore	3	1.27%
Georgia	2	0.84%	South Africa	3	1.27%
Germany	**64**	**27.00%**	Spain	1	0.42%
Ghana	1	0.42%	Sudan	2	0.84%
Indonesia	3	1.27%	Switzerland	5	2.11%
Iraq	5	2.11%	Thailand	3	1.27%
Israel	2	0.84%	Uganda	1	0.42%
Italy	18	7.59%	Ukraine	4	1.69%
Japan	22	9.28%	United Arab Emir.	1	0.42%
Jordan	2	0.84%	United Kingdom	6	2.53%
Kazakhstan	1	0.42%	Zambia	1	0.42%
Kenya	4	1.69%			

* (Percent of attorneys outside the U.S.)

Administrative Law Judges

Note: The maximum 2009 rate of $162,900 shown in these tables was increased to $165,300 in 2010.

U.S. Agency	Positions	Males	Females	Avg. Salary
Commodity Futures Trading Comm.	2	2	-	$162,900
Dept. of Agriculture	4	3	1	$162,900
Dept. of Education	1	1	-	$162,900
Dept. of Energy	14	9	5	$162,900
Dept. of Health & Human Services	73	57	16	$151,582
Dept. of Homeland Security	6	6	-	$162,342
Dept. of Housing & Urban Dev.	2	2	-	$158,942
Dept. of Justice	4	1	3	$162,900
Dept. of Labor	44	35	9	$161,015
Dept. of the Interior	9	9	-	$161,970
Dept. of the Treasury	1	1	-	$162,900
Dept. of Transportation	3	3	-	$162,900
Dept. of Veterans Affairs[2]	59	34	25	$160,907
Environmental Protection Agency[1]	4	2	2	$162,900
Federal Communications Comm.	1	1	-	$162,900
Federal Labor Relations Auth.	3	2	1	$162,900
Federal Maritime Commission	1	1	-	$162,900
Federal Mine Safety & Health Rev.	11	9	2	$161,307
Federal Trade Commission	1	1	-	$162,900
National Labor Relations Board	39	34	5	$162,400
National Transportation Safety Bd.	4	4	-	$162,900
Occ. Safety & Health Rev. Comm.	12	10	2	$162,900
Securities & Exchange Commission	4	2	2	$162,900
Social Security Administration	1,298	995	303	$152,839
U.S. International Trade Comm.	6	6	-	$158,661
TOTAL	**1,606**	**1,231**	**376**	**$154,061**
Percent of Positions		**77%**	**23%**	

[1] Only 1 salary reported for the EPA.

[2] Includes personnel classified as General Attorney by the Board of Veterans Appeals with AL-2 and AL-3 salary codes.

Total AL-1 positions	6	Avg. Salary: $162,900
Total AL-2 positions	38	Avg. Salary: $162,900
Total AL-3 positions	1,562	Avg. Salary: $153,558

ALJs in U.S. Agencies	Positions	Males	Females	Average/Total
Cabinet Level Agencies	165	129	36	$161,256
Large Independent Agencies	1,388	1,046	353	$154,485
Medium Independent Agencies	16	14	2	$163,459
Small Independent Agencies	27	22	5	$163,627
Average Salary (all Locations)	1,607	$157,388	$149,410	$155,424
Average Salary (United States)	1,596	$157,620	$149,595	$155,641
Average Salary (U.S. Territories)	11	$126,409	$112,941	$123,960
Average Length of Service (years)	1,607	21.2	17.1	20.2

* Data as of June, 2010.

Average Salary History

ALJs	Sept 2005	Sept 2006	Sept 2007	Sept 2008	Sept 2009	June 2010
Positions	1,432	1,402	1,353	1,467	1,547	1,607
Avg Salary	$140,511	$144,834	$148,607	$149,659	$153,800	$155,424

ALJs: Total Non-Minority	88.23%
American Indian and Alaskan Native	1.00%
Asian	1.18%
Black/African American	5.67%
Native Hawaiian or Pacific Islander	0.00%
Not H/L & Of More Than One Race	0.25%
Hispanic/Latino (H/L)	2.99%
H/L & American Indian and Alaskan Native	0.00%
H/L & Asian	0.00%
H/L & Black/African American	0.00%
H/L & Native Hawaiian or Pacific Islander	0.00%
H/L & White	0.68%
H/L & Of More Than One Race	0.00%
Total Minority	**11.77%**
Total Unspecified	0.00%
TOTAL	**100.00%**

* Data as of June, 2010.

General Attorneys

U.S. Agency	Positions	Males	Females	Average/Total
Cabinet Level Agencies	24,038	13,558	10,480	$130,912
Large Independent Agencies	8,868	4,304	4,564	$130,340
Medium Independent Agencies	1,087	582	505	$139,151
Small Independent Agencies	103	47	56	$130,298
Average Salary (all Locations)	34,096	$134,411	$127,008	$131,024
Average Salary (United States)	33,704	$134,746	$127,181	$131,276
Average Salary (U.S. Territories)	152	$107,609	$104,424	$106,079
Average Salary (Foreign Countries)	238	$111,081	$111,986	$111,336
Average Length of Service (years)	34,096	14.4	12.1	13.4

* Data as of June, 2010.

Average Salary History

Attorneys	Sept 2005	Sept 2006	Sept 2007	Sept 2008	Sept 2009	June 2010
Positions	28,983	29,764	29,845	30,928	33,101	34,096
Avg Salary	$114,460	$116,591	$119,124	$124,139	$127,928	$131,024

General Attorneys: Total Non-Minority	81.43%
American Indian and Alaskan Native	0.45%
Asian	5.11%
Black/African American	8.49%
Native Hawaiian or Pacific Islander	0.05%
Not H/L & Of More Than One Race	0.43%
Hispanic/Latino (H/L)	3.30%
H/L & American Indian and Alaskan Native	0.02%
H/L & Asian	0.01%
H/L & Black/African American	0.04%
H/L & Native Hawaiian or Pacific Islander	0.00%
H/L & White	0.51%
H/L & Of More Than One Race	0.04%
Total Minority	**18.45%**
Total Unspecified	0.12%
TOTAL	**100.00%**

* Data as of June, 2010.

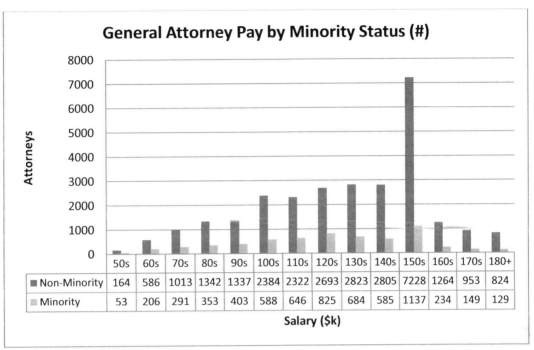

General Attorney Pay by Minority Status (#)

	50s	60s	70s	80s	90s	100s	110s	120s	130s	140s	150s	160s	170s	180+
Non-Minority	164	586	1013	1342	1337	2384	2322	2693	2823	2805	7228	1264	953	824
Minority	53	206	291	353	403	588	646	825	684	585	1137	234	149	129

Salary ($k)

* Data as of June, 2010.

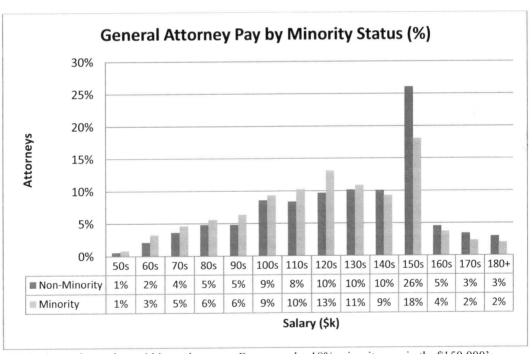

General Attorney Pay by Minority Status (%)

	50s	60s	70s	80s	90s	100s	110s	120s	130s	140s	150s	160s	170s	180+
Non-Minority	1%	2%	4%	5%	5%	9%	8%	10%	10%	10%	26%	5%	3%	3%
Minority	1%	3%	5%	6%	6%	9%	10%	13%	11%	9%	18%	4%	2%	2%

Salary ($k)

(Table above shows data within each group. For example, 18% minority pay in the $150,000's means 18% of all minorities are employed in this pay range while 26% of all non-minorities are employed in this pay range.). Data as of June, 2010.

Hearing and Appeals

U.S. Agency	Positions	Males	Females	Avg. Salary
Dept. of Agriculture – Civil Rights	6	2	4	$102,865
Dept. of Agriculture – Food & Nutrition	7	5	2	$111,088
Dept. of Agriculture – Natl. Appeals Div	60	35	25	$105,903
Dept. of Commerce – National Oceanic & Atmospheric Admin	2	1	1	$88,588
Dept. of Homeland Security – Bur of Citizenship and Immigration Svcs.	439	174	265	$92,801
Dept. of Labor – Ofc. of Sec of Labor	1	1	-	unspecified
Dept. of Interior – Mineral Mgmt Svc.	3	2	1	$114,690
Dept. of Treasury – Internal Revenue Sv	897	480	417	$108,919
Dept. of Veterans Affairs – Dep Asst Sec for Info & Technology	1	1	-	$98,518
Dept. of Veterans Affairs – Veterans Benefits Administration	433	197	236	$93,359
Pension Benefit Guaranty Corporation	3	2	1	$150,466
Railroad Retirement Board	8	4	4	$126,375
TOTAL	1,860	904	957	$101,504
Percent of Positions		49%	51%	

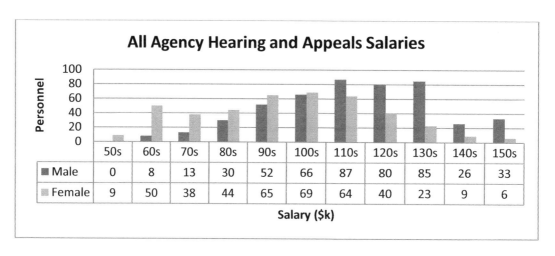

Average Salary History

Hearing/App	Sept 2005	Sept 2006	Sept 2007	Sept 2008	Sept 2009	June 2010
Positions	1,719	1,685	1,688	1,756	1,860	1,980
Avg Salary	$90,845	$93,364	$94,893	$97,994	$101,504	$102,627

Hearings & Appeals: Total Non-Minority	**73.12%**
American Indian and Alaskan Native	0.51%
Asian	6.52%
Black/African American	11.42%
Native Hawaiian or Pacific Islander	0.00%
Not H/L & Of More Than One Race	0.51%
Hispanic/Latino (H/L)	7.33%
H/L & American Indian and Alaskan Native	0.00%
H/L & Asian	0.00%
H/L & Black/African American	0.00%
H/L & Native Hawaiian or Pacific Islander	0.00%
H/L & White	0.25%
H/L & Of More Than One Race	0.00%
Total Minority	**26.53%**
Total Unspecified	0.35%
TOTAL	**100.00**

* Data as of June, 2010.

Cabinet Level Agencies

Department	Attorneys	Admin. Law Judges	Law Clerks	Average Salary	2009 Est. Annual Salary Exp.
Agriculture	246	4	-	$124,928	$31,231,911
Commerce	1,008	-	1	$126,040	$126,922,201
Defense	643	-	11	$130,665	$85,454,908
- Air Force	477	-	1	$120,633	$57,662,568
- Army	1,418	-	12	$112,740	$161,218,046
- Navy	745	-	8	$127,410	$95,939,650
Education	348	1	1	$117,286	$41,050,228
Energy	586	14	10	$128,200	$78,201,854
Health & Human Services	674	73	1	$120,207	$89,914,789
Homeland Security	1,881	6	2	$120,111	$226,890,599
Housing & Urban Development	399	2	21	$117,551	$49,606,561
Interior	403	9	3	$125,180	$51,949,676
Justice	10,398	4	76	$134,389	$1,408,127,053
Labor	590	44	12	$126,424	$81,669,591
State	203	-	5	$135,076	$27,960,709
Transportation	533	3	4	$128,709	$69,502,796
Treasury	2,327	1	39	$125,364	$296,737,466
Veterans Affairs	907	-	21	$109,657	$101,652,168
TOTAL	**23,786**	**161**	**228**	**$127,495**	$3,081,692,774

* Tables do not include 1,849 personnel classified as GS-930 "Hearing and Appeal" who had an average salary of $101,317 in 2009. Attorneys includes patent attorneys.

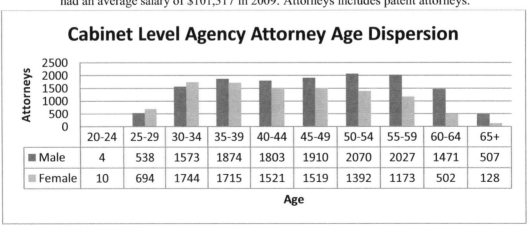

Cabinet Level Agency Attorney Age Dispersion

	20-24	25-29	30-34	35-39	40-44	45-49	50-54	55-59	60-64	65+
Male	4	538	1573	1874	1803	1910	2070	2027	1471	507
Female	10	694	1744	1715	1521	1519	1392	1173	502	128

Cabinet Level Agency – General Attorney Minority Status

Department	Non-Minority	Minority
Agriculture	81%	19%
Commerce	75%	25%
Defense	89%	11%
- Air Force	90%	10%
- Army	88%	12%
- Navy	87%	13%
Education	67%	33%
Energy	80%	20%
Health & Human Services	74%	26%
Homeland Security	79%	21%
Housing & Urban Development	65%	35%
Interior	84%	16%
Justice	84%	16%
Labor	83%	17%
State	89%	11%
Transportation	79%	21%
Treasury	86%	14%
Veterans Affairs	80%	20%
TOTAL	83%	17%

* Data for both tables as of June, 2010.

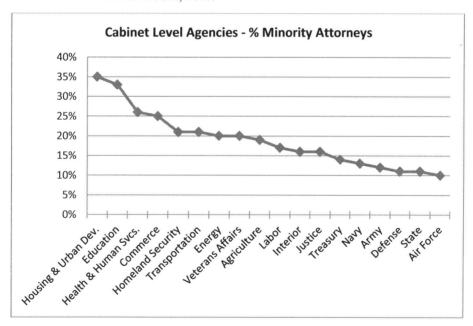

Department of Agriculture

Description:
The Department of Agriculture works to improve and maintain farm income and to develop and expand markets abroad for agricultural products. The Department helps to curb and cure poverty, hunger, and malnutrition. It works to enhance the environment and to maintain production capacity by helping landowners protect the soil, water, forests, and other natural resources. The Department, through inspection and grading services, safeguards and ensures standards of quality in the daily food supply.

The Department of Agriculture (USDA) was created by act of May 15, 1862 (7 U.S.C. 2201). In carrying out its work in the program mission areas, USDA relies on the support of departmental administration staff, as well as the Office of the Chief Financial Officer, Office of the Chief Information Officer, Office of Communications, Office of Congressional and Intergovernmental Relations, Office of the Inspector General, and the Office of the General Counsel. USDA's rural development mission is to assist rural Americans to increase their economic opportunities and improve their quality of life. To accomplish this, USDA works to foster new cooperative relationships among Government, industry, and communities. As a capital investment bank, USDA provides financing for rural housing and community facilities, business and cooperative development, telephone and high-speed Internet access, electric, water, and sewer infrastructure. Approximately 800 rural development field offices, staffed by 7,000 employees, provide frontline delivery of rural development loan and grant programs at the local level.

Address: U.S. Department of Agriculture
1400 Independence Ave., S.W.
Washington, DC 20250

Website: www.usda.gov   **Phone**:   202-720-2791

Department of Agriculture	Avg. Salary	Attorneys	Hearings/Appeals
Civil Rights	-	-	6
Departmental Administration	$150,408	7 (4 ALJs)	-
Food and Nutrition Service	$111,088	-	7
National Appeals Division	$162,900	1	60
Office of the Inspector General	$122,401	9	
Office of the General Counsel	$124,097	233 (2 patent)	-
TOTAL	**$124,928**	**250**	**73**

* Personnel categorized as Hearings and Appeal had an average salary of $106,150.

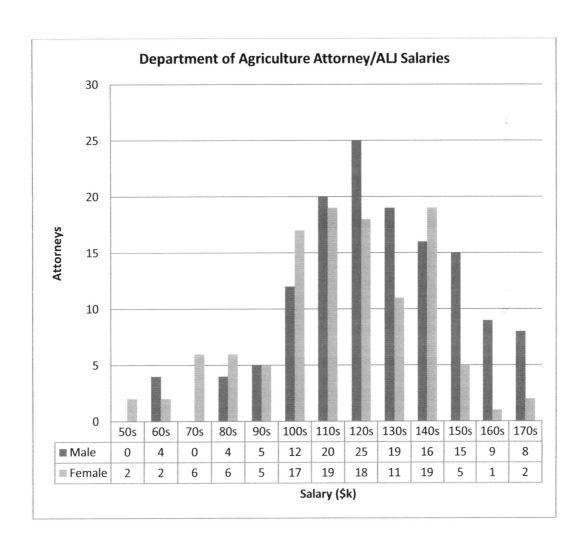

	50s	60s	70s	80s	90s	100s	110s	120s	130s	140s	150s	160s	170s
Male	0	4	0	4	5	12	20	25	19	16	15	9	8
Female	2	2	6	6	5	17	19	18	11	19	5	1	2

Department of Agriculture Attorney/ALJ Salaries

Attorneys

Salary ($k)

Civil Rights
(6 hearing and appeals, www.ascr.usda.gov)

The Office of the Assistant Secretary for Civil Rights provides overall leadership, coordination, and direction for USDA's civil rights programs, including matters related to program delivery, compliance and equal employment opportunity. They ensure compliance with applicable Federal civil rights laws, and are a resource for customers or employees who wish to file complaints of discrimination.

Food and Nutrition Service
(7 attorneys, www.fns.usda.gov)

The Food and Nutrition Service (FNS) administers the USDA food assistance programs. These programs, which serve one in six Americans, represent the Nation's commitment to the principle that no one in this United States should fear hunger or experience want. They provide a Federal safety net to people in need. The goals of the programs are to provide needy persons with access to a more nutritious diet, to improve the eating habits of the Nation's children, and to help America's farmers by providing an outlet for distributing foods purchased under farmer assistance authorities.

The Service works in partnership with the States in all its programs. State and local agencies determine most administrative details regarding distribution of food benefits and eligibility of participants, and FNS provides commodities and funding for additional food and to cover administrative costs.

National Appeals Division
(1 attorney, 60 hearing and appeals, www.nad.usda.gov)

The National Appeals Division (NAD) reports directly to the Secretary of Agriculture and is independent of other parts of USDA. Its sole mission is to provide fair and timely hearings and appeals to USDA program participants. Any person who receives an adverse program decision from USDA's Farm Service Agency, Risk Management Agency, Natural Resources Conservation Service, or the three USDA Rural Development agencies may file an appeal with NAD. NAD employs a two-stage appeal process. A participant has a right to a hearing in his state of residence before a NAD hearing officer. Thereafter, either the appellant or the agency may ask the NAD Director to reverse the hearing officer's determination.

Office of General Counsel

(233 attorneys)

The Office of the General Counsel (OGC) is an independent legal agency within the USDA. OGC provides legal advice and services to the Secretary of Agriculture and to all other officials and agencies of the Department with respect to all USDA programs and activities. All legal services are centralized within OGC and the General Counsel reports directly to the Secretary.

The General Counsel is assisted by a Deputy General Counsel, a Senior Counsel, six Associate General Counsel, a Director of Administration and Resource Management and Regional Attorneys.

Inspector General's Office

(9 attorneys, www.usda.gov/oig/)

The Office of Inspector General was established in 1978. The Inspector General is required to independently and objectively perform audits and investigations of the Department's programs and operations. The Office works with the Department's management team in activities that promote economy, efficiency, and effectiveness or that prevent and detect fraud and abuse in programs and operations, both within USDA and in non-Federal entities that receive USDA assistance. The Office also reports OIG activities to the Secretary and Congress semiannually.

Department of Commerce

Herbert Hoover Building. Photo: Carol M. Highsmith Photography, Inc.

Description:

The Department of Commerce encourages, serves, and promotes the Nation's international trade, economic growth, and technological advancement. The Department provides a wide variety of programs through the competitive free enterprise system. It offers assistance and information to increase America's competitiveness in the world economy; administers programs to prevent unfair foreign trade competition; provides social and economic statistics and analyses for business and government planners; provides research and support for the increased use of scientific, engineering, and technological development; works to improve the understanding and benefits of the Earth's physical environment and oceanic resources; grants patents and registers trademarks; develops policies and conducts research on telecommunications; provides assistance to promote domestic economic development; and assists in the growth of minority businesses.

The General Counsel is the chief legal officer of the Department and legal advisor to the Secretary, Secretarial Officers, and other officers of the Department, including heads of operating units. He/she directs the operation of ten offices that report directly to him/her and also provides legal and policy direction to four additional legal offices that receive their funding and personnel allocations from their bureaus.

Department of Commerce – Office of General Counsel

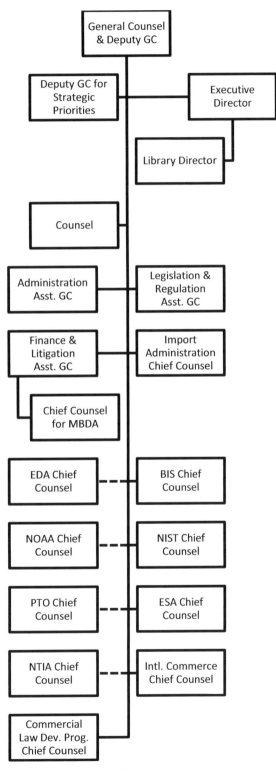

Address: U.S. Department of Commerce
1401 Constitution Avenue, NW
Washington, DC 20230

Website: www.commerce.gov   **Phone**:   202-482-2000

Department of Commerce	Avg. Salary	Attorneys
Economic Development Administration	$129,456	13
National Oceanic & Atmospheric Admin	$129.361	104
National Telecommunications and Info Admin	$135,201	6
Office of the Inspector General	$126,520	6
Office of the Secretary	$122,276	158 (1 law clerk)
Patent and Trademark Office	$119,683	722 (147 patent)
TOTAL	**$121,633**	**1,009**

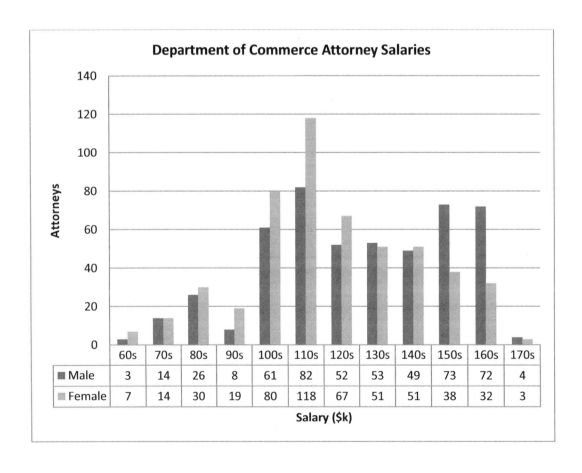

Department of Commerce Attorney Salaries

	60s	70s	80s	90s	100s	110s	120s	130s	140s	150s	160s	170s
Male	3	14	26	8	61	82	52	53	49	73	72	4
Female	7	14	30	19	80	118	67	51	51	38	32	3

Salary ($k)

Economic Development Administration
(13 attorneys, www.eda.gov)

The Economic Development Administration (EDA) was created in 1965 under the Public Works and Economic Development Act (42 U.S.C. 3121) as part of an effort to target Federal resources to economically distressed areas and to help develop local economies in the United States. It was mandated to assist rural and urban communities that were outside the mainstream economy and that lagged in economic development, industrial growth, and personal income.

EDA provides grants to States, regions, and communities across the Nation to help create wealth and minimize poverty by promoting a favorable business environment to attract private capital investment and higher skill, higher wage jobs through capacity building, planning, infrastructure, research grants, and strategic initiatives. Through its grant program, EDA utilizes public sector resources to create an environment where the private sector risks capital and job opportunities are created.

The EDA Chief Counsel is responsible for legal review of matters under EDA's statutory authority.

National Oceanic and Atmospheric Administration
(104 attorneys, www.noaa.gov)

The National Oceanic and Atmospheric Administration (NOAA) was formed on October 3, 1970, by Reorganization Plan No. 4 of 1970 (5 U.S.C. app.). NOAA's mission entails environmental assessment, prediction, and stewardship. It is dedicated to monitoring and assessing the state of the environment in order to make accurate and timely forecasts to protect life, property, and natural resources, as well as to promote the economic well-being of the United States and to enhance its environmental security. NOAA is committed to protecting America's ocean, coastal, and living marine resources while promoting sustainable economic development.

The NOAA Office of General Counsel provides legal advice and counsel for NOAA. The General Counsel is appointed by the Secretary of Commerce, with the approval of the President. The NOAA General Counsel serves as the chief legal officer for NOAA and as legal advisor to the Under Secretary of Commerce for Oceans and Atmosphere and other NOAA senior officials. With more than 100 lawyers in thirteen primary subdivision offices across the Nation, the NOAA GC supports the various offices that execute NOAA's mission.

NOAA – Office of General Counsel

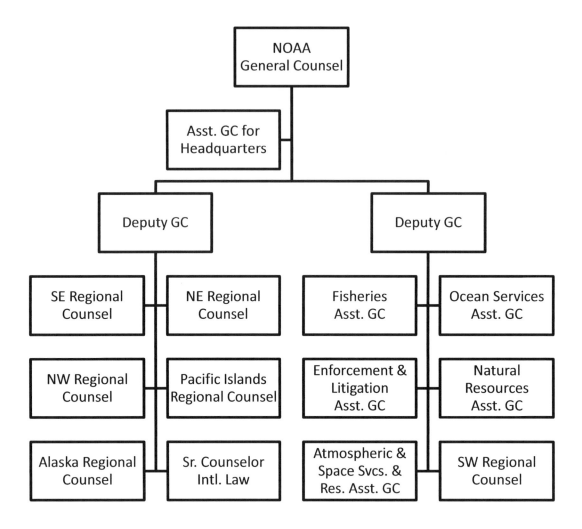

National Telecommunications and Information Administration
(6 attorneys, www.ntia.doc.gov)

The National Telecommunications and Information Administration (NTIA) was established in 1978 by Reorganization Plan No. 1 of 1977 (5 U.S.C. app.) and Executive Order 12046 of March 27, 1978 (3 CFR, 1978 Comp., p. 158), by combining the Office of Telecommunications Policy of the Executive Office of the President and the Office of Telecommunications of the Department of Commerce to form a new agency reporting to the Secretary of Commerce. NTIA operates under the authority of the National Telecommunications and Information Administration Organization Act (47 U.S.C. 901).

NTIA's principal responsibilities and functions include:

- serving as the principal executive branch adviser to the President on telecommunications and information policy;
- developing and presenting U.S. plans and policies at international communications conferences and related meetings;
- prescribing policies for and managing Federal use of the radio frequency spectrum;
- serving as the principal Federal telecommunications research and engineering laboratory, through NTIA's Institute for Telecommunication Sciences;
- administering Federal programs to assist telecommunication facilities, public safety organizations, and the general public with the transition to digital broadcasting;
- providing grants through the Broadband Technology Opportunities Program to increase broadband accessibility in underserved areas of the United States; and
- providing grants through the Public Telecommunications Facilities Program to extend delivery or public telecommunications services to U.S. citizens, to increase ownership and management by women and minorities, and to strengthen the capabilities of existing public broadcasting stations to provide telecommunications services.

The NTIA Office of Chief Counsel (OCC) is headed by the Chief Counsel of NTIA who has full responsibility for the development and administration of the NTIA legal program. OCC provides legal advice and general counseling to the Administrator, Deputy Administrator and all components of NTIA with regard to the powers, duties, and responsibilities of NTIA and its relationship with other government departments and agencies (particularly, the Federal Communications Commission), Congress, business, industry, and private organizations; and the development and administration of NTIA policies and programs.

OCC prepares and reviews legislative proposals and statements concerning pending legislation or oversight to be made before committees of Congress, and prepares or reviews regulatory proposals and comments before regulatory agencies. OCC also carries out additional policy development functions with significant legal orientation in coordination with other components of NTIA as the Administrator directs.

Patent and Trademark Office

(722 attorneys, www.uspto.gov)

The United States Patent and Trademark Office (USPTO) was established by the act of July 19, 1952 (35 U.S.C. 1) "to promote the progress of science and the useful arts by securing for limited times to inventors the exclusive right to their respective discoveries for a certain period of time" (Article I, Section 8 of the United States Constitution). The registration of trademarks is based on the commerce clause of the U.S. Constitution. USPTO examines and issues patents. There are three major patent categories: utility patents, design patents, and plant patents. USPTO also issues statutory invention registrations and processes international patent applications.

Through the registration of trademarks, USPTO assists businesses in protecting their investments, promoting goods and services, and safeguarding consumers against confusion and deception in the marketplace. A trademark includes any distinctive word, name, symbol, device, or any combination thereof adopted and used or intended to be used by a manufacturer or merchant to identify his goods or services and distinguish them from those manufactured or sold by others. Trademarks are examined by the Office for compliance with various statutory requirements to prevent unfair competition and consumer deception.

The USPTO Office of the General Counsel consists of five organizations that are concerned with legal review of agency decisions, defense of agency decisions in court and administrative tribunals, internal agency legal advice, and regulation of persons practicing before the USPTO. These five organizations are the Office of the Solicitor, the Office of General Law, the Board of Patent Appeals and Interferences, the Trademark Trial and Appeal Board, and the Office of Enrollment and Discipline.

The Office of the Solicitor serves as legal counsel to the USPTO on intellectual property law matters. The Solicitor's Office also works in collaboration with the Department of Commerce on interagency intellectual property law matters.

Department of Defense

Description:
The Department of Defense (DOD) is responsible for providing the military forces needed to deter war and protect the security of the United States. The National Security Act Amendments of 1949 redesignated the National Military Establishment as the Department of Defense and established it as an executive department (10 U.S.C. 111), headed by the Secretary of Defense.

The major elements of these forces are the Army, Navy, Marine Corps, and Air Force, consisting of about 1.3 million men and women on active duty. They are backed, in case of emergency, by the 825,000 members of the Reserve and National Guard. In addition, there are about 600,000 civilian employees in the Defense Department.

Under the President, who is also Commander in Chief, the Secretary of Defense exercises authority, direction, and control over the Department, which includes the separately organized military departments of Army, Navy, and Air Force, the Joint Chiefs of Staff providing military advice, the combatant commands, and defense agencies and field activities established for specific purposes.

Address: Department of Defense
                 The Pentagon
                 Washington, DC 20301-1155

Website: www.defense.gov   **Phone**:   703-545-6700

Department of Defense	Attorneys	Male	Female	Avg Salary
Business Transformation Agency	1		1	$160,860
Defense Advanced Research Projects Agency	3	2	1	$151,538
Defense Commissary Agency	11	7	4	$117,971
Defense Contract Audit Agency	6	3	3	$142,825
Defense Contract Management Agency	88	49	39	$130,012
Defense Finance & Accounting Service	38	23	15	$108,027
Defense Human Resources Activity	4	2	2	$157,458
Defense Information Systems Agency	14	6	8	$130,274
Defense Legal Services Agency	173	118	55	$135,376
Defense Logistics Agency	125	77	48	$116,964
Defense Media Activity	2	2	-	$149,805
Defense POW/Missing Personnel Office	1	1	-	$160,084
Defense Security Cooperation Agency	9	8	1	$130,917
Defense Security Service	6	5	1	$105,980
Defense Technology Security Admin	1	1	-	$160,860
Defense Threat Reduction Agency	8	6	2	$151,295
Department of Defense Education Activity	11	5	6	$129,990
Missile Defense Agency	19	16	3	$150,603
National Defense University	1	-	1	$126,877
Office of the Inspector General	11	8	3	$159,476
Office of the Secretary of Defense	42	29	13	$158,862
Tricare Management Activity	25 (1 law clerk)	17	8	$126,924
U.S. Court of Appeals for the Armed Forces	35 (8 law clerks)	24	11	$118,929
Washington Headquarters Services	20	14	6	$140,959
TOTAL	654	423	231	$130,665
Percent of Positions		65%	35%	
Average Salary		$133,249	$125,933	

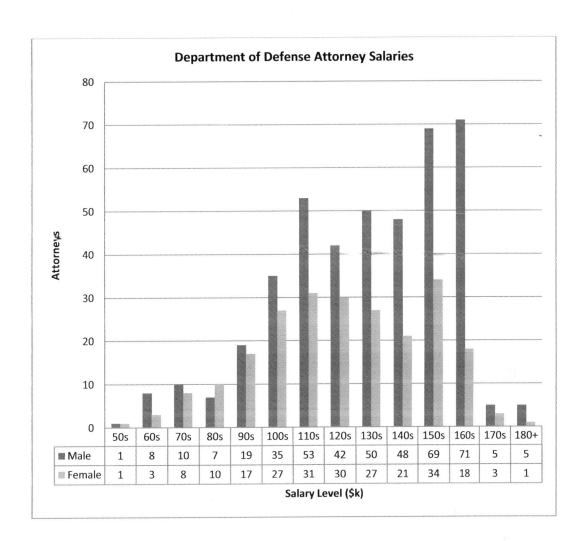

Department of Defense Attorney Salaries

	50s	60s	70s	80s	90s	100s	110s	120s	130s	140s	150s	160s	170s	180+
Male	1	8	10	7	19	35	53	42	50	48	69	71	5	5
Female	1	3	8	10	17	27	31	30	27	21	34	18	3	1

Salary Level ($k)

Office of the Secretary of Defense (Office of the General Counsel)
(258 attorneys, www.dod.gov/dodgc/)

The DOD Office of the General Counsel (OGC) is part of the Office of the Secretary of Defense (OSD). The DOD General Counsel is appointed by the President and confirmed by the Senate and serves as the Chief Legal Officer of DOD, the legal advisor to the Secretary of Defense, and the Director of the Defense Legal Services Agency (in which capacity he or she oversees the General Counsel Offices of over two dozen Defense Agencies and DOD Field Activities). The DOD OGC is the highest level legal organization in DOD. The DOD as a whole has over 10,000 full-time and part-time civilian and military attorneys.

The DOD OGC is responsible for advising high level policy makers in OSD. In addition, the Office works closely with senior attorneys and policy makers from the military departments, as well as the White House, Departments of Justice, State, Treasury, and other Government agencies. The Office also frequently works on special projects for OSD.

► Office of the Secretary of Defense Honors Legal Internship Program
www.dod.gov/dodgc/contact.html

Business Transformation Agency
(1 attorney, www.bta.mil)

The mission of the Business Transformation Agency is to guide the transformation of business operations throughout the DOD and to deliver enterprise-level capabilities that align to warfighter needs.

Defense Advanced Research Projects Agency
(3 attorneys, www.darpa.mil)

The Defense Advanced Research Projects Agency (DARPA) is the research and development office for the DOD. DARPA's mission is to maintain technological superiority of the U.S. military and prevent technological surprise from harming national security. It also creates technological surprise for adversaries. DARPA funds unique and innovative research through the private sector, academic and other non-profit organizations as well as government labs. DARPA research runs the gamut from conducting scientific investigations in a laboratory, to building full-scale prototypes of military systems. DARPA funds research in biology, medicine, computer science, chemistry, physics, engineering, mathematics, material sciences, social sciences, neuroscience, and other disciplines.

Defense Commissary Agency
(11 attorneys, www.commissaries.com)

The Defense Commissary Agency headquartered at Fort Lee, Virginia, operates a worldwide chain of commissaries providing groceries to military personnel, retirees and their families in a safe and secure shopping environment. Authorized patrons purchase items at cost plus a 5 percent surcharge, which covers the costs of building new commissaries and modernizing existing ones. Commissaries are considered a core military family support element and a valued part of military pay and benefits, contributing to family readiness and enhancing the quality of life for America's military and their families.

Defense Contract Audit Agency
(6 attorneys, www.dcaa.mil)

The Defense Contract Audit Agency (DCAA), while serving the public interest as its primary customer, performs all necessary contract audits for the DOD and provides accounting and financial advisory services regarding contracts and subcontracts to all DOD Components responsible for procurement and contract administration. These services are provided in connection with negotiation, administration, and settlement of contracts and subcontracts to ensure taxpayer dollars are spent on fair and reasonable contract prices. The DCAA provides contract audit services to other Federal agencies as appropriate.

Defense Contract Management Agency
(88 attorneys, www.dcma.mil)

The Defense Contract Management Agency (DCMA) is the DOD component that works directly with Defense suppliers to help ensure that DOD, Federal, and allied government supplies and services are delivered on time, at projected cost, and meet all performance requirements. DCMA directly contributes to the military readiness of the United States and its allies. DCMA professionals serve as "information brokers" and in-plant representatives for military, Federal, and allied government buying agencies - both during the initial stages of the acquisition cycle and throughout the life of the resulting contracts.

Defense Finance and Accounting Service

(38 attorneys, www.dfas.mil)

In 1991, the Secretary of Defense created the Defense Finance and Accounting Service (DFAS) to standardize, consolidate, and improve accounting and financial functions throughout the DOD. The intent was to reduce the cost of the Department's finance and accounting operations while strengthening its financial management. DFAS pays all DOD military and civilian personnel, retirees and annuitants, as well as major DOD contractors and vendors. DFAS also supports customers outside the DOD in support of electronic government initiatives.

Defense Human Resource Activity

(4 attorneys, www.dhra.mil)

The Defense Human Resource Activity oversees an array of DOD-mandated human resource programs, policies, and initiatives.

Defense Information Systems Agency

(14 attorneys, www.disa.mil)

Defense Information Systems Agency, a combat support agency, engineers and provides command and control capabilities and enterprise infrastructure to continuously operate and assure a global net-centric enterprise in direct support to joint warfighters, national level leaders, and other mission and coalition partners across the full spectrum of operations.

Defense Legal Services Agency

(173 attorneys)

The Defense Legal Services Agency (DLSA) provides legal services to the Office of the Secretary of Defense, DOD Field Activities, and the Defense Agencies.

The largest component of DLSA, the Defense Office of Hearings and Appeals (DOHA), adjudicates numerous types of cases that arise from all Military Departments and Defense Agencies. The DOHA provides hearings and issues decisions in personnel security clearance cases for contractors performing classified work for all DOD components and numerous other Federal Agencies, and conducts personal appearances and issues decisions in security clearance cases for DOD civilian employees and military personnel. The DOHA also conducts hearings and issues decisions in cases involving claims for DOD Dependents Schools Activity benefits and TRICARE payment for medical services. The DOHA's claims function includes review of uniformed service and carrier claims for loss or damage of household goods and review of waiver applications. The DOHA provides support to the Deputy General Counsel Legal Counsel and is the point of contact for selection of third party neutrals in DOHA alternative dispute resolution processes.

Defense Logistics Agency

(125 attorneys, www.dla.mil)

The Defense Logistics Agency DLA is under the authority, direction, and control of the Under Secretary of Defense for Acquisition, Technology, and Logistics. It supports both the logistics requirements of the military services and their acquisition of weapons and other materiel. The Agency provides logistics support and technical services to all branches of the military and to a number of Federal agencies. Agency supply centers consolidate the requirements of the military services and procure the supplies in sufficient quantities to meet their projected needs. The Agency manages supplies in eight commodity areas: fuel, food, clothing, construction material, electronic supplies, general supplies, industrial supplies, and medical supplies.

Defense Media Activity

(2 attorneys, www.dma.mil)

The Defense Media Activity provides a broad range of high quality multimedia products and services to inform, educate, and entertain DOD audiences around the world.

Defense POW/Missing Personnel Office

(1 attorney, www.dtic.mil/dpmo/)

The Defense POW/Missing Personnel Office is responsible for establishing and overseeing policies on the rescue of living Americans and the recovery of the remains of those who are missing in action from foreign battle fields.

Defense Security Service

(6 attorneys, www.dss.mil)

The Defense Security Service (DSS) is an agency of the DOD located in Alexandria, Virginia with field offices throughout the United States. The Under Secretary of Defense for Intelligence provides authority, direction and control over DSS. DSS provides the military services, Defense Agencies, numerous Federal agencies and thousands of cleared contractor facilities with security support services. DSS supports national security and the warfighter, secures the technological base of the U.S., and oversees the protection of U.S. and foreign classified information in the hands of industry.

Defense Technology Security Administration
(1 attorney, www.dtsa.mil)

The Defense Technology Security Administration DTSA administers the development and implementation of DOD technology security policies on international transfers of defense-related goods, services and technologies. It ensures that critical U.S. military technological advantages are preserved; transfers that could prove detrimental to U.S. security interests are controlled and limited; proliferation of weapons of mass destruction and their means of delivery is prevented; diversion of defense-related goods to terrorists is prevented; military interoperability with foreign allies and friends is supported; and the health of the U.S. defense industrial base is assured.

Department of Defense Education Activity
(11 attorneys, www.dodea.edu)

The Department of Defense Education Activity (DODEA) is a civilian agency that oversees schools on certain military bases. DODEA operates 194 schools in 14 districts located in 12 foreign countries, seven States, Guam, and Puerto Rico. All schools within DODEA are fully accredited by U.S. accreditation agencies. Approximately 8,700 educators serve more than 86,000 DODEA students.

Missile Defense Agency
(19 attorneys, www.mda.mil)

The Missile Defense Agency (MDA) is a research, development, and acquisition agency within the DOD. Its workforce includes government civilians, military service members, and contractor personnel in multiple locations across the United States.

As MDA develops, tests, and fields an integrated Ballistic Missile Defense System (BMDS), it works closely with the Combatant Commanders (e.g. Pacific Command, Northern Command, etc.) who will rely on the system to protect the United States, its forward deployed forces, and its friends and allies from hostile ballistic missile attack. MDA works with the Combatant Commanders to ensure the development of a robust BMDS technology and development program to address the challenges of an evolving threat. MDA also increases international cooperation by supporting mutual security interests in missile defense.

National Defense University
(1 attorney, www.ndu.edu)

The National Defense University is a center for Joint Professional Military Education and is under the direction of the Chairman, Joint Chiefs of Staff. The University's main campus is on Fort Lesley J. McNair in Washington, D.C. The Joint Forces Staff College is located in Norfolk, Virginia. The National Defense University is accredited by the Commission on Higher Education of the Middle States Association of Colleges and Schools.

Office of the Inspector General
(11 attorneys, www.dodig.mil)

The mission of the DOD Office of the Inspector General is to promote integrity, accountability, and improvement of DOD personnel, programs and operations to support the Department's mission and serve the public interest.

Tricare Management Activity
(25 attorneys, www.tricare.mil)

The TRICARE Management Activity (TMA) is a field activity of the Undersecretary of Defense for Personnel and Readiness, and was formally established under DOD Directive 5136.12 on May 31, 2001. Since February 1998, TMA leadership has managed the TRICARE health care program for active duty members and their families, retired service members and their families, National Guard/Reserve members and their families, survivors and others entitled to DOD medical care.

TMA has operational offices located in Falls Church, Virginia and Aurora, Colorado. Additionally, TMA is organized into six geographic health service regions, each with its own TRICARE Regional Office and Regional Director. The overseas regions are referred to as "areas." Each region/area:
- Provides oversight of regional operations and health plan administration at the regional level;

- Manages the contracts with regional contractors;
- Supports military treatment facility (MTF) Commanders;
- Develops business plans for non-MTF areas (e.g. remote areas); and
- Funds regional initiatives to optimize and improve delivery of health care.

U.S. Court of Appeals for the Armed Forces
(35 attorneys, www.armfor.uscourts.gov)

The United States Court of Appeals for the Armed Forces exercises worldwide appellate jurisdiction over members of the armed forces on active duty and other persons subject to the Uniform Code of Military Justice. The Court is composed of five civilian judges appointed for 15-year terms by the President with the advice and consent of the Senate.

Cases on the Court's docket address a broad range of legal issues, including constitutional law, criminal law, evidence, criminal procedure, ethics, administrative law, and national security law. Decisions by the Court are subject to direct review by the Supreme Court of the United States.

▶ U.S. Court of Appeals for the Armed Forces Clerkships
www.armfor.uscourts.gov/Clerkships.htm

Washington Headquarters Service
(19 attorneys, www.whs.mil)

Washington Headquarters Services (WHS) is a DOD Field Activity, created on October 1, 1977. WHS provides consolidated administrative and operational support to several Defense Agencies, DOD Field Activities, the headquarters and various elements of the military departments, the White House, and to some degree, Congress.

Department of the Air Force

Description:

The Department of the Air Force (USAF) is responsible for defending the United States through control and exploitation of air and space.

The USAF was established as part of the National Military Establishment by the National Security Act of 1947 (61 Stat. 502) and came into being on September 18, 1947. The National Security Act Amendments of 1949 redesignated the National Military Establishment as the Department of Defense, established it as an executive department, and made the Department of the Air Force a military department within the Department of Defense (63 Stat. 578). The Department of the Air Force is separately organized under the Secretary of the Air Force. It operates under the authority, direction, and control of the Secretary of Defense (10 U.S.C. 8010). The Department consists of the Office of the Secretary of the Air Force, the Air Staff, and field organizations.

The General Counsel is the chief legal officer and ethics official of the Air Force. The General Counsel provides oversight, guidance and direction for legal advice provided by more than 2,600 Department of the Air Force military and civilian lawyers worldwide.

Address: Department of the Air Force
                 1690 Air Force Pentagon
                 Washington, DC 20330-1670

Website: www.af.mil   **Phone**:   703-697-6061

Air Force Department	Attorneys	Male	Female	Avg Salary
Engineering & Services Center	1	-	1	$99,378
Office of Special Investigations	3	1	2	$129,314
Operational Test and Eval. Ctr.	1	-	1	$128,554
AF – Wide Support Element	12 (1 law clerk)	7	5	$132,909
Air Combat Command	14	11	3	$99,587
Air Education & Training Command	19	16	3	$95,598
Air Force Communications Agency	3	3	-	$124,349
Air Force Ctr. for Environmental Excellence	10	7	3	$120,114
Air Force District of Washington	10	6	4	$106,692
Air Force Elements, other than Europe	1	-	1	$140,660
U.S. Central Command	2	2	-	$129,490
U.S. Northern Command	5	4	1	$120,788
U.S. Special Operations Command	5	4	1	$126,808
U.S. Strategic Command	1	1	-	$133,591
U.S. Transportation Command	11	10	1	$119,325
Intelligence, Surveillance & Recon Agency	2	2	-	$110,483
Air Force Legal Services Center	97 (1 patent)	74	23	$127,672
Air Force Manpower Agency	1	1	-	$103,953
Air Force Materiel Command	135 (13 patent)	111	24	$116,579
Air Force Medical Services	1	-	1	$153,096
Morale, Welfare & Rec. Center	6	6	-	$109,597
Personnel Center	3	3	-	$112,139
Air Force Real Property Agency	11	8	3	$124,790
Air Force Review Boards Office	2	2	-	$160,860
Air Force Special Operations Command	1	1	-	$80,402
Air Force Supply Center	1	1	-	$111,555
Air Mobility Command	12	10	2	$105,113
Air National Guard Support Center	7	7	-	$130,157
Air National Guard Units (Title 32)	3	2	1	$105,688
Headquarters, Air Force Reserve	3	3	-	$112,586
Headquarters, USAF	45	34	11	$148,061
Pacific Air Forces	8	8	-	$85,463
Space Command	28	22	6	$121,677
U.S. Air Force Academy	4	4	-	$103,927
U.S. Air Forces, Europe	10	9	1	$104,593
TOTAL	**478**	**380**	**98**	**$120,633**
Percent of Positions		**79%**	**21%**	
Average Salary		**$121,545**	**$117,098**	

Department of the Army

Description:

The mission of the Department of the Army is to organize, train, and equip active duty and reserve forces for the preservation of peace, security, and the defense of the United States. As part of the U.S. national military team, the Army focuses on land operations; its soldiers must be trained with modern arms and equipment and be ready to respond quickly. The Army also administers programs aimed at protecting the environment, improving waterway navigation, flood and beach erosion control, and water resource development. It provides military assistance to Federal, State, and local government agencies, including natural disaster relief assistance.

The American Continental Army, now called the United States Army, was established by the Continental Congress on June 14, 1775, more than a year before the Declaration of Independence. The Department of War was established as an executive department at the seat of government by act approved August 7, 1789 (1 Stat. 49). The Secretary of War was established as its head. The National Security Act of 1947 (50 U.S.C. 401) created the National Military Establishment, and the Department of War was designated the Department of the Army. The title of its Secretary became Secretary of the Army (5 U.S.C. 171). The National Security Act Amendments of 1949 (63 Stat. 578) provided that the Department of the Army be a military department within the Department of Defense.

The General Counsel is responsible for determining the Army's position on any legal question. The General Counsel serves as legal counsel to the Secretary, Under Secretary, five Assistant Secretaries, and other members of the Army Secretariat. The General Counsel also exercises technical supervision over the Office of the Judge Advocate General, the Office of the Command Counsel, Army Materiel Command, and the Office of the Chief Counsel, Corps of Engineers.

Address: Department of the Army
             The Pentagon
             Washington, DC 20310

Website: www.army.mil   **Phone**:   703-695-6518

Army Department	Attorneys	Male	Female	Avg Salary
Army National Guard Units (Title 32)	38	32	6	$81,107
Eighth U.S. Army	1	-	1	$80,000
Fld Op AG of Army Staffed Res. OA-22	81	60 (3 patent)	21	$133,439
Fld Operating Agencies of the Army Staff	2	2	-	$123,174
Fld Operating Ofc of Ofc of Sec of Army	6	3	3	$135,446
Headquarters, AMC	18	12	6	$139,526
Cmd-in-Chief US Army Eur & Sev Army	31	26	5	$89,318
Ofc of Chief of Staff of Army	16	10	6	$147,317
Joint Activities	18	15	3	$111,353
Jt Serv & Act Sup by Ofc, Sec of Army	37	24	13	$150,611
Ofc of Chief of National Guard Bureau	1	1	-	$133,543
Office of the Secretary of the Army	38	26	12	$147,070
Space & Miss Def Cmd/Forces Strat. Cmd	9	6	3 (1 patent)	$125,563
U.S. Army Contracting Command	40	25	15	$122,575
U.S. Army Accessions Command	11	9	2	$99,845
U.S. Army Acquisition Support Center	5	3	2	$124,926
U.S. Army Aviation and Missile Command	55	36 (4 patent)	19 (1 patent)	$112,761
U.S. Army Central	3	1	2	$94,830
U.S. Army Chemical Materials Agency	4	3	1	$130,851
U.S. Army Corps of Engineers	444	257 (1 patent; 5 l cl)	187 (5 law clerk)	$108,093
U.S. Army Criminal Inv.Command	6	3	3	$135,070
U.S. Army Element Shape	1	1	-	$108,483
U.S. Army Forces Command	36	29	7	$105,827
U.S. Army Installation Mgmt Command	195	139	56	$100,213
U.S. Army Joint Munitions Command	5	5	-	$98,993
U.S. Army Medical Command	68	45	23 (1 patent)	$103,844
U.S. Army Mil Surf Deploy & Destr Cmd	7	3	4	$118,883
U.S. Army Netcom/9th Army Signal Cmd	9	9	-	$100,952
U.S. Army North	3	3	-	$100,762
U.S. Army Res., Dev & Engineering Cmd	45 (11 patent)	38	7	$139,921
U.S. Amy Security Assistance Command	2	2	-	$129,680
U.S. Army South	3	2	1	$122,625
U.S. Army Sustainment Command	33 (1 law clerk)	17	16	$108,519
U.S. Army Tank-Autom & Armament Cmd	55 (1 patent;1 l cl)	31	24	$103,898
U.S. Army Test and Evaluation Command	9	8	1	$126,583
U.S. Army Training and Doctrine Command	17	12	5	$110,034
U.S. Army, Pacific	5	3	2	$95,656
U.S. Military Academy	5	3	2	$106,730
U.S. Military Entrance Processing Cmd	2	1	1	$110,997
U.S. Special Operations Cmd (Army)	3	3	-	$105,157
U.S. Army Comm. Electronics Cmd	50 (6 patent)	26	24	$123,916
U.S. Army Intelligence and Security Adm	6	4	2	$140,706
U.S. Army Mil District of Washington	7	6	1	$114,975
TOTAL	**1,430**	**944**	**486**	**$112,740**
Percent of Positions		**66%**	**34%**	
Average Salary		**$115,186**	**$107,989**	

Department of the Navy

Description:
The primary mission of the Department of the Navy is to protect the United States, as directed by the President or the Secretary of Defense, by the effective prosecution of war at sea including, with its Marine Corps component, the seizure or defense of advanced naval bases; to support, as required, the forces of all military departments of the United States; and to maintain freedom of the seas.

The United States Navy was founded on October 13, 1775, when Congress created the Continental Navy of the American Revolution. The Department of the Navy and the Office of Secretary of the Navy were established by act of April 30, 1798 (10 U.S.C. 5011, 5031). For 9 years prior to that date, by act of August 7, 1789 (1 Stat. 49), the conduct of naval affairs was under the Secretary of War.

The National Security Act Amendments of 1949 provided that the Department of the Navy be a military department within the Department of Defense (63 Stat. 578). The Secretary of the Navy is appointed by the President as the head of the Department of the Navy and is responsible to the Secretary of Defense for the operation and efficiency of the Navy (10 U.S.C. 5031).

The General Counsel of the Navy is the department's chief legal and ethics officer, managing over 700 attorneys in 140 offices worldwide, assisting in the oversight of the Naval Criminal Investigative Service, and advising senior Navy and Marine Corps officials on litigation, acquisition, contractual, fiscal, environmental, property, personnel, legislative, ethics, and intelligence law issues. The General Counsel is also the debarring authority on acquisition matters for the Department of the Navy.

Address: Department of the Navy
The Pentagon
Washington, DC 20350

Website: www.navy.mil   **Phone**:   703-697-7391

Department of Navy	Attorneys	Male	Female	Avg Salary
Asst for Admin, Under Sec of Navy	145	88 (1 law clerk)	57 (1 law clerk)	$136,879
Commander, Navy Installations	39	23	16	$123,280
Ofc of Chief of Naval Operations	30	20 (1 patent)	10 (1 patent)	$112,962
Military Sealift Command	25	14 (1 law clerk)	11	$119,418
Naval Air Systems Command	73	40 (1 patent)	33 (1 patent)	$121,201
Naval Education & Training Comm.	9	4	5	$121,174
Naval Facilities Engineering Comm.	98	59 (1 law clerk)	39	$123,405
Naval Intelligence Command	1	1	-	$149,782
Naval Medical Command	16	8 (2 patent)	8 (1 patent)	$124,456
Naval Reserve Force	1	1	-	$147,814
Naval Sea Systems Command	86	47 (14 patent)	39 (2 patent)	$134,901
Naval Special Warfare Command	1	-	1	$112,293
Naval Supply Systems Command	53	37	16 (1 law clerk)	$116,817
Office of Naval Research	32	24 (10 patent; 1 law clerk)	8 (4 patent)	$138,428
Space & Naval Warfare Systems Command	42	29 (8 patent)	13 (1 law clerk)	$129,216
Strategic Systems Programs Office	11	9 (2 patent)	2 (1 law clerk)	$138,519
U.S. Atlantic Fleet, Commander in Chief	16	12	4	$125,473
U.S. Marine Corps	63	50 (1 patent)	13	$124,492
U.S. Pacific Fleet, Commander in Chief	12	7	5	$121,090
TOTAL	753	474	281	$127,410
Percent of Positions		63%	37%	
Average Salary		$130,695	$121,860	

Department of Education

Description:
The Department of Education establishes policy for, administers, and coordinates most Federal assistance to education. Its mission is to ensure equal access to education and to promote educational excellence throughout the United States.

The Department of Education was created by the Department of Education Organization Act (20 U.S.C. 3411) and is administered under the supervision and direction of the Secretary of Education.

Address: U.S. Department of Education
400 Maryland Avenue, SW
Washington, D.C. 20202

Website: www.ed.gov   **Phone**:   800-872-5327

Department of Education	Attorneys	Male	Female	Avg Salary
Office for Civil Rights	256 (1 L Clerk)	81	175 (1 L Clerk)	$108,795
Office of the Inspector General	3	1	2	$149,453
Office of Management	10 (1 ALJ)	7 (1 ALJ)	3	$140,918
Office of the General Counsel	81	32	49	$140,016
TOTAL	350	121	229	$117,286
Percent of Positions		35%	65%	

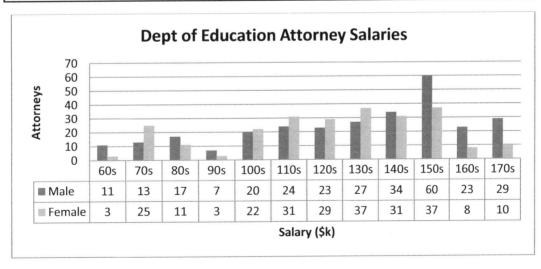

Dept of Education Attorney Salaries

Salary ($k)	60s	70s	80s	90s	100s	110s	120s	130s	140s	150s	160s	170s
Male	11	13	17	7	20	24	23	27	34	60	23	29
Female	3	25	11	3	22	31	29	37	31	37	8	10

Office for Civil Rights

(256 attorneys, www2.ed.gov/about/offices/list/ocr/)

The mission of the Office for Civil Rights (OCR) is to ensure equal access to education and to promote educational excellence throughout the United States through vigorous enforcement of civil rights.

The Office serves student populations facing discrimination and the advocates and institutions promoting systemic solutions to civil rights problems. An important responsibility is resolving complaints of discrimination. Agency-initiated cases, typically called compliance reviews, permit OCR to target resources on compliance problems that appear particularly acute. OCR also provides technical assistance to help institutions achieve voluntary compliance with the civil rights laws that OCR enforces. An important part of OCR's technical assistance is partnerships designed to develop creative approaches to preventing and addressing discrimination.

Office of the General Counsel

(81 attorneys, www2.ed.gov/about/offices/list/ogc/)

The General Counsel serves as principal adviser to the Secretary on all legal matters affecting Departmental programs and activities. The Office directs, coordinates, and recommends policy for activities that are designed to:

- Provide legal advice and services to the Secretary, Deputy Secretary, Principal Officers of the Department, or any other authorized person.
- Prepare or review for legal form and effect public documents, rules, regulations issued by the Department.
- Represent the Secretary, the Department, or any of its officers or units in court or administrative litigation, except for administrative proceedings initiated by the Office for Civil Rights.
- Serve as liaison to other Federal agencies in connection with legal matters involving the Department.
- Draft legislative proposals originating in the Department and review the legal aspects of proposed or pending legislation.
- Prepare or review pleadings, briefs, memoranda, and other legal documents for proceedings involving the Department or requested by other Government agencies for use in proceedings except for administrative proceedings initiated by the Office for Civil Rights.

Department of Education – Office of General Counsel

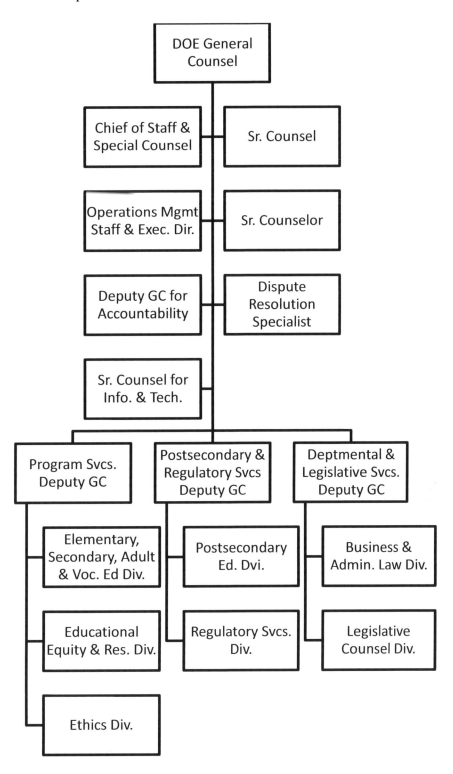

Office of the Inspector General
(3 attorneys, www2.ed.gov/about/offices/list/oig/)

The Office of the Inspector General promotes the efficiency, effectiveness, and integrity of the Department's programs and operations. The office conducts independent and objective audits, investigations, inspections, and other activities.

Office of Management
(10 attorneys, www2.ed.gov/about/offices/list/om/)

The mission of the Office of Management is to transform the Department of Education into a high-performance, customer-focused organization by providing services to its customers that help them do a better job of managing their people, processes, and overall strategy. The Assistant Secretary for Management serves as the principal adviser to the Secretary on Departmental administrative matters.

Department of Energy

Description:
The Department of Energy's mission is to foster a secure and reliable energy system that is environmentally and economically sustainable; to be a responsible steward of the Nation's nuclear weapons; to clean up the Department's facilities; to lead in the physical sciences and advance the biological, environmental, and computational sciences; and to provide premier scientific instruments for the Nation's research enterprise.

The Department of Energy (DOE) was established by the Department of Energy Organization Act (42 U.S.C. 7131), effective October 1, 1977, pursuant to Executive Order 12009 of September 13, 1977. The act consolidated the major Federal energy functions into one Cabinet-level Department.

The Office of the General Counsel provides legal advice, counsel, and support to the Secretary, Deputy Secretary, and all Departmental elements, except the National Nuclear Security Administration and the Federal Energy Regulatory Commission. The Office assures that the Department operates in compliance with all pertinent laws and regulations.

Address: U.S. Department of Energy
1000 Independence Avenue, SW
Washington, DC 20585

Website: www.energy.gov

Phone: 202-586-5000   **Fax**:   202-586-4403

► **DOE General Counsel Law Student Intern Program**
http://gc.energy.gov/1101.htm

Dept. of Energy	General Attorneys	Patent Attorneys	ALJs	Law Clerks	TOTAL
Positions	562	24	14	10	607
Avg. Salary	$128,759	$123,525	$162,900	$59,429	$128,200

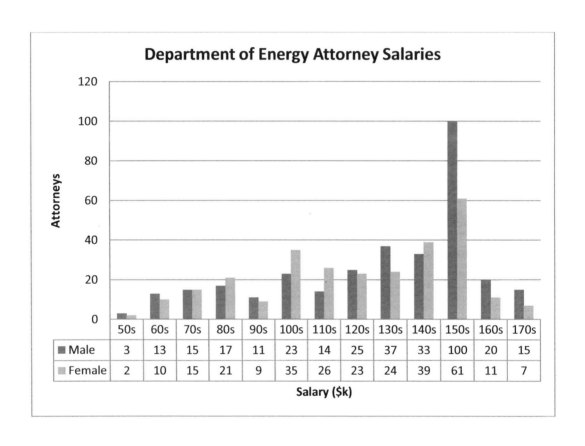

Department of Energy Attorney Salaries

Salary ($k)	50s	60s	70s	80s	90s	100s	110s	120s	130s	140s	150s	160s	170s
Male	3	13	15	17	11	23	14	25	37	33	100	20	15
Female	2	10	15	21	9	35	26	23	24	39	61	11	7

Department of Health and Human Services

Description:
The Department of Health and Human Services (HHS) is the United States Government's principal agency for protecting the health of all Americans and providing essential human services, especially for those who are least able to help themselves. HHS was created as the Department of Health, Education, and Welfare on April 11, 1953 (5 U.S.C. app.).

HHS represents almost a quarter of all Federal outlays, and it administers more grant dollars than all other Federal agencies combined. HHS' Medicare program is the nation's largest health insurer, handling more than one billion claims per year. Medicare and Medicaid together provide health care insurance for one in four Americans.

HHS works closely with State and local governments, and many HHS-funded services are provided at the local level by State or county agencies, or through private sector grantees. The Department's programs are administered by eleven operating divisions, including eight agencies in the U.S. Public Health Service and three human services agencies. The department includes more than 300 programs, covering a wide spectrum of activities. In addition to the services they deliver, the HHS programs provide for equitable treatment of beneficiaries nationwide, and they enable the collection of national health and other data.

Address: U.S. Department of Health and Human Services
200 Independence Avenue, SW
Washington, DC 20201

Website: www.hhs.gov   **Phone**:   202-619-0257

▶ **HHS Office of the General Counsel Legal Opportunities**
www.hhs.gov/ogc/careers/career.html

▶ **HHS Departmental Appeals Board Internship/Externship Program**
www.hhs.gov/dab/about/internships/intern.html

Dept. of Health & Human Services	Attorneys/ Avg. Salary	ALJs/ Avg. Salary	Law Clerks/ Avg. Salary
Center for Disease Control & Prevention	12 $129,797	-	-
Center for Medicare & Medicaid Services	10 $114,813	-	-
Food and Drug Administration	93 $120,641	1 $162,900	-
National Institutes of Health (NIH)	9 $57,972	-	-
Office of the Secretary of HHS	550 $116,984	72 $151,425	1 $60,989
Total Attorneys: 748			
Overall Average Salary: $120,207			

* 8 of the attorneys in the NIH were classified as "Intermittent Nonseasonal".

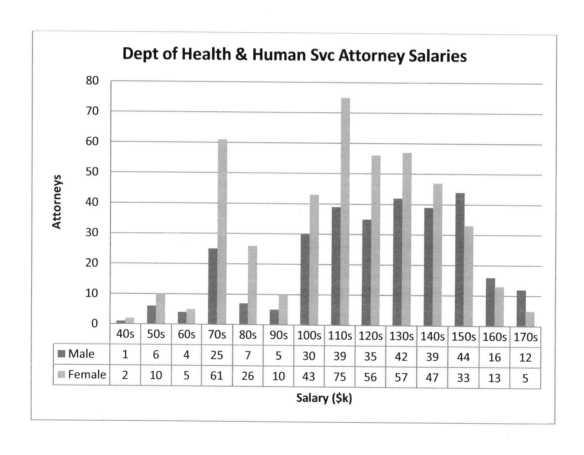

Dept of Health & Human Svc Attorney Salaries

Salary ($k)	40s	50s	60s	70s	80s	90s	100s	110s	120s	130s	140s	150s	160s	170s
Male	1	6	4	25	7	5	30	39	35	42	39	44	16	12
Female	2	10	5	61	26	10	43	75	56	57	47	33	13	5

Centers for Disease Control and Prevention
(12 attorneys, www.cdc.gov)

The Centers for Disease Control and Prevention (CDC), as part of the Public Health Service, is charged with protecting the public health of the Nation by providing leadership and direction in the prevention of and control of diseases and other preventable conditions and responding to public health emergencies. Within the CDC, there are four coordinating centers, two coordinating offices, and the National Institute for Occupational Safety and Health.

Centers for Medicare & Medicaid Services
(10 attorneys, www.cms.gov)

The Centers for Medicare and Medicaid Services, formerly known as the Health Care Financing Administration, was created to administer the Medicare, Medicaid, and related Federal medical care programs.

Food and Drug Administration
(94 attorneys, www.fda.gov)

The Food and Drug Administration (FDA) is responsible for protecting the public health by ensuring the safety, efficacy, and security of human and veterinary drugs, biological products, medical devices, the Nation's food supply, cosmetics, and products that emit radiation. FDA is also responsible for advancing the public health by accelerating innovations to make medicines more effective and providing the public with accurate, science-based information on medicines and food to improve their health. FDA plays a significant role in addressing the Nation's counterterrorism capability and ensuring the security of the food supply.

The Office of the Chief Counsel (OCC), which is the Food and Drug Division of the HHS Office of the General Counsel, is composed of litigators, counselors, and support staff. Litigators handle both civil and criminal enforcement cases, and defend challenges to provisions of the Federal Food, Drug, and Cosmetic Act (FDCA), the implementing regulations, and FDA policies, initiatives, and decisions. The litigators work closely with agency compliance personnel to ensure an adequate evidentiary foundation for enforcement matters, prepare referrals to the Department of Justice, draft memoranda setting out the agency's interpretation of the law, develop case strategy, conduct negotiations, prepare and respond to discovery, and are key participants in hearings, trials, and appellate proceedings. The litigators act as the liaison to the Department of Justice during active litigation, and in many criminal prosecutions have been asked to work as Special Assistant United States Attorneys, assuming primary responsibility for prosecuting violations of the FDCA or related statutes. The litigators frequently work closely with senior officials at the Department of Justice and play an active role in all of FDA's cases, including matters before the United States District Courts, the Courts of Appeal, and the Supreme Court of the United States.

The counselors provide legal services to FDA and HHS officials on matters involving FDA-regulated products, such as drugs, biologics, food, medical devices, cosmetics, veterinary products, radiation-emitting products, and tobacco products. Such services include, for example, review and revision of draft and final regulations, draft and final guidance documents, responses to citizen petitions, draft legislation, press materials, and correspondence. In addition, the counselors advise agency officials on complex medical product approvals and safety issues and food safety and nutrition issues. During emergencies, such as foodborne illness outbreaks, novel influenza epidemics, or potential bioterrorism attacks, the counselors provide legal services essential to the government's effective immediate response.

In addition, the counselors have active roles in agency activities related to Congress. For example, the counselors review agency officials' written congressional testimony and congressional correspondence, analyze pending FDA-related legislation, and help FDA respond to congressional requests for technical assistance or other briefings. The counselors help FDA implement new, as well as longstanding, legislation, which often involves complex legal analyses of intricate statutory provisions. The counselors also participate in FDA's interactions with other Federal agencies (e.g., USDA, EPA, FTC) and with State public health agencies. The counselors also advise FDA officials on their interactions with stakeholders, such as members of the public, health care providers and institutions, regulated firms, and associations representing a broad range of interest groups. The counselors also contribute significantly to the transparency of the agency's actions through interpretation and implementation of the Freedom of Information Act, the Federal Advisory Committee Act, the Administrative Procedure Act, and other administrative law activities.

The OCC litigators and counselors also have central roles in FDA's administrative proceedings, such as clinical investigator disqualification hearings, hearings on product approval withdrawals, and civil money penalty hearings. The litigators and counselors also advise agency enforcement officials on pending compliance issues and review certain warning letters sent to firms and individuals believed to have violated the FDCA or related laws. Support staff assist with all OCC activities through applying their technical skills.

▶ **FDA Attorney Positions**
www.fda.gov/AboutFDA/WorkingatFDA/CareerDescriptions/ucm112708.htm

National Institutes of Health
(9 attorneys, www.nih.gov)

The National Institutes of Health supports biomedical and behavioral research domestically and abroad, conducts research in its own laboratories and clinics, trains research scientists, and develops and disseminates credible, science-based health information to the public.

Department of Homeland Security

Description:
The Department of Homeland Security (DHS) leads the unified national effort to secure the United States. It prevents and deters terrorist attacks and protects against and responds to threats and hazards to the United States. The Department ensures safe and secure borders, welcomes lawful immigrants and visitors, and promotes the free-flow of commerce.

DHS was established by the Homeland Security Act of 2002, (6 U.S.C. 101 note). The Department came into existence on January 24, 2003, and is administered under the supervision and direction of the Secretary of Homeland Security.

The Office of General Counsel integrates lawyers from throughout the Department into a full-service legal team and comprises a headquarters office with subsidiary divisions and the legal programs for eight Department components. The Office of the General Counsel includes the ethics division for the Department.

Address: U.S. Department of Homeland Security
245 Murray Drive, SW
Washington, DC 20528

Website: www.dhs.gov   **Phone**:   202-282-8000

▶ **DHS Office of the General Counsel Honors Program**
www.dhs.gov/xabout/careers/gc_1192223920159.shtm#2

▶ **DHS Office of the General Counsel Summer Law Intern Program**
www.dhs.gov/xabout/careers/gc_1192223920159.shtm#3

▶ **DHS Office of the General Counsel Legal Intern/Extern Program**
www.dhs.gov/xabout/careers/gc_1192223920159.shtm#4

DHS Department	Attorneys	Male	Female	Avg Salary
Bur of Citizenship & Immigration Svc	138	63	75	$136,205
Bur of Customs & Border Enf.	348 (2 L Clerks)	171	177 (2L Clerks)	$107,567
Bur of Immigration & Customs Enf.	896	439	457	$116,011
DHS Headquarters	95	58	37	$133,964
Federal Emergency Management Ag.	67	32	35	$120,319
Fed. Law Enforcement Training Ctr.	24	17	7	$100,734
Office of the Inspector General	9	3	6	$138,534
Transportation Security Admin.	190	94	96	$139,040
U.S. Coast Guard	101 (6 ALJs)	70 (6 ALJs)	31	$120,388
U.S. Secret Service	21	6	15	$126,267
TOTAL	**1,889**	**953**	**936**	**$120,111**

* Table does not include 439 personnel classified as "Hearing and Appeals" with an average salary of $92,801.

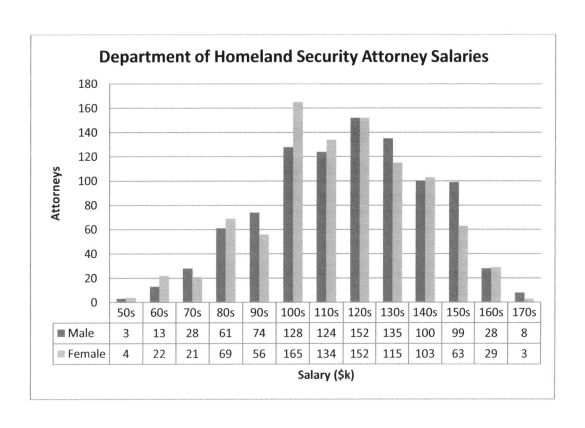

Department of Homeland Security Attorney Salaries

Salary ($k)	50s	60s	70s	80s	90s	100s	110s	120s	130s	140s	150s	160s	170s
Male	3	13	28	61	74	128	124	152	135	100	99	28	8
Female	4	22	21	69	56	165	134	152	115	103	63	29	3

Coast Guard

(101 attorneys, www.uscg.mil)

The United States Coast Guard was established by act of January 28, 1915 (14 U.S.C. 1) and became a component of the Department of Transportation on April 1, 1967, pursuant to the Department of Transportation Act of October 15, 1966. Following the enactment of the Homeland Security Act of 2002, The Coast Guard was transferred from Department of Transportation to the Department of Homeland Security on March 1, 2003 (116 Stat. 2135).

The Coast Guard protects the public, the environment, and U.S. economic interests in the Nation's ports and waterways, along the coast, on international waters, or in any maritime region, as required, to support national security. Among its duties are: search and rescue operations in and over the high seas and navigable waters, maritime law enforcement, marine inspection and licensing, pilotage of the Great Lakes, protection of the marine environment by enforcing the Federal Water Pollution Control Act, ensuring the safety and security of ports and anchorages, maintaining the management of waterways, providing navigational aids, and regulating the construction, maintenance and operation of bridges and causeways across navigable waters.

The Coast Guard Legal Program is a full-service legal support organization, providing legal advice and counsel for any and all requirements placed on service members. This is done within ten general legal practice areas: Criminal Law/Military Justice, Operations, International Activities, Civil Advocacy, Environmental Law, Procurement Law, Internal Organizational Law, Regulations and Administrative Law, Legislative Support and Legal Assistance.

Federal Emergency Management Agency

(67 attorneys, www.fema.gov)

The Federal Emergency Management Agency (FEMA) coordinates the Federal Government's role in preparing for, preventing, mitigating the effects of, responding to, and recovering from all domestic disasters, whether natural or man-made, including acts of terror. FEMA can trace its beginnings to the Congressional Act of 1803. This act, generally considered the first piece of disaster legislation, provided assistance to a New Hampshire town following an extensive fire. In the century that followed, ad hoc legislation was passed more than 100 times in response to hurricanes, earthquakes, floods and other natural disasters.

66

In 2001, the terrorist attacks of September 11th focused the agency on issues of national preparedness and homeland security. The agency coordinated its activities with the newly formed Office of Homeland Security, and FEMA's Office of National Preparedness was given responsibility for helping to ensure that the Nation's first responders were trained and equipped to deal with weapons of mass destruction.

In March 2003, FEMA joined 22 other Federal agencies, programs and offices in becoming the Department of Homeland Security. The new department brought a coordinated approach to national security from emergencies and disasters - both natural and man made. The Post Katrina Emergency Reform Act significantly reorganized FEMA and provided it substantial new authority to remedy gaps that became apparent in the response to Hurricane Katrina in August 2005.

The FEMA Office of Chief Counsel advises the Administrator and all of FEMA's directorates on legal matters related to agency programs and operations.

Federal Law Enforcement Training Center
(24 attorneys, www.fletc.gov)

The Federal Law Enforcement Training Center (FLETC) serves as an interagency law enforcement training organization for dozens of Federal agencies. The FLETC also provides services to State, local, tribal, and international law enforcement agencies. The FLETC is headquartered at Glynco, Georgia.

In addition to Glynco, the FLETC operates two other residential training sites in Artesia, New Mexico and Charleston, South Carolina. The FLETC also operates a non-residential in-service re-qualification and advanced training facility in Cheltenham, Maryland, for use by agencies with large concentrations of personnel in the Washington, D.C. area.

The FLETC has oversight and program management responsibilities at the International Law Enforcement Academies (ILEA) in Gaborone, Botswana, and Bangkok, Thailand. The FLETC also supports training at other ILEAs in Hungary and El Salvador.

Secret Service

(21 attorneys, www.secretservice.gov)

The Secret Service protects the President and other high-level officials and investigates counterfeiting and other financial crimes, including financial institution fraud, identity theft, and computer fraud and computer-based attacks on the financial, banking, and telecommunications infrastructure of the United States.

Transportation Security Administration

(190 attorneys, www.tsa.gov)

The Transportation Security Administration (TSA) was created in the wake of 9/11 to strengthen the security of the nation's transportation systems while ensuring the freedom of movement for people and commerce. Originally established as a sub-agency of the Department of Transportation, TSA was transferred to the Department of Homeland Security in March of 2003. TSA employs a risk-based strategy to secure U.S. transportation systems, working closely with stakeholders in aviation, rail, transit, highway, and pipeline sectors, as well as the partners in the law enforcement and intelligence community.

The TSA Chief Counsel advises senior officials on all legal matters relating to protection of the Nation's transportation systems.

U.S. Citizenship and Immigration Services

(138 attorneys, www.uscis.gov)

On March 1, 2003, U.S. Citizenship and Immigration Services (USCIS) officially assumed responsibility for the immigration service functions of the Federal government. The USCIS was formed to enhance the security and improve the efficiency of national immigration services by exclusively focusing on the administration of benefit applications. Immigration and Customs Enforcement and Customs and Border Protection, components within DHS, handle immigration enforcement and border security functions.

U.S. Customs and Border Protection

(348 attorneys, www.cbp.gov)

The U.S. Customs and Border Protection (CBP) was established on March 1, 2003 in the Directorate for Border and Transportation Security, Department of Homeland Security.

CBP is responsible for guarding nearly 7,000 miles of land border the United States shares with Canada and Mexico and 2,000 miles of coastal waters surrounding the Florida peninsula and off the coast of Southern California. The agency also protects 95,000 miles of maritime border in partnership with the United States Coast Guard.

CBP's priority mission is to prevent terrorists and terrorist weapons from entering the United States and ensuring the security of America's borders and ports of entry. CPB strives to maintain this line of defense while allowing legitimate travel and trade that is vital to the economy.

CBP is responsible for apprehending individuals attempting to enter the United States illegally; stemming the flow of illegal drugs and other contraband; protecting agricultural and economic interests from harmful pests and diseases; protecting American businesses from theft of their intellectual property; and regulating and facilitating international trade, collecting import duties, and enforcing U.S. trade laws.

U.S. Immigrations and Customs Enforcement
(896 attorneys, www.ice.gov)

U.S. Immigration and Customs Enforcement (ICE) is the largest investigative agency in the DHS. Formed in 2003 as part of the Federal Government's response to the 9/11 attacks, ICE's primary mission is to protect national security, public safety and the integrity of the U.S. borders through the criminal and civil enforcement of Federal laws governing border control, customs, trade and immigration.

ICE has approximately 19,000 employees in over 400 offices worldwide and an annual budget of more than $5 billion. The agency's law enforcement authorities encompass more than 400 Federal statutes that ICE is responsible for enforcing in its commitment to ensuring national security and public safety.

Attorneys based across the country are responsible for representing ICE in removal proceedings before immigration courts and the Board of Immigration Appeals. In addition, the ICE legal program handles numerous enforcement components on issues ranging from customs law to Fourth Amendment search and seizure issues.

▶ **ICE Office of the Principal Legal Advisor Externship Program**
www.ice.gov/doclib/about/offices/opla/pdf/externship.pdf

Department of Housing and Urban Development

Robert C. Weaver Federal Building. Photos: U.S. GSA by Ben Schnall

Description:

The Department of Housing and Urban Development (HUD) is the principal Federal agency responsible for programs concerned with the Nation's housing needs, fair housing opportunities, and improvement and development of the Nation's communities.

HUD was established in 1965 by the Department of Housing and Urban Development Act (42 U.S.C. 3532–3537). It was created to:

- administer the principal programs that provide assistance for housing and for the development of the Nation's communities;
- encourage the solution of housing and community development problems through States and localities; and
- encourage the maximum contributions that may be made by vigorous private homebuilding and mortgage lending industries, both primary and secondary, to housing, community development, and the national economy.

Address: Department of Housing and Urban Development
451 Seventh Street SW
Washington, DC 20410

Website: www.hud.gov   **Phone**:   202-708-1422

Dept. of Housing & Urban Dev.	Attorneys	Male	Female	Avg Salary
Asst. Secy. for Policy Dev. & Res.	1	1	-	$126,693
Ofc. of Sr. Coord. for Great Plains	16	10	6	$104,199
Ofc. of Sr. Coord. for Mid-Atlantic	22	12	10	$114,569
Ofc. of Sr. Coord. for Midwest	36 (2 L Clerk)	17	19	$115,008
Ofc. of Sr. Coord. for New England	19 (1 L Clerk)	11	8	$119,834
Ofc. of Sr. Coord. for NY/NJ	24	12	12	$122,619
Ofc. of Sr. Coord. for Northwest/AL	11	3	8	$111.486
Ofc. of Sr. Coord. for Pacific/Hawaii	28 (1 L Clerk)	9	19	$114,658
Ofc. of Sr. Coord. for Rocky Mount.	12	5	7	$110,923
Ofc. of Sr. Coord. for Southeast/Carib	37 (1 L Clerk)	12	25	$111,400
Ofc. of Sr. Coord. for Southwest	27 (1 L Clerk)	15	12	$116,394
Office of the General Counsel	176 (12 L Clerk)	78	98	$120,745 Atty:$125,117 LC: $60,989
Office of the Inspector General	4	4	-	$129,282
Office of the Chief Financial Officer	3	3	-	$126,627
Office of the Secretary of HUD	6 (2 ALJ) (2 L Clerk)	4	2	$120,300 Atty:$140,970 ALJ:$158,942 LC: $60,989
TOTAL	**422**	**196**	**226**	**$117,551**

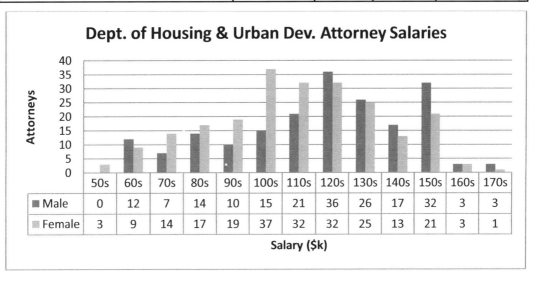

Dept. of Housing & Urban Dev. Attorney Salaries

	50s	60s	70s	80s	90s	100s	110s	120s	130s	140s	150s	160s	170s
Male	0	12	7	14	10	15	21	36	26	17	32	3	3
Female	3	9	14	17	19	37	32	32	25	13	21	3	1

Salary ($k)

Office of General Counsel

(176 attorneys, www.hud.gov/offices/ogc/)

The Office of General Counsel (OGC) helps HUD accomplish its mission of assuring decent and affordable housing, enabling all Americans to achieve homeownership, providing resources for communities to build strong neighborhoods, preventing homelessness, and enforcing fair housing laws. OGC attorneys provide legal opinions, advice and services with respect to all departmental programs and activities. The OGC also includes the Enforcement Center.

The Departmental Enforcement Center (DEC) focuses on assuring the highest standards of ethics, management and accountability in the resolution of HUD's troubled properties. The DEC is comprised of the Office of the Director, the Compliance Division, the Operations Division and Satellite Offices.

▶ HUD Legal Honors Program

www.hud.gov/offices/ogc/   202-708-0290   Legalhonors@hud.gov

Office of the Inspector General

(4 attorneys, www.hud.gov/offices/oig/)

The Office of Inspector General's mission is independent and objective reporting to the Secretary and the Congress for the purpose of bringing about positive change in the integrity, efficiency, and effectiveness of HUD operations.

Office of the Chief Financial Officer

(4 attorneys, www.hud.gov/offices/cfo/)

HUD is tasked with employing sound financial management practices to help meet the Department's mission to promote adequate and affordable housing, economic opportunity, and a suitable living environment free from discrimination.

Office of the Chief Financial Officer (CFO) staff functions include: accounting, budget, and financial management for HUD's budget appropriation. In addition, CFO financial systems process millions of transactions annually to support HUD projects.

Department of the Interior

Description:
The Department of the Interior (DOI) protects and provides access to the Nation's natural and cultural heritage and honors the Nation's trust responsibilities to tribes and its commitments to island communities.

The Department of the Interior was created by act of March 3, 1849 (43 U.S.C. 1451), which transferred to it the General Land Office, the Office of Indian Affairs, the Pension Office, and the Patent Office. It was reorganized by Reorganization Plan No. 3 of 1950, as amended (5 U.S.C. app.).

The Department manages the Nation's public lands and minerals, national parks, national wildlife refuges, and western water resources and upholds Federal trust responsibilities to Indian tribes and Alaskan natives. It is also responsible for migratory wildlife conservation; historic preservation; endangered species conservation; surface-mined lands protection and restoration; mapping geological, hydrological, and biological science for the Nation; and for financial and technical assistance for the insular areas. The insular areas include the territories of American Samoa, Guam, and the U.S. Virgin Islands and the Freely Associated States of Micronesia, the Republic of the Marshall Islands, and the Republic of Palau.

The Solicitor is the chief general counsel for Interior and represents the Department in administrative and judicial litigation and meetings, negotiations and other contracts with Congress, Federal agencies, States, tribes and the public.

Address: U.S. Department of the Interior
1849 C Street, NW
Washington, DC 20240

Website: www.doi.gov   **Phone**:   202-208-3100

Department of the Interior	Attorneys	Male	Female	Avg Salary
Office of the Inspector General	9	4	5	$141,644
Office of the Secretary of the Interior	79	41	38	$133,204
Office of the Solicitor	327	166	161	$122,788
TOTAL	**415**	**211**	**204**	**$125,180**

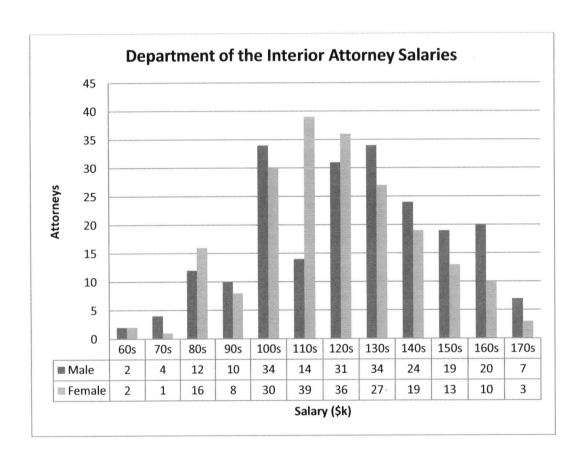

	60s	70s	80s	90s	100s	110s	120s	130s	140s	150s	160s	170s
Male	2	4	12	10	34	14	31	34	24	19	20	7
Female	2	1	16	8	30	39	36	27	19	13	10	3

Office of the Inspector General
(9 attorneys, www.doioig.gov)

The mission of the Office of the Inspector General (OIG) is to provide independent oversight in order to promote integrity, accountability, effectiveness, and efficiency within the programs, operations, and management of DOI. The OIG accomplishes its mission by performing audits, investigations, evaluations, inspections, and other reviews of the Department's programs and operations. It independently and objectively identifies risks and vulnerabilities that directly affect, or could impact, DOI's mission and the vast responsibilities of its bureaus and entities. The office targets its resources by identifying and developing solutions for the Department's most serious management and program challenges.

Office of the Solicitor
(327 attorneys, www.doi.gov/solicitor/)

With an emphasis on high ethical standards, excellence in public service and the delivery of quality legal services, the Office performs the legal work for the United States Department of the Interior, manages the Department's Ethics Office and resolves Freedom of Information Act appeals. With more than four hundred total employees, three hundred of which are attorneys licensed in forty States, the Office strives to provide sound legal services to fulfill the Department's diverse and wide-ranging mission.

▶ DOI Office of the Solicitor Honors Attorney Program
www.doi.gov/solicitor/honors_attorney.html   202-208-5764

Department of Justice

Description:
The Department of Justice (DOJ) serves as counsel on behalf of the citizens of the United States. It represents them in enforcing the law in the public interest. Through its thousands of lawyers, investigators, and agents, the Department plays the key role in protection against criminals and subversion, ensuring healthy business competition, safeguarding the consumer, and enforcing drug, immigration, and naturalization laws.

The DOJ was established by act of June 22, 1870 (28 U.S.C. 501, 503, 509 note), with the Attorney General as its head. The affairs and activities of the DOJ are generally directed by the Attorney General.

The Judiciary Act of 1789 created the Office of the Attorney General which evolved over the years into the head of the DOJ and chief law enforcement officer of the Federal Government. The Attorney General represents the United States in legal matters generally and gives advice and opinions to the President and to the heads of the executive departments of the Government when so requested. In matters of exceptional gravity or importance the Attorney General appears in person before the Supreme Court. Since the 1870 Act that established the DOJ as an executive department of the government of the United States, the Attorney General has guided the one of the world's largest legal organizations and the central agency for enforcement of Federal laws.

Address: U.S. Department of Justice
950 Pennsylvania Avenue, NW
Washington, DC 20530-0001

Website: www.justice.gov   **Phone**:   202-514-2000

▶ **DOJ Antitrust Div – Legal Internships & Attorney General's Honors Prog.**
www.justice.gov/atr/contact/jobs_attorneys.htm

▶ **DOJ Civil Division – Volunteer Internships**
www.justice.gov/civil/studentopportunities/volunteers.htm   202-307-0261

▶ **DOJ Civil Rights Division – Volunteer Internship Opportunities**
www.justice.gov/crt/vol_intern_opps.php

▶ **DOJ Community Relations Service**
www.justice.gov/crs/crsinternship.htm

▶ **DOJ Criminal Division – Volunteer Legal Internships**
www.justice.gov/criminal/employment/internships.html

▶ **DOJ Environmental & Natural Resources Division – Attorney Employment**
www.justice.gov/enrd/3008.htm

▶ **DOJ Environmental & Natural Resources Division – Legal Internships**
www.justice.gov/enrd/3004.htm

▶ **DOJ Exec. Office for Immigration Review, Attorney General's Honors Program**
www.justice.gov/eoir/Honor&SLIOCIJ.htm

▶ **DOJ Ofc. of Legal Counsel– Attorney-Advisors & Summer Law Internships**
www.justice.gov/olc/opportunities.htm

▶ **DOJ Office of Legal Policy –Volunteer / Work-Study Law Clerk Positions**
www.justice.gov/olp/lawclerk.htm

▶ **DOJ Office of the Solicitor General – Attorney Assistants**
www.justice.gov/osg/opportunities.html

▶ **DOJ Office of the Solicitor General – Bristol Fellowships**
www.justice.gov/osg/opportunities.html#bristow

▶ **DOJ Office of the Solicitor General – Summer Legal Internship Program**
www.justice.gov/osg/opportunities.html#summer

▶ **DOJ Professional Responsibility Advisory Office – Legal Internships**
www.justice.gov/prao/internship.htm

Department of Justice	Attorneys	Male	Female	Avg Salary
Alcohol, Tobacco, Firearms & Explosives	72	36	36	$128,683
Bureau of Prisons / Fed Prison System	166	85	81	$117,509
Community Relations Service	2	1	1	$137,015
Drug Enforcement Agency	94	52	42	$140,912
Exec Ofc US Attorney & Off US Atty	5,805	3,713	2,092	$132,646
Exec Ofc for Immigration Review	508	255	253	$138,204
Federal Bureau of Investigation	181	101	80	$136,385
Office of Justice Programs	34	15	19	$132,943
Office of the Inspector General	18	12	6	$152,594
Offices, Boards & Divisions	3,290	1,930	1,360	$137,733
U.S. Marshals Service	18	12	6	$148,078
U.S. Trustee Program	290	158	132	$130,533
TOTAL	10,478	6,370	4,108	$134,389
Percent of Positions		61%	39%	

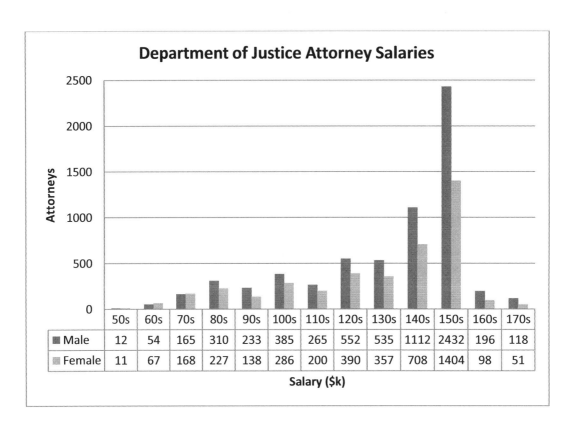

	50s	60s	70s	80s	90s	100s	110s	120s	130s	140s	150s	160s	170s
Male	12	54	165	310	233	385	265	552	535	1112	2432	196	118
Female	11	67	168	227	138	286	200	390	357	708	1404	98	51

Bureau of Alcohol, Tobacco, Firearms & Explosives
(72 attorneys, www.atf.gov)

The Bureau of Alcohol, Tobacco, Firearms and Explosives (ATF) is responsible for enforcing Federal criminal laws and regulating the firearms and explosives industries. ATF was initially established by Department of Treasury Order No. 221, effective July 1, 1972, which transferred the functions, powers, and duties arising under laws relating to alcohol, tobacco, firearms, and explosives from the Internal Revenue Service to ATF. The Homeland Security Act of 2002 (6 U.S.C. 531) transferred certain functions and authorities of ATF to the Department of Justice and established it under its current name. ATF works, directly and through partnerships, to investigate and reduce violent crime involving firearms and explosives, acts of arson, and illegal trafficking of alcohol and tobacco products.

The Bureau provides training and support to its Federal, State, local, and international law enforcement partners and works primarily in 23 field divisions across the 50 States, Puerto Rico, the U.S. Virgin Islands, and Guam. It also has foreign offices in Mexico, Canada, Colombia, and France.

ATF Office of Chief Counsel attorneys provide legal advice and services to the Bureau nationwide in support of programs and operations. A number of attorneys are located in ATF Headquarters in Washington D.C., where they provide legal advice and strategic guidance to Bureau leadership. Headquarters attorneys are divided into four practice groups, including: Litigation; Administration and Ethics; Disclosure, Forfeiture and Criminal Law; and Firearms, Explosives, and Arson. ATF lawyers also are based in field offices, where they work directly with ATF agents and industry operations investigators on active cases.

▶ ATF Office of Chief Counsel - Attorneys and Summer Law Intern Program
www.atf.gov/careers/attorneys/

Bureau of Prisons / Federal Prison System
(166 attorneys, www.bop.gov)

The mission of the Bureau of Prisons is to protect society by confining offenders in the controlled environments of prisons and community-based facilities that are safe, humane, cost-efficient, and appropriately secure, and that provide work and other self-improvement opportunities to assist offenders in becoming law-abiding citizens. The Bureau has its Central Office in Washington, DC. The Central Office is divided into nine divisions, including the National Institute of Corrections.

▶ **BOP Office of Legal Service Recruitment Video**
www.bop.gov/common/movies/Legal_sm.wmv

▶ **Federal Bureau of Prisons – Summer Law Intern Program**
www.bop.gov/jobs/students/index.jsp

Drug Enforcement Agency
(94 attorneys, www.justice.gov/dea/index.htm)

The Drug Enforcement Administration (DEA) is the lead Federal agency in enforcing narcotics and controlled substances laws and regulations. The DEA also enforces the Federal money laundering and bulk currency smuggling statutes when the funds involved in the transactions or smuggling are derived from the sale of narcotics. It was created in July 1973 by Reorganization Plan No. 2 of 1973 (5 U.S.C. app.).

The DEA enforces the provisions of the controlled substances and chemical diversion and trafficking laws and regulations of the United States, and operates on a worldwide basis. It presents cases to the criminal and civil justice systems of the United States, or any other competent jurisdiction, on those significant organizations and their members involved in cultivation, production, smuggling, distribution, laundering of proceeds, or diversion of controlled substances appearing in or destined for illegal traffic in the United States. The DEA disrupts and dismantles these organizations by arresting their members, confiscating their drugs, and seizing their assets; and creates, manages, and supports enforcement-related programs, domestically and internationally, aimed at reducing the availability of and demand for illicit controlled substances.

▶**DEA Professional Career Opportunities (including attorneys)**
www.justice.gov/dea/resources/careers/opportunity/professional-and-admin.html

Executive Office for U.S. Attorney & U.S. Attorneys Offices
(5,805 attorneys, www.justice.gov/usao/eousa/)

The Executive Office for United States Attorneys (EOUSA) was created on April 6, 1953, by AG Order No. 8-53 to provide for close liaison between the DOJ in Washington, D.C., and the 93 United States Attorneys located throughout the 50

States, the District of Columbia, Guam, the Marianas Islands, Puerto Rico, and the U. S. Virgin Islands.

The United States Attorneys serve as the Nation's principal litigators under the direction of the Attorney General. United States Attorneys are appointed by, and serve at the discretion of, the President, with advice and consent of the Senate. One United States Attorney is assigned to each of the judicial districts, with the exception of Guam and the Northern Mariana Islands where a single United States Attorney serves in both districts. Each United States Attorney is the chief Federal law enforcement officer of the United States within his or her particular jurisdiction.

United States Attorneys conduct most of the trial work in which the United States is a party. The United States Attorneys have three statutory responsibilities under Title 28, Section 547 of the United States Code:
- the prosecution of criminal cases brought by the Federal government;
- the prosecution and defense of civil cases in which the United States is a party; and
- the collection of debts owed the Federal government which are administratively uncollectible.

Although the distribution of caseload varies between districts, each has every category of cases and handles a mixture of simple and complex litigation. Each United States Attorney exercises wide discretion in the use of his/her resources to further the priorities of the local jurisdictions and needs of their communities.

►U.S. Attorneys Employment & Attorney General's Honors Program
www.justice.gov/usao/employment/index.html

Executive Office for Immigration Review
(508 attorneys, www.justice.gov/eoir/)

The Executive Office for Immigration Review, under a delegation of authority from the Attorney General, is charged with adjudicating matters brought under various immigration statutes to its three administrative tribunals: the Board of Immigration Appeals, the Office of the Chief Immigration Judge, and the Office of the Chief Administrative Hearing Officer.

► Office of the Chief Immigration Judge – Attorney General's Honors Program & Summer Law Intern Program

Federal Bureau of Investigation

(181 attorneys, www.fbi.gov)

The Federal Bureau of Investigation (FBI) is the principal investigative arm of the DOJ. It is primarily charged with gathering and reporting facts, locating witnesses, and compiling evidence in cases involving Federal jurisdiction. It also provides law enforcement leadership and assistance to State and international law enforcement agencies.

The FBI was established in 1908 by the Attorney General, who directed that DOJ investigations be handled by its own staff. The Bureau is charged with investigating all violations of Federal law except those that have been assigned by legislative enactment or otherwise to another Federal agency. Its jurisdiction includes a wide range of responsibilities in the national security, criminal, and civil fields. Priority has been assigned to areas such as counterterrorism, counterintelligence, cyber-crimes, internationally and nationally organized crime/drug matters, and financial crimes.

The FBI also offers cooperative services to local, State, and international law enforcement agencies. These services include fingerprint identification, laboratory examination, police training, the Law Enforcement Online communication and information service for use by the law enforcement community, the National Crime Information Center, and the National Center for the Analysis of Violent Crime.

The Office of General Counsel (OGC) provides timely and comprehensive advice to the Director, other FBI officials and divisions, and field offices on all aspects of law, particularly in the areas of national security law, the Foreign Intelligence Surveillance Act process, criminal investigative law, forfeiture law, information law and policy, procurement and contracting law, fiscal law and policy, and all areas of litigation to which the FBI is involved.

In addition to providing legal advice as requested, OGC reviews the legal sufficiency of sensitive Title III affidavits, ensures that electronic surveillance techniques are used in compliance with the FISA, and supports Federal criminal prosecutions. OGC coordinates the defense of the FBI and its employees in civil actions which arise out of the FBI's investigative mission and personnel matters.

OGC also provides legal training for the FBI, the National Academy, and other law enforcement groups.

▶Federal Bureau of Investigations Honors Internship Program
www.fbi.gov/jobs (click on Internship Programs)

Office of Justice Programs
(34 attorneys, www.ojp.usdoj.gov)

The Office of Justice Programs (OJP) provides innovative leadership to Federal, State, local, and tribal justice systems, by disseminating state-of-the art knowledge and practices across America, and providing grants for the implementation of these crime fighting strategies. Because most of the responsibility for crime control and prevention falls to law enforcement officers in States, cities, and neighborhoods, the Federal government can be effective in these areas only to the extent that it can enter into partnerships with these officers. Therefore, OJP does not directly carry out law enforcement and justice activities. Instead, OJP works in partnership with the justice community to identify the most pressing crime-related challenges confronting the justice system and to provide information, training, coordination, and innovative strategies and approaches for addressing these challenges.

Office of the Inspector General
(18 attorneys, www.justice.gov/oig/)

The Office of the Inspector General (OIG) consists of an immediate office, which is comprised of the Inspector General, the Deputy Inspector General, and the Office of the General Counsel and five major components. Each of the Divisions is headed by an Assistant Inspector General. The five OIG divisions include Audit, Investigations, Evaluations and Inspections, Oversight and Review, and Management and Planning.

U.S. Marshals Service
(18 attorneys, www.usmarshals.gov)

The U.S. Marshals Service is the Nation's oldest Federal law enforcement agency. Federal Marshals have served the country since 1789, oftentimes in unseen but critical ways. To this day, the Marshals Service occupies a central position in the Federal justice system. It is the enforcement arm of the Federal courts, and as such, it is involved in most Federal law enforcement initiatives.

Presidentially appointed, U.S. Marshals direct the activities of 94 districts — one for each Federal judicial district. More than 3,000 Deputy U.S. Marshals and Criminal Investigators form the backbone of the agency. Among their many duties, they apprehend Federal fugitives, protect the Federal judiciary, operate the Witness Security Program, transport Federal prisoners and seize property acquired by criminals through illegal activities.

U.S. Trustee Program
(290 attorneys, www.justice.gov/ust/)

The United States Trustee Program is a component of the Department of Justice that seeks to promote the efficiency and protect the integrity of the Federal bankruptcy system. To further the public interest in the just, speedy and economical resolution of cases filed under the Bankruptcy Code, the Program monitors the conduct of bankruptcy parties and private estate trustees, oversees related administrative functions, and acts to ensure compliance with applicable laws and procedures. It also identifies and helps investigate bankruptcy fraud and abuse in coordination with United States Attorneys, the FBI, and other law enforcement agencies.

► Advertisements of Vacancies for Private Bankruptcy Estate Trustees
www.justice.gov/ust/eo/private_trustee/vacancies/index.htm
(Qualifications: http://cfr.vlex.com/vid/58-qualification-membership-trustees-19677744)

Department of Labor

Description:

The Department of Labor (DOL) fosters and promotes the welfare of the job seekers, wage earners, and retirees of the United States, by improving their working conditions, advancing their opportunities for profitable employment, protecting their retirement and health care benefits, helping employers find workers, strengthening free collective bargaining, and tracking changes in employment, prices, and other national economic measurements. In carrying out this mission, the Department administers a variety of Federal labor laws including those that guarantee workers' rights to safe and healthful working conditions; a minimum hourly wage and overtime pay; freedom from employment discrimination; unemployment insurance; and other income support.

The DOL was created by act of March 4, 1913 (29 U.S.C. 551). A Bureau of Labor was first created by Congress by act of June 24, 1884, in the Interior Department. The Bureau of Labor later became independent as a Department of Labor without executive rank by act of June 13, 1888. It again returned to bureau status in the Department of Commerce and Labor, which was created by act of February 14, 1903 (15 U.S.C. 1501; 29 U.S.C. 1 note).

Address: U.S. Department of Labor
200 Constitution Avenue, NW
Washington, DC 20210

Website: www.dol.gov   **Phone**:   866-487-2365

Department of Labor	Attorneys	Male	Female	Avg Salary
Office of the Secretary of Labor	153	74 (35 ALJ)	79 (9 ALJ)	$123,543 Atty: $125,193 ALJ: $161,015 Clerk:$59,972
Office of the Inspector General	4	2	2	$144,766
Office of the Solicitor	489	233 (2 L Clerk)	256 (1 L Clerk)	$127,175 Atty: $127,587 Clerk: $60,378
TOTAL	646	309	337	$126,424
Percent of Positions		48%	52%	

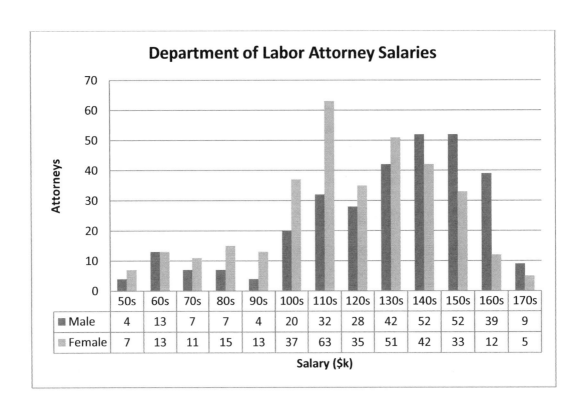

Department of Labor Attorney Salaries

	50s	60s	70s	80s	90s	100s	110s	120s	130s	140s	150s	160s	170s
Male	4	13	7	7	4	20	32	28	42	52	52	39	9
Female	7	13	11	15	13	37	63	35	51	42	33	12	5

Salary ($k)

Office of Inspector General
(4 attorneys, www.oig.dol.gov)

The Office of Inspector General (OIG) at the DOL conducts audits and evaluations to review the effectiveness, efficiency, economy, and integrity of all DOL programs and operations, including those performed by its contractors and grantees. This work is conducted in order to determine whether: the programs and operations are in compliance with the applicable laws and regulations; DOL resources are efficiently and economically being utilized; and DOL programs achieve their intended results.

In addition, the OIG is unique among Inspectors General because it has an "external" program function to conduct criminal investigations to combat the influence of labor racketeering and organized crime in the Nation's labor unions. It conducts labor racketeering investigations in three areas: employee benefit plans, labor-management relations, and internal union affairs.

Office of the Solicitor
(489 attorneys, www.dol.gov/sol/)

The Office of the Solicitor's mission is to meet the legal service demands of the entire DOL. As the Secretary of Labor and other Department officials seek to accomplish the Department's overall mission and to further specific priorities, the Office of the Solicitor (SOL) provides legal advice regarding how to achieve those goals. In doing so, SOL ensures that the Nation's labor laws are forcefully and fairly applied to protect the Nation's workers.

SOL fulfills its mission by representing the Secretary and the client agencies in all necessary litigation, including both enforcement actions and defensive litigation, and in alternative dispute resolution activities; by assisting in the development of regulations, standards and legislative proposals; and by providing legal opinions and advice concerning all the Department's activities.

▶ **DOL Office of the Solicitor – Attorney Positions**
www.dol.gov/sol/resumes.htm

▶ **DOL Office of the Solicitor Honors Program**
www.dol.gov/sol/honorsprogram.htm

Department of State

Harry S. Truman Federal Building. Photo: Carol M. Highsmith Photography, Inc.

Description:

The Department of State advises the President in the formulation and execution of foreign policy and promotes the long-range security and well-being of the United States. The Department determines and analyzes the facts relating to American overseas interests, makes recommendations on policy and future action, and takes the necessary steps to carry out established policy. In so doing, the Department engages in continuous consultations with the American public, the Congress, other U.S. departments and agencies, and foreign governments; negotiates treaties and agreements with foreign nations; speaks for the United States in the United Nations and other international organizations in which the United States participates; and represents the United States at international conferences.

The Department of State was established by act of July 27, 1789, as the Department of Foreign Affairs and was renamed Department of State by act of September 15, 1789 (22 U.S.C. 2651 note).

The Office of the Legal Adviser furnishes advice on all legal issues, domestic and international, arising in the course of the Department's work. This includes assisting Department principals and policy officers in formulating and implementing the foreign policies of the U.S., and promoting the adherence to and development of international law and its institutions as a fundamental element of those policies.

Attorneys in the Office are at the forefront of the important international issues faced by our country, whether they are working to respond to humanitarian crises, to prevent human rights abuses, to promote international trade and resolve international disputes, to create a more livable world, or to help foster peace and security. They work directly with high-level U.S. and foreign officials, the Congress, and the White House staff. While almost all of the Office's attorneys are based in Washington, their work may require them to travel overseas on a "temporary duty" basis to most anywhere in the world for bilateral and multilateral negotiations, dispute resolution efforts, or an unlimited range of other diplomatic missions.

Attorneys negotiate, draft and interpret international agreements involving a wide range of matters, such as peace initiatives, arms control discussions, trade-liberalization agreements, international commodity agreements, consular conventions, and private law conventions on subjects such as judicial cooperation and recognition of foreign judgments. They also work with Department officials on legislative initiatives and draft and interpret domestic statutes, Departmental regulations, Executive Orders, and other legal documents. They represent or assist in representing the U.S. in meetings of international organizations and conferences and many UN programs and represent the U.S. before international tribunals such as the International Court of Justice and the Iran-U.S. Claims Tribunal, as well as in international arbitrations. The attorneys work closely with the Department of Justice in litigation in the U.S. and foreign countries affecting the Department's interests and have had increasing opportunities to represent the Department in domestic courts and administrative courts before the Foreign Service Grievance Board, the Merit Systems Protection Board, the Equal Opportunity Employment Commission, and in contract disputes, Boards of Contract Appeals.

The Office is comprised of approximately 175 permanent attorneys and about 100 support staff, including paralegal specialists, treaty analysts, secretaries, and general administrative personnel. Although all are stationed in Washington, DC, attorneys from the Office also fill the Legal Counsel and Deputy Attorney positions at U.S. Missions in Geneva and The Hague. On occasion, the office provides attorneys for other overseas posts.

Address: U.S. Department of State
2201 C Street, NW
Washington, DC 20520

Website: www.state.gov   **Phone**:   202-647-4000

▶ **Practicing Law in the Office of the Legal Adviser**
www.state.gov/s/l/3190.htm

▶ **Office of the Legal Adviser –Law Student Summer Intern Program**
www.state.gov/s/l/3190.htm#summer

▶ **Office of the Legal Adviser –Law Student Work-Study (Extern) Program**
www.state.gov/s/l/3190.htm#work

Contact the Offices below for other opportunities for law students:
▶ Office of the Inspector General – Internships (2L)
▶ Office of Civil Rights – Internships
▶ Office of War Crimes Issues – Internships

▶ **Programs for Graduate & Post-Graduate Students (including law):**
http://careers.state.gov/students/gpg_students.html

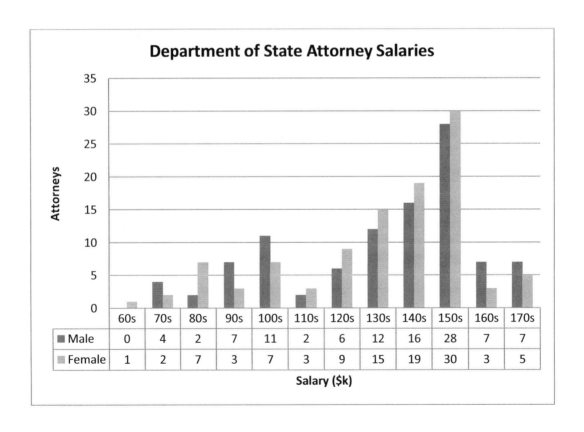

Department of State Attorney Salaries

	60s	70s	80s	90s	100s	110s	120s	130s	140s	150s	160s	170s
Male	0	4	2	7	11	2	6	12	16	28	7	7
Female	1	2	7	3	7	3	9	15	19	30	3	5

Salary ($k)

Department of Transportation

Description:

The U.S. Department of Transportation (DOT) establishes the Nation's overall transportation policy. Under its umbrella are eleven administrations whose jurisdictions include highway planning, development, and construction; motor carrier safety; urban mass transit; railroads; aviation; and the safety of waterways, ports, highways, and oil and gas pipelines. Decisions made by the Department in conjunction with the appropriate State and local officials strongly affect other programs such as land planning, energy conservation, scarce resource utilization, and technological change.

The DOT was established by act of October 15, 1966, as amended (49 U.S.C. 102 and 102 note), "to assure the coordinated, effective administration of the transportation programs of the Federal Government" and to develop "national transportation policies and programs conducive to the provision of fast, safe, efficient, and convenient transportation at the lowest cost consistent therewith." It became operational in April 1967 and was comprised of elements transferred from eight other major departments and agencies.

The General Counsel serves as the Chief Legal Officer of the Department, with final authority on questions of law. The General Counsel is the legal advisor to the Secretary, and is responsible for the supervision, coordination and review of the legal work of the lawyers throughout DOT. The General Counsel is responsible for the Office of Aviation Consumer Protection and Enforcement, and also coordinates the Department's legislative efforts, regulatory program, and involvement in legal proceedings before other agencies, as well as various operational and international legal matters.

Address: U.S. Department of Transportation
1200 New Jersey Avenue, SE
Washington, DC 20590

Website: www.dot.gov   **Phone**:   202-366-4000

U.S. Department of Transportation - Office of General Counsel

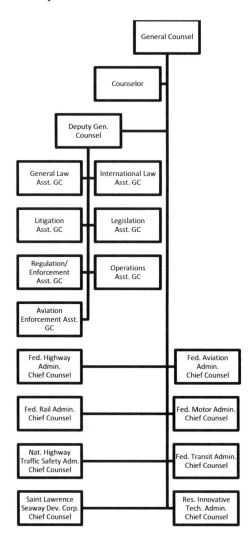

▶ **DOL Honors Attorney Program**
www.dot.gov/ost/ogc/HONORS/

▶ **DOT –Law Student Internships**
www.dot.gov/ost/ogc/org/interns.html

> ▶ Office of General Law
> ▶ Office of International Law
> ▶ Office of Litigation
> ▶ Office of Legislation
> ▶ Office of Regulation and Enforcement
> ▶ Office of Aviation Enforcement and Proceedings
> ▶ Center for Dispute Resolution

► **DOT - Agency Opportunities for Students and Recent Graduates**
http://careers.dot.gov/stuopp.html

► **DOT – Cooperative Education Program**
http://careers.dot.gov/stu_coop.html

Department of Transportation	Attorneys	Male	Female	Avg Salary
Federal Aviation Administration	197	107	90	$131,700
Federal Highway Administration	52	20	32 (2 L Clerk)	$127,954
Federal Motor Carrier Safety Admin.	27	17	10	$121,505
Federal Railroad Administration	34	19	15	$117,662
Federal Transit Administration	23	10	13	$129,967
Maritime Administration	20	12	8	$127,214
Natl. Highway Traffic Safety Adm	26	17	9	$115,748
Ofc. of the Secy. of Transportation	66	38 (3 ALJ) (1 L Clerk)	28 (1 L Clerk)	$140,623
Office of Inspector General	12	8	4	$115,142
Pipeline/Hazardous Materials Safety Adm.	27	12	15	$105,805
Research & Innovative Tech. Adm	7	5	2	$128,452
St. Lawrence Seaway Dev. Corp.	1	-	1	$134,113
Surface Transportation Board	48	24	24	$135,985
TOTAL	540	289	251	$128,709
Percent of Positions		54%	46%	

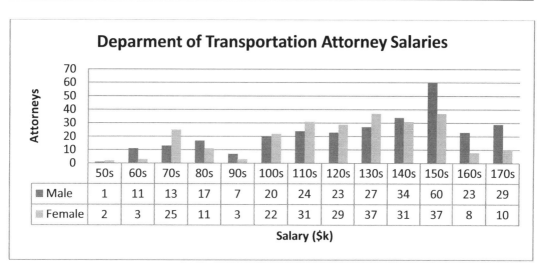

Federal Aviation Administration

(197 attorneys, www.faa.gov)

The mission of the Federal Aviation Administration (FAA) is to provide the safest, most efficient aerospace system in the world.

The FAA Office of the Chief Counsel supports the Agency's mission by furnishing timely and responsive legal services to the FAA Administrator and all Agency organizations at the Headquarters, Regional and Center levels. The principal areas of the Chief Counsel's legal practice include:

- Airports and Environmental Law
- Enforcement & Compliance
- Ethics
- International Affairs & Legal Policy
- Legislation
- Litigation & General Legal Services
- Office of Dispute Resolution for Acquisition
- Personnel & Labor Law
- Procurement
- Regulations

Components of the Office also serve as the FAA Administrator's adjudicative forums for civil penalty and acquisition disputes. Attorneys represent the agency before a variety of forums, including:

- National Transportation Safety Board
- Merit Systems Protection Board
- Equal Employment Opportunity Commission
- FAA's Office of Dispute Resolution for Acquisition
- United States Federal courts

The Counsel's office also works closely with the Office of the General Counsel of the DOT on issues that are common to modal administrations or that are of national significance to the aviation industry.

▶ FAA Office of the Chief Counsel Law Honors Intern Program
www.faa.gov/about/office_org/headquarters_offices/agc/intern/

Federal Highway Administration

(52 attorneys, www.fhwa.dot.gov)

The Federal Highway Administration (FHWA) is charged with the broad responsibility of ensuring that America's roads and highways continue to be the safest and most technologically up-to-date. Although State, local, and tribal governments own most of the Nation's highways, FHWA provides financial and technical support to them for constructing, improving, and preserving America's highway system. FHWA's annual budget of more than $30 billion is funded by fuel and motor vehicle excise taxes. The budget is primarily divided between two programs: Federal-aid funding to State and local governments; and Federal Lands Highways funding for national parks, national forests, Indian lands, and other land under Federal stewardship.

The FHWA Office of Chief Counsel provides legal advice and services regarding all aspects of FHWA's programs and the representation of FHWA in legal or administrative proceedings. The Office of Chief Counsel works with State and local government transportation attorneys and other customers to enhance the understanding and application of Federal laws and procedures relating to transportation.

Federal Motor Carrier Safety Administration

(27 attorneys, www.fmcsa.dot.gov)

The Federal Motor Carrier Safety Administration's primary mission is to prevent commercial motor vehicle-related fatalities and injuries. Activities of the Administration contribute to ensuring safety in motor carrier operations through strong enforcement of safety regulations; targeting high-risk carriers and commercial motor vehicle drivers; improving safety information systems and commercial motor vehicle technologies; strengthening commercial motor vehicle equipment and operating standards; and increasing safety awareness. To accomplish these activities, the Administration works with Federal, State, and local enforcement agencies, the motor carrier industry, labor safety interest groups, and others.

Federal Railroad Administration

(34 attorneys, www.fra.dot.gov)

The Federal Railroad Administration (FRA) was created by the Department of Transportation Act of 1966 (49 U.S.C. 103, Section 3(e)(1)). The purpose of FRA is to: promulgate and enforce rail safety regulations; administer railroad assistance programs; conduct research and development in support of improved railroad safety and national rail transportation policy; provide for the rehabilitation of Northeast Corridor rail passenger service; and consolidate government support of rail transportation activities.

The Safety Law Division of the Office of Chief Counsel develops and drafts the agency's safety regulations, assesses civil penalties for violations of the rail safety statutes and FRA safety regulations, and provides other legal support for FRA's safety program. The General Law Division provides legal services to FRA's various offices on all legal issues other than safety law, including Freedom of Information Act, Federal Tort Claims Act, and Surface Transportation Board matters.

Federal Transit Administration
(23 attorneys, www.fta.dot.gov)

The Federal Transit Administration (FTA) provides stewardship of combined formula and discretionary programs totaling more than $10B to support a variety of locally planned, constructed, and operated public transportation systems throughout the United States. Transportation systems typically include buses, subways, light rail, commuter rail, streetcars, monorail, passenger ferry boats, inclined railways, or people movers.

The FTA Office of Chief Counsel provides legal advice and support to the Administrator and FTA management and coordinates with and supports the Department of Transportation General Counsel on FTA legal matters. The office also is responsible for reviewing development and management of FTA-sponsored projects, representing the Administration before civil courts and administrative agencies, and drafting and reviewing legislation and regulations to implement the Administration's programs.

Maritime Administration
(20 attorneys, www.marad.dot.gov)

The Maritime Administration is the agency within the DOT dealing with waterborne transportation. Its programs promote the use of waterborne transportation and its seamless integration with other segments of the transportation system, and the viability of the U.S. merchant marine. The Maritime Administration works in many areas involving ships and shipping, shipbuilding, port operations, vessel operations, national security, environment, and safety. The Maritime Administration is also charged with maintaining the health of the merchant marine, since commercial mariners, vessels, and intermodal facilities are vital for supporting national security, and so the agency provides support and information for current mariners, extensive support for educating future mariners, and programs to educate America's young people about the vital role the maritime industry plays in the lives of all Americans.

The Maritime Administration also maintains a fleet of cargo ships in reserve to provide surge sealift during war and national emergencies, and is responsible for disposing of ships in that fleet, as well as other non-combatant Government ships, as they become obsolete.

National Highway Traffic Safety Administration
(26 attorneys, www.nhtsa.gov)

The National Highway Traffic Safety Administration (NHTSA) was established by the Highway Safety Act of 1970 (23 U.S.C. 401 note) to help reduce the number of deaths, injuries, and economic losses resulting from motor vehicle crashes on the Nation's highways. The Administration carries out programs relating to the safety performance of motor vehicles and related equipment; administers the State and community highway safety program with the FHWA; regulates the Corporate Average Fuel Economy program; investigates and prosecutes odometer fraud; carries out the National Driver Register Program to facilitate the exchange of State records on problem drivers; conducts studies and operates programs aimed at reducing economic losses in motor vehicle crashes and repairs; performs studies, conducts demonstration projects, and promotes programs to reduce impaired driving, increase seat belt use, and reduce risky driver behaviors; and issues theft prevention standards for passenger and non-passenger motor vehicles.

Office of Inspector General
(12 attorneys, www.oig.dot.gov)

The Office of Inspector General was established by law in 1978 to provide the Secretary and Congress with independent and objective reviews of the efficiency and effectiveness of DOT operations and programs and to detect and prevent fraud, waste, and abuse.

▶ OIG Office of Legal Counsel Law-Student Clerkship
www.oig.dot.gov/internship-programs#law-student-clerkship

Pipeline/Hazardous Materials Safety Administration
(27 attorneys, www.phmsa.dot.gov)

The Pipeline and Hazardous Materials Safety Administration (PHMSA) works to protect the American public and the environment by ensuring the safe and secure movement of hazardous materials to industry and consumers by all transportation modes, including the Nation's pipelines. PHMSA was created under the Norman Y. Mineta Research and Special Programs Improvement Act (P.L. 108-426) of 2004, which was signed into law on November 20, 2004. The creation of PHMSA provides the Department a modal administration focused solely on its pipeline and hazardous materials transportation programs. Through PHMSA, the Department develops and enforces regulations for the safe, reliable, and environmentally sound operation of the Nation's 2.3 million mile pipeline transportation system and the nearly 1 million daily shipments of hazardous materials by land, sea, and air.

Responsibilities of the PHMSA Chief Counsel include:
- Serving as legal advisor to the Administrator.
- Overseeing PHMSA's comprehensive legal programs and services with regard to proposed legislation, applicable laws, rules, regulations and orders.
- Recommending or completing enforcement actions for violations of pipeline safety or hazardous materials transportation safety laws and regulations.

Research & Innovative Tech. Administration
(7 attorneys, www.rita.dot.gov)

The Research and Innovative Technology Administration (RITA) was created under the Norman Y. Mineta Research and Special Programs Improvement Act (49 U.S.C. 101 note). RITA coordinates, facilitates, and reviews the Department's research and development programs and activities; performs comprehensive transportation statistics research, analysis, and reporting; and promotes the use of innovative technologies to improve our Nation's transportation system. RITA brings together important DOT data, research, and technology transfer assets and provides strategic direction and oversight of DOT's Intelligent Transportation Systems Program. RITA is composed of the staff from the Office of Research, Development, and Technology, the Volpe National Transportation Systems Center, the Transportation Safety Institute, and the Bureau of Transportation Statistics.

St. Lawrence Seaway Development Corporation

(1 attorney, www.rita.dot.gov)

The Saint Lawrence Seaway Development Corporation was established by the Saint Lawrence Seaway Act of May 13, 1954 (33 U.S.C. 981-990), and became an operating administration of the Department of Transportation in 1966. The Corporation, working cooperatively with the Saint Lawrence Seaway Management Corporation (SLSMC) of Canada, is dedicated to operating and maintaining a safe, reliable, and efficient deep draft waterway between the Great Lakes and the Atlantic Ocean. It ensures the safe transit of commercial and noncommercial vessels through the two U.S. locks and the navigation channels of the Saint Lawrence Seaway System. The Corporation works jointly with SLSMC on all matters related to rules and regulations, overall operations, vessel inspections, traffic control, navigation aids, safety, operating dates, and trade development programs.

Surface Transportation Board

(48 attorneys, www.stb.dot.gov)

The Surface Transportation Board (STB) was created in the Interstate Commerce Commission Termination Act of 1995 and is the successor agency to the Interstate Commerce Commission. The STB is an economic regulatory agency that Congress charged with the fundamental missions of resolving railroad rate and service disputes and reviewing proposed railroad mergers. The STB is decisionally independent, although it is administratively affiliated with the DOT.

The STB serves as both an adjudicatory and a regulatory body. The agency has jurisdiction over railroad rate and service issues and rail restructuring transactions (mergers, line sales, line construction, and line abandonments); certain trucking company, moving van, and non-contiguous ocean shipping company rate matters; certain intercity passenger bus company structure, financial, and operational matters; and rates and services of certain pipelines not regulated by the Federal Energy Regulatory Commission.

The STB Office of the General Counsel (OGC) responds to questions on a variety of legal issues. However, its primary mission is two-fold: to defend the STB's decisions in court and to assess the defensibility of agency decisions that might be challenged in court. Unlike most Federal agencies, the STB has independent litigating authority (49 U.S.C. 703d). Under the Hobbs Act (28 U.S.C. 2323), when an STB order or decision is challenged in the U.S. Court of Appeals, both the STB (represented by the agency's own attorneys) and the United States (represented by U.S. Department of Justice (DOJ) attorneys) must be named as "respondents" (defendants), and both have authority to appear in court in such cases. STB and DOJ attorneys, in most cases, jointly defend the agency's decisions, with the STB's attorneys preparing written briefs (in consultation with DOJ attorneys) and presenting oral arguments on behalf of the Federal Government.

In performing defensibility assessments, OGC attorneys meet with other STB staff to discuss cases before draft decisions are prepared. Defensibility assessments are key to issuing sound decisions that are less likely to be challenged and, if challenged, are more likely to be upheld.

Department of the Treasury

Description:
The Department of the Treasury performs four basic functions: formulating and recommending economic, financial, tax, and fiscal policies; serving as financial agent for the U.S. Government; enforcing the law; and manufacturing coins and currency.

The Treasury Department was created by act of September 2, 1789 (31 U.S.C. 301 and 301 note). Many subsequent acts have figured in the development of the Department, delegating new duties to its charge and establishing the numerous bureaus and divisions that now comprise the Treasury.

The Office of General Counsel provides legal and policy advice to the Secretary and other senior Departmental officials. The General Counsel also is the head of the Treasury Legal Division, a separate bureau within the Department that is composed of the approximately 2,000 attorneys and 1,500 support staff who are located in Treasury Departmental Offices and in Treasury bureaus.

General Counsel
The Treasury Department General Counsel is a statutory officer appointed by the President with the advice and consent of the Senate. The General Counsel serves as senior legal and policy adviser to the Secretary, the Deputy Secretary and other senior Departmental officials. As head of the Treasury Legal Division, the General Counsel has responsibility for all legal work in the Department. There also is a Principal Deputy General Counsel and a Deputy General Counsel who is supervised by the General Counsel and through whom the General Counsel operates the Legal Division. The Counselor to the General Counsel assists the General Counsel and the Deputy General Counsel by coordinating issues of general interest within the Legal Division and undertakes special assignments as requested by the General Counsel or the Deputy General Counsel. The General Counsel also is assisted by one or more Senior Advisors.

In Treasury Departmental Offices, senior officials reporting to the General Counsel through the Principal Deputy General Counsel and the Deputy General Counsel include: the Assistant General Counsel for Banking and Finance; the Assistant General Counsel for Enforcement and Intelligence; the Assistant General Counsel for General Law, Ethics and Regulation; the Assistant General Counsel for

International Affairs; the International Tax Counsel; the Tax Legislative Counsel; and the Benefits Tax Counsel.

Chief and Legal Counsel for Treasury bureaus generally report to the General Counsel, Principal Deputy General Counsel and Deputy General Counsel through an Assistant General Counsel. The Chief Counsel for the Internal Revenue Service (IRS) reports to the General Counsel and the IRS Commissioner. The Chief Counsels of two other Treasury bureaus, the Office of the Comptroller of the Currency and the Office of Thrift Supervision (OTS), work with the General Counsel and other members of the Legal Division but report directly to the Comptroller and the OTS Director, respectively.

Counselor to the General Counsel
The Counselor to the General Counsel is in the immediate office of the General Counsel and acts as a technical expert on legal and other matters to assist the General Counsel and the Deputy General Counsel on the formulation of policies and practices governing the Treasury Department as a whole and the Legal Division in particular. The Counselor to the General Counsel acts in an advisory capacity to top officials of the Department, and represents the General Counsel and the Deputy General Counsel at meetings and conferences where policy is developed or determined. The Counselor to the General Counsel performs special assignments as requested by the General Counsel that often cut across organizational divisions, including matters relating to Internal Revenue Service policies, corporate and securities law issues, and Departmental litigation.

Assistant General Counsel for Banking and Finance
The Assistant General Counsel for Banking and Finance (B&F) supervises the Deputy Assistant General Counsel B&F, staff attorneys, support staff, the Chief Counsels of the Bureau of the Public Debt and the Financial Management Service, and the Legal Counsels of the Community Development Financial Institutions Fund and the Terrorism Risk Insurance Program. The principal clients of the office include the Under Secretary for Domestic Finance, the Assistant Secretary for Financial Markets, the Assistant Secretary for Financial Institutions, the Fiscal Assistant Secretary, and the Assistant Secretary for Economic Policy.

The Office of the Assistant General Counsel B&F is responsible for providing legal advice on a broad range of issues arising in connection with Treasury's financing of the operations of the U.S. Government. The office is the Department's legal adviser on Treasury's borrowing authorities and debt issuing activities, including the national debt limit; Federal debt collection; Treasury's cash investment activities; Federal investment policy; Federal credit policy and programs, including Treasury's participation on inter-agency loan guarantee boards; and Federal payment systems, including e-commerce initiatives. The office also provides legal advice on the issues relating to financial markets oversight and the regulation of the government securities market.

The Office of the Assistant General Counsel B&F also is responsible for providing legal advice on issues affecting the financial services industry, with an emphasis on insured depository institutions and government-sponsored enterprises. As the Department's legal adviser on matters involving financial institutions, the office is involved in matters affecting bank and bank holding companies, savings associations and their holding companies, nonbank banks, the banking regulatory agencies, and government-sponsored enterprises. The office also provides legal advice on Treasury's funding programs for community development financial institutions, Treasury's terrorism risk insurance program, financial-sector critical infra-structure protection, financial privacy, and financial education.

Assistant General Counsel for Enforcement and Intelligence
The mission of the Office of the Assistant General Counsel for Enforcement and Intelligence (E&I) is to formulate and provide legal and policy-related advice to the Under Secretary for Terrorism and Financial Intelligence, the Assistant Secretary for Terrorist Financing and Financial Crimes and the Assistant Secretary for Intelligence and Analysis. Additionally, the Assistant General Counsel E&I directly supervises the provision of legal advice to the Financial Crimes Enforcement Network, the Office of Foreign Assets Control and the Treasury Executive Office for Asset Forfeiture.

The Assistant General Counsel E&I is supported by a Deputy Assistant General Counsel, staff attorneys and administrative staff. Additionally, the Chief Counsel's Office for the Financial Crimes Enforcement Network, the Chief Counsel's Office for the Office of Foreign Assets Control and the Legal Counsel of the Executive Office for Asset Forfeiture provide legal support to their respective clients.

The Assistant General Counsel (E&I) provides legal advice concerning a wide range of issues impacting the Department's intelligence and enforcement functions. In particular, the Assistant General Counsel (E&I) provides legal advice on financial intelligence matters focused on the twin aims of safeguarding the financial system against illicit use and combating rogue nations, terrorists, weapons of mass destruction proliferation, money laundering, narcotics kingpins and other national security threats. The office works with counsel from the Department of Justice, the Internal Revenue Service (Criminal Investigation) and counsel from other intelligence and enforcement agencies regarding litigation, intelligence and law enforcement matters.

Assistant General Counsel for General Law, Ethics and Regulation
The Assistant General Counsel for General Law, Ethics and Regulation (GLER) supervises the Deputy Assistant General Counsel for General Law, the Deputy Assistant General Counsel for Ethics, the Senior Counsel for Regulatory Affairs, staff attorneys, support staff, and the Chief Counsels of the U.S. Mint, the Bureau of Engraving and Printing, and the Alcohol and Tobacco Tax and Trade Bureau.

The Office of the Assistant General Counsel GLER provides legal advice concerning a wide range of issues at Treasury, including issues concerning government contracts, regulations, Departmental organization, appropriations, budget formulation and execution, disclosure, labor management relations, equal employment opportunity and personnel law. The office represents the Department in administrative litigation before the Government Accountability Office, the Civilian Board of Contract Appeals, the Merit Systems Protection Board, the Equal Employment Opportunity Commission, and the Federal Labor Relations Authority. GLER counsel also assist the Department of Justice in litigation before Federal district and appellate courts.

The office is responsible for managing the Department's ethics program, which requires an in-depth knowledge of the complex statutes, regulations, and precedents in this field, and which includes reviewing Presidential appointments to the Department pending Senate confirmation. In addition, the office is responsible for clearance of regulations issued by the Department and its bureaus, including tax regulations issued by the IRS. In this role, the office works with the Office of Information and Regulatory Affairs at the Office of Management and Budget and the Small Business Administration. In the area of disclosure law, the office provides legal guidance to the Department on Freedom of Information Act and Privacy Act requests and on document requests from Congress.

Assistant General Counsel for International Affairs

The Office of the Assistant General Counsel for International Affairs (IA), which includes the Assistant General Counsel for International Affairs, a deputy, staff attorneys, and support staff, principally advises the Under Secretary for International Affairs and the Assistant Secretaries for International Affairs.

The Office of the Assistant General Counsel IA provides legal advice in connection with a broad range of international economic and financial matters, including third world debt problems, issues involving the International Monetary Fund (IMF), the World Bank and other multilateral development banks, international trade and trade finance issues, the Committee on Foreign Investment in the United States CFIUS which the Secretary of the Treasury chairs, international investment, and international banking and securities issues.

Office of the Benefits Tax Counsel

The Office of the Benefits Tax Counsel (BTC) develops and reviews policy, legislation, regulations, and revenue rulings dealing with all aspects of employee benefits taxation and related matters including qualified retirement plans, Employee Stock Ownership Plans, employee welfare plans, health and long term care benefits, social security taxes, and executive compensation.

BTC is responsible for advising the Assistant Secretary (Tax Policy) and other Treasury officials in the formulation of the Administration's employee benefits taxation policy: for formulating, analyzing, and reviewing employee benefits taxation legislation and for preparing the Administration's testimony on such legislation. BTC assists Congressional staff in drafting legislation and in documenting the legislative history of employee benefits legislation.

In consultation with IRS, BTC is responsible for review of all Treasury regulations and IRS revenue rulings relating to the taxation of employee benefits. Such regulations and rulings play a crucial role in the development of tax policy and implementation of tax law.

Office of Tax Legislative Counsel

The Office of the Tax Legislative Counsel (TLC) develops and reviews policy, legislation, regulations, revenue rulings, revenue procedures, and other published guidance dealing with all aspects of domestic Federal income tax law other than employee benefits taxation matters handled by the Office of the Benefits Tax Counsel.

TLC is responsible for advising the Assistant Secretary (Tax Policy) and other Treasury officials in connection with the formulation of the Administration's domestic taxation policy, for formulating, analyzing, and reviewing domestic taxation legislation, and for preparing the Administration's testimony on such legislation. TLC assists congressional staff in drafting legislation and in documenting the legislative history of domestic tax legislation.

In consultation with IRS, TLC is responsible for review of all Treasury regulations and IRS revenue rulings, revenue procedures, and other published guidance relating to domestic tax issues. Such regulations and rulings play a crucial role in the development of tax policy and implementation of tax law.

Office of the International Tax Counsel
The Office of the International Tax Counsel (ITC) performs for international tax matters the same functions that Tax Legislative Counsel performs for domestic tax issues. In addition, the office is responsible for negotiating and reviewing income tax and estate and gift tax treaties with foreign countries and coordinating tax treaty matters with the State Department and the Congress. Two important purposes of these treaties are to help reduce international double taxation and thereby facilitate a freer movement of trade and capital flows and to improve taxpayer compliance.

ITC attorneys develop international tax legislation proposals, review and assess all international tax bills, prepare background information, produce testimony for Treasury officials, and coordinate with Congressional staffs and other agencies on matters related to U.S. international tax policy.

The ITC staff works closely with the International Taxation Division of the Office of Tax Analysis in the preparation of detailed technical analyses and the publication of congressionally mandated reports on various international tax issues. ITC works with the IRS in designing and finalizing regulations to implement international tax aspects of Congressional acts. ITC attorneys provide technical advice on interpretation of the Code and regulations issued. ITC attorneys serve as the official representative of the United States in various international organizations such as the Organisation for Economic Cooperation and Development and the Group of Seven. Meetings in these international fora contribute to the search for common approaches to addressing current and important tax problems for which international consensus can be very valuable.

Legal Counsel, Community Development Financial Institutions Fund
The Legal Counsel Office of the Community Development Financial Institutions (CDFI) Fund is responsible for providing legal advice to the Director of the CDFI Fund and other CDFI Fund officials. The Legal Counsel supervises a staff of two attorneys and one paralegal. The CDFI Fund, including the Legal Counsel Office, is located in Washington, D.C.

The CDFI Fund, a wholly owned government corporation within the Department of the Treasury, promotes economic revitalization and development in distressed urban and rural communities throughout the United States. By providing strategic investments and leveraging private sector funds, the Fund promotes access to capital and local economic growth. The CDFI Fund also encourages economic opportunity by advancing the role of microenterprise development in the United States.

The Legal Counsel Office is responsible for providing all legal services pertaining to the operations and functions of the CDFI Fund, including advice pertaining to investment of funds in community development financial institutions, Federal legislation, regulations and policy, various organizational matters, representation of the Fund before regulatory and oversight agencies and committees, and contractual and administrative matters.

Legal Counsel, Terrorism Risk Insurance Program
The Legal Counsel, Terrorism Risk Insurance Program, is the legal advisor to the Executive Director, Terrorism Risk Insurance Program, and supervises and directs the legal staff advising the Terrorism Risk Insurance Program. This Legal Counsel reports to and is supervised by the Assistant General Counsel B&F.

Legal Counsel, Treasury Executive Office of Asset Forfeiture
The Legal Counsel and a staff attorney provide legal advice to the Executive Office for Asset Forfeiture. That office administers the Treasury Forfeiture Fund and oversees related activities that promote the strategic use of asset forfeiture by Treasury law enforcement bureaus to disrupt and dismantle criminal enterprises.

Office of the General Counsel
Department of the Treasury

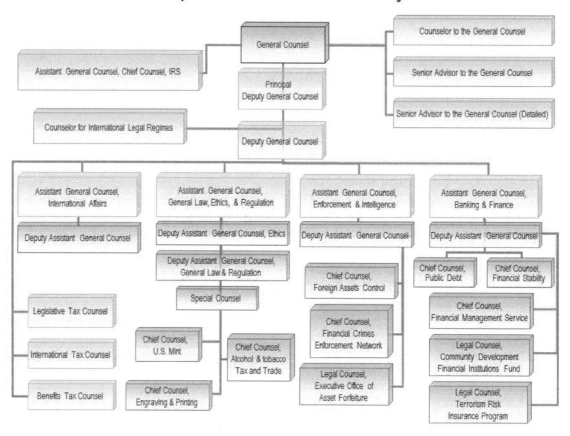

Address: Department of the Treasury
1500 Pennsylvania Avenue, NW
Washington, DC 20220

Website: www.treasury.gov   **Phone**:   202-622-2000

▶ **General Counsel's Summer Honors Program**
www.treasury.gov/offices/general-counsel/honors.shtml

Department of the Treasury	Attorneys	Male	Female	Avg Salary
Alcohol & Tobacco Tax Trade Bur.	16	10	6	$135,273
Bureau of Engraving & Printing	12	6	6	$125,546
Bureau of the Public Debt	14	7	7	$124,532
Departmental Offices	111	73	38	$142,009
Financial Crimes Enforcement Net	11	6	5	$135,498
Financial Management Service	16	7	9	$139,765
Internal Revenue Service[1]	1,983 (35 L Clerk)	1,079 (18 L Clerk)	904 (17 L Clerk)	$120,643
Comptroller of the Currency	133 (4 L Clerk)	75 (3 L Clerk)	58 (1 L Clerk)	$162,266
Inspector General for Tax Admin.	14	6	8	$130,110
Office of Inspector General	1	1	-	$158,743
Office of Thrift Supervision	42 (1 ALJ)	25 (1 ALJ)	17	$169,345
U.S. Mint	10	5	5	$133,823
Unspecified	4	3	1	$146,229
TOTAL	2,367	1,303	1064	$125,364
Percent of Positions		55%	45%	

[1] Does not include 897 personnel classified as "Hearing and Appeals" in the IRS with an average salary of $108,919. (Range $56,411 - $153,200).

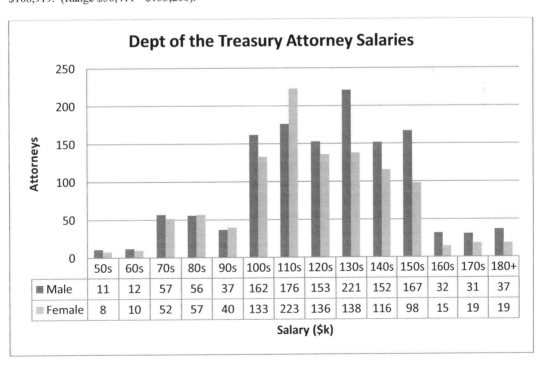

Dept of the Treasury Attorney Salaries

	50s	60s	70s	80s	90s	100s	110s	120s	130s	140s	150s	160s	170s	180+
Male	11	12	57	56	37	162	176	153	221	152	167	32	31	37
Female	8	10	52	57	40	133	223	136	138	116	98	15	19	19

Salary ($k)

Alcohol and Tobacco Tax Trade Bureau
(16 attorneys, www.ttb.gov)

The Alcohol and Tobacco Tax and Trade Bureau (TTB) was established under the Homeland Security Act of 2002 (the Act) on January 24, 2003. Rendering the functions of the Bureau of Alcohol, Tobacco and Firearms (ATF) into two new organizations with separate functions, the Act created a new tax and trade bureau within the Department of the Treasury, and shifted certain law enforcement functions of ATF to the Department of Justice. The Act called for the tax collection functions to remain with the Department of the Treasury; and the new organization was called the Alcohol and Tobacco Tax and Trade Bureau.

The mission of TTB is to collect alcohol, tobacco, firearms, and ammunition excise taxes that are rightfully due; to protect the consumer of alcohol beverages through compliance programs that are based upon education and enforcement of the industry to ensure an effectively regulated marketplace; and to assist industry members to understand and comply with Federal tax, product, and marketing requirements associated with the regulated commodities.

The TTB Chief Counsel supervises a Deputy Chief Counsel and other attorneys in Washington, D.C., and in field offices around the country. The Office of the Chief Counsel provides legal advice to TTB officials across the full range of their responsibilities.

TTB is responsible for enforcement of Federal laws related to alcohol and tobacco, and the collection of excise taxes on firearms, ammunition, alcohol and tobacco. These issues involve interpretations of the Federal Alcohol Administration Act, Webb Kenyon Act, and the Internal Revenue Code of 1986.

The Office of Chief Counsel attorneys advise TTB on issues related to the regulated industries concerning licensing, product labeling, international trade and regulatory inspections. Legal advice is provided on tax issues related to the products that TTB regulates. Attorneys also represent TTB in alcohol and tobacco permit revocation and other administrative proceedings.

The Office of the Chief Counsel also provides advice concerning ethics, labor relations, equal employment opportunity, personnel, fiscal, contract and disclosure law, and represents TTB before the Merit Systems Protection Board, the Equal Employment Opportunity Commission, the Federal Labor Relations Authority and the Board of Contract Appeals. Attorneys review and advise on claims and suits by and against TTB and its employees in areas such as the Federal Tort Claims Act and employee claims.

Bureau of Engraving & Printing
(12 attorneys, www.moneyfactory.gov)

The Bureau of Engraving and Printing (BEP) operates on basic authorities conferred by act of July 11, 1862 (31 U.S.C. 303), and additional authorities contained in past appropriations made to the Bureau that are still in force. Operations are financed by a revolving fund established in 1950. The Bureau is headed by a Director who is selected by the Secretary of the Treasury.

The Bureau designs, prints, and finishes all of the Nation's paper currency and many other security documents, including White House invitations and military identification cards. It also is responsible for advising and assisting Federal agencies in the design and production of other Government documents that, because of their innate value or for other reasons, require security or counterfeit-deterrence characteristics.

The Chief Counsel of the BEP is responsible for providing legal advice and assistance to the Bureau's Director and other Bureau officials. BEP has a headquarters and stamp and currency production facility located in Washington, D.C., and also has a currency production facility in Fort Worth, TX. The BEP Chief Counsel office includes attorneys plus support staff in the Washington, D.C. and Fort Worth offices. The Office of the Chief Counsel provides advice to BEP in areas including labor-management and employee relations, Government contract law, Federal employee ethics, environmental law, occupational safety and health, and administrative law. In addition, the Chief Counsel's Office plays a primary role in all litigation arising before administrative tribunals and the courts where BEP is a party.

Bureau of the Public Debt
(14 attorneys, www.publicdebt.treas.gov)

The Bureau of the Public Debt (BPD) was established on June 30, 1940, pursuant to the Reorganization Act of 1939 (31 U.S.C. 306). The Bureau's mission is to borrow the money needed to operate the Federal Government, account for the resulting public debt, and provide reimbursable support to Federal agencies. The Bureau fulfills its mission through five programs: wholesale securities, Government agency investment, retail securities services, summary debt accounting, and franchise services.

The Bureau auctions and issues Treasury bills, notes, and bonds and manages the U.S. Savings Bond Program. It issues, services, and redeems bonds through a nationwide network of issuing and paying agents. It provides daily and other periodic reports to account for the composition and size of the debt. In addition, the Bureau implements the regulations for the Government securities market. These regulations provide for investor protection while maintaining a fair and liquid market for Government securities.

The Chief Counsel of the BPD, along with Deputy Chief Counsels, staff attorneys, and support staff, provides legal advice to BPD's Commissioner and other officials of the Bureau. This can involve areas such as contract and commercial law, securities law and regulation, electronic payments, trusts and estates, privacy/disclosure, ethics, and administrative law. In addition, the Chief Counsel's Office plays a central role in any regulatory activity, legislative proposals or litigation in BPD's area of responsibility.

Financial Crimes Enforcement Network
(11 attorneys, www.fincen.gov)

The U.S. Department of the Treasury established the Financial Crimes Enforcement Network (FINCEN) in 1990 to provide a government-wide multisource financial intelligence and analysis network. The organization's operation was broadened in 1994 to include regulatory responsibilities for administering the Bank Secrecy Act (BSA), one of the Nation's most potent weapons for preventing corruption of the U.S. financial system. The USA PATRIOT Act of 2001, enacted shortly after the 9/11 attacks in America, broadened the scope of the BSA to focus on terrorist financing as well as money laundering. The Act also gave the FINCEN additional responsibilities and authorities in both important areas, and established the organization as a bureau within the Treasury Department.

The Chief Counsel of the FINCEN supervises attorneys and support staff. The Office of Chief Counsel provides legal advice to FINCEN officials across the full range of their responsibilities. Members of the Office of Chief Counsel advise FINCEN on issues relating to the terms and interpretation of the BSA, domestic and

112

international aspects of information law, inter-agency information-sharing, the use of information in enforcement operations and proceedings, international law relating to counter-money laundering efforts, and administrative law.

▶ FINCEN Student Volunteer Program
www.fincen.gov/careers/unpaid_student_volunteer_program.html

Internal Revenue Service
(1,093 attorneys, www.irs.gov)

The Office of the Commissioner of Internal Revenue was established by act of July 1, 1862 (26 U.S.C. 7802). The Internal Revenue Service (IRS) is responsible for administering and enforcing the internal revenue laws and related statutes, except those relating to alcohol, tobacco, firearms, and explosives. Its mission is to collect the proper amount of tax revenue, at the least cost to the public, by efficiently applying the tax law with integrity and fairness.

The Chief Counsel of the IRS supervises the attorneys who are assigned among the IRS National Office and the major operational divisions of the agency. The principal client of the Office of the Chief Counsel is the Commissioner of the IRS. The Chief Counsel's Office plays a central role in the administration of the Federal tax laws. Its attorneys provide guidance on the correct legal interpretation of the tax laws, represent the IRS in litigation, and provide all other legal support the IRS needs to carry out its mission of serving American taxpayers. For example, the Chief Counsel's Office drafts regulations, rulings, and other published legal guidance; handles tens of thousands of cases per year in the U.S. Tax Court and bankruptcy courts and works closely with the Department of Justice on other tax litigation in other Federal courts; and provides specific legal advice and determinations to taxpayers and to various IRS offices both before and after taxes are filed.

▶ IRS Office of Chief Counsel Honors Program
http://jobs.irs.gov/student/occ-law-students-recent-grads.html#honorsprogram

▶ IRS Office of Chief Counsel Summer Legal Intern Program
http://jobs.irs.gov/student/occ-law-students-recent-grads.html#legalintern

▶ IRS Office of Chief Counsel Volunteer Legal Externship Program
http://jobs.irs.gov/student/occ-law-students-recent-grads.html#extern

▶ IRS Tax Law Specialist Hiring

http://jobs.irs.gov/student/tax-law-specialist.html

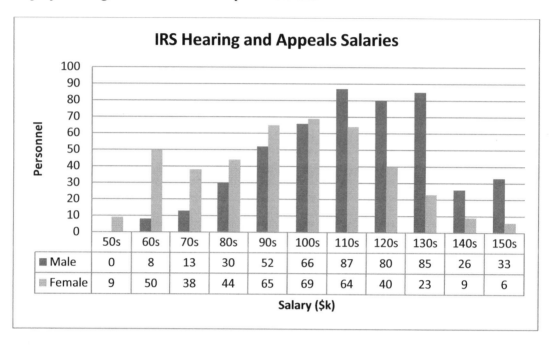

IRS Hearing and Appeals Salaries

	50s	60s	70s	80s	90s	100s	110s	120s	130s	140s	150s
■ Male	0	8	13	30	52	66	87	80	85	26	33
▦ Female	9	50	38	44	65	69	64	40	23	9	6

Salary ($k)

Comptroller of the Currency

(133 attorneys, www.occ.gov)

The Office of the Comptroller of the Currency (OCC) was created February 25, 1863 (12 Stat. 665), as a bureau of the Department of the Treasury. Its primary mission is to regulate national banks. The Office is headed by the Comptroller, who is appointed for a 5-year term by the President with the advice and consent of the Senate.

The Office regulates national banks by its power to examine banks; approves or denies applications for new bank charters, branches, or mergers; takes enforcement action--such as bank closures--against banks that are not in compliance with laws and regulations; and issues rules, regulations, and interpretations on banking practices.

The Office supervises approximately 2,100 national banks, including their trust activities and overseas operations. Each bank is examined annually through a nationwide staff of approximately 1,900 bank examiners supervised in 4 district offices. The Office is independently funded through assessments of the assets of national banks.

The Chief Counsel of the OCC supervises the attorneys in the Washington headquarters and in the four District offices. The Office of the Chief Counsel consists of seven legal practice areas located in the Washington headquarters office and four general practice offices in each of the four district office locations. The Bank Activities and Structure Division is responsible for corporate and operational issues relating to banking organizations such as branching, mergers, lending, and ownership of real and personal property. The Community and Consumer Law Division provides legal interpretation and advice on consumer protection, fair lending and community reinvestment issues. The Enforcement and Compliance Division is responsible for handling enforcement actions, including civil money penalties, suspensions and removals cease and desist orders, and other administrative enforcement actions to assure compliance with Federal banking laws by national banks and officials.

The Legislative and Regulatory Activities Division prepares and reviews proposed banking legislation and regulations and advise on related legal issues and is the focal point for legal issues relating to foreign banks' operations in the United States, U.S. banks' operations abroad. The Litigation Division is primarily responsible for representing the Comptroller and OCC employees in Federal and, where necessary, State court proceedings. The Securities and Corporate Practices Division administers and enforces the Federal securities and national banking laws that affect the securities and corporate activities of national banks relating to securities, insurance, annuities, derivatives, corporate governance, shareholder rights, and fiduciary activities of national banks. The Administrative and Internal Law Division is responsible for matters relating to the OCC's operation as a Federal agency.

▶ OCC Office of the Chief Counsel Employment Program
www.occ.gov/jobs/lawjob.htm

Treasury Inspector General for Tax Administration
(14 attorneys, www.ustreas.gov/tigta/)

The Treasury Inspector General for Tax Administration (TIGTA) was established under the IRS Restructuring and Reform Act of 1998 to provide independent oversight of IRS activities. TIGTA promotes the economy, efficiency, and effectiveness in the administration of the internal revenue laws. It is also committed to the prevention and detection of fraud, waste, and abuse within the IRS and related entities.

Office of Inspector General

(1 attorneys, www.ustreas.gov/inspector-general/)

The Department of the Treasury's Office of Inspector General (OIG) was established in 1989 in accordance with the Inspector General Act Amendments of 1998. The OIG is headed by an Inspector General who is appointed by the President with the advice and consent of the Senate. The Inspector General reports to the Secretary of the Treasury through the Deputy Secretary and provides the Secretary with independent and objective reviews of the department's operations. The Inspector General is required to keep both the Secretary and the Congress fully and currently informed about the problems and deficiencies relating to the administration of department programs and operations and the necessity for corrective action. Serving with the Inspector General in the Immediate Office is a Deputy Inspector General.

Office of Thrift Supervision

(42 attorneys, www.ots.treas.gov)

The Office of Thrift Supervision (OTS) regulates Federal- and State-chartered savings institutions. Created by the Financial Institutions Reform, Recovery, and Enforcement Act of 1989, its mission is to effectively and efficiently supervise Thrift institutions in a manner that encourages a competitive industry to meet housing and other credit and financial services needs and ensure access to financial services for all Americans.

The Chief Counsel of the OTS supervises the attorneys, paralegals, investigators and secretaries in the agency's Washington, D.C. headquarters and in five regional offices. The Office of Chief Counsel consists of five divisions in Washington and five general practice offices in each of the agency's five regional offices in Jersey City, Atlanta, Chicago, Dallas, and San Francisco. The Litigation Division represents OTS in all matters before State or Federal courts. The Enforcement Division is responsible for handling enforcement actions, including civil money penalties, suspensions and removals, cease and desist orders, and other administrative enforcement actions to assure compliance with Federal laws by savings associations, related entities and officials of savings associations. The Regulations and Legislation Division drafts regulations and legal opinions interpreting the laws and regulations that govern the activities of savings associations. The Business Transactions Division provides legal advice on mergers, acquisitions, and other activities proposed in applications submitted by savings

116

associations and holding companies and implements and supervises compliance with the securities statutes that apply to publicly traded savings associations. The General Law Division provides legal guidance for most internal OTS administrative matters including ethics, procurement, information disclosure and employment issues.

United States Mint

(10 attorneys, www.usmint.gov)

The establishment of a mint was authorized by act of April 2, 1792 (1 Stat. 246). The Bureau of the Mint was established by act of February 12, 1873 (17 Stat. 424), and recodified on September 13, 1982 (31 U.S.C. 304, 5131). The name was changed to United States Mint by Secretarial order dated January 9, 1984.

The primary mission of the Mint is to produce an adequate volume of circulating coinage for the Nation to conduct its trade and commerce. The Mint also produces and sells numismatic coins, American Eagle gold and silver bullion coins, and national medals. In addition, the Fort Knox Bullion Depository is the primary storage facility for the Nation's gold bullion.

The Chief Counsel of the United States Mint supervises a Deputy Chief Counsel, staff attorneys, and support staff. The Chief Counsel's Office is located in Washington, D.C. and is responsible for providing legal advice and assistance to Mint headquarters and field facilities concerning the functions and activities of the Mint. The Chief Counsel's Office conducts legal research and develops recommendations and conclusions on all laws applicable to the Mint's operations. It is a general practice of law, whose principal subject areas of work include contracting, legislation, advertising, litigation, personnel, administration and fiscal matters. The Chief Counsel's office also represents the Mint in various third party proceedings, such as hearings before the Merit System Protection Board and Equal Employment Opportunity Commission.

Department of Veterans Affairs

Description:
The Department of Veterans Affairs (VA) operates programs to benefit veterans and members of their families. Benefits include compensation payments for disabilities or death related to military service; pensions; education and rehabilitation; home loan guaranty; burial; and a medical care program incorporating nursing homes, clinics, and medical centers.

The VA was established as an executive department by the Department of Veterans Affairs Act (38 U.S.C. 201 note). It is comprised of three organizations that administer veterans' programs: the Veterans Health Administration, the Veterans Benefits Administration, and the National Cemetery Administration. Each organization has field facilities and a central office component. Staff offices support the overall function of the Department and its Administrations.

▶ **VA Legal Careers**
www4.va.gov/JOBS/career_types/legal.asp

Address: U.S. Department of Veterans Affairs
810 Vermont Avenue, NW
Washington, DC 20420

Website: www.va.gov   **Phone**:   202-273-4800

Department of Veterans Affairs	Attorneys	Male	Female	Avg Salary
Board of Veterans Appeals	429	186 (9 L Clerk)	243 (9 L Clerk)	$103,824
Dep Asst Sec for Resolution Mgmt	1	1	-	$144,997
Dep Asst Sec Human Resource Mgmt & Labor Relations	1	-	1	$112,995
General Counsel Office	475	239 (2 L Clerk)	236 (1 L Clerk)	$114,024
Inspector General Office	4	2	2	$140,862
Office of the Secretary	14	6	8	$129,461
Veterans Benefits Administration	3	1	2	$99,692
Veterans Health Administration	1	1	0	$120,983
TOTAL	928	436	492	$109,657
Percent of Positions		47%	53%	

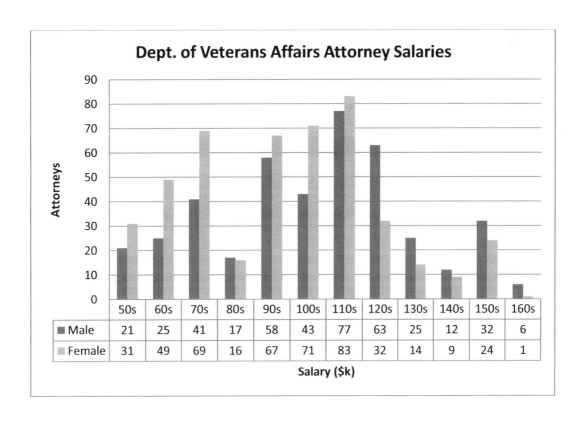

Dept. of Veterans Affairs Attorney Salaries

Salary ($k)	50s	60s	70s	80s	90s	100s	110s	120s	130s	140s	150s	160s
Male	21	25	41	17	58	43	77	63	25	12	32	6
Female	31	49	69	16	67	71	83	32	14	9	24	1

Office of the General Counsel

(475 attorneys, www4.va.gov/ogc/)

The mission of the Office of General Counsel (OGC) is to identify and meet the legal needs of the VA. Its primary objective is to ensure the just and faithful execution of the laws, regulations and policies that the Secretary has responsibility for administering, and by so doing enable the Department to accomplish its mission of service to our Nation's veterans.

The General Counsel issues written legal opinions having precedential effect in adjudications and appeals involving veterans' benefits under laws administered by VA. The General Counsel's interpretations on legal matters, contained in such opinions, are conclusive as to all VA officials and employees not only in the matter at issue but also in future adjudications and appeals, in the absence of a change in controlling statute or regulation, Court decision, or a superseding written legal opinion of the General Counsel. VA provides these opinions in order to give the public notice of those interpretations of the General Counsel that must be followed in future benefit matters and to assist veterans' benefit claimants and their representatives in the prosecution of benefit claim.

Board of Veterans Appeals

(429 attorneys, www.bva.va.gov)

The Board was established in 1933 and consists of a Chairman, Vice Chairman, Principal Deputy Vice Chairman, 60 Veterans Law Judges (VLJs), 8 Senior Counsel, hundreds of staff counsel, and other administrative and clerical staff. The Chairman reports directly to the Secretary of Veterans Affairs. The Board is comprised of four Decision Teams with jurisdiction over appeals arising from the VA Regional Offices (RO) and Medical Centers in one of four geographical regions: Northeast, Southeast, Midwest, and West (including the Philippines). Each Decision Team includes a Deputy Vice Chairman, two Chief VLJs, 12 line Judges, 2 Senior Counsel, and 75 staff counsel. Staff counsel review the record on appeal, research the applicable law, and prepare comprehensive draft decisions or remand orders for review by a VLJ who reviews the draft and issues the final decision or appropriate preliminary order in the appeal. The Board has jurisdiction over a wide variety of issues and matters, but the vast majority of appeals considered (95%) involve claims for disability compensation or survivor benefits. Examples of other types of claims that are addressed by the Board include fee basis medical care, waiver of recovery of overpayments, reimbursements for emergency medical treatment expenses, education assistance benefits, vocational rehabilitation training, burial benefits, and insurance benefits.

The Board published the Veterans Law Review: www.bva.va.gov/VLR.asp

Office of Inspector General
(4 attorneys, www4.va.gov/oig/)

Office of the Inspector General works with the VA management team to identify and address issues that are important to them and the veterans served. The OIG is organized into three line elements; the Offices of Investigations, Audit, and Healthcare Inspections, plus the Office of Contract Review and the Office of Management & Administration.

Large Independent Agencies

(1,000 or more employees)

Agency	Attorneys	Admin. Law Judges	Law Clerks	Avg. Salary
Agency for Intl. Development	80	-	-	$134,017
Broadcasting Board of Governors	8	-	-	$130,015
Court Services & Offender Supervision Agency for DC	5	-	-	$125,680
Environmental Protection Agency	1,087 (3 Patent)	4	12	$130,251
Equal Employment Opportunity Commission	484	-	5	$118,867
Fed. Communications Commission	546	1	2	$142,545
Federal Deposit Insurance Corp.	376	-	5	$162,227
Federal Trade Commission	586	1	3	$138,158
General Services Administration	153	-	1	$130,539
Government Printing Office	9	-	-	$130,899
National Aeronautics & Space Adm.	132 (19 Patent)	-	1	$136,421
National Archives & Records Admin	11	-	-	$117,163
National Credit Union Admin.	25	-	-	$155,564
National Labor Relations Board	672	39	13	$127,635
National Science Foundation	19	-	-	$146,925
Nuclear Regulatory Commission	109	-	13	$128,177
Office of Personnel Management	28	-	-	$132,933
Securities & Exchange Commission	1,526	4	9	$167,532
Small Business Administration	281	-	-	$103,437
Smithsonian Institution	25	-	-	$126,032
Social Security Administration	2,346	1,298	17	$112,262
TOTAL	**8,508**	**1,347**	**81**	**$130,431**

Large Independent Agency – General Attorney Minority Status

Agency	Non-Minority	Minority
Agency for International Development	77%	23%
Broadcasting Board of Governors	100%	0%
Court Services & Offender Sup. Agency for DC	NA	NA
Environmental Protection Agency	79%	21%
Equal Employment Opportunity Commission	61%	39%
Federal Communications Commission	79%	21%
Federal Deposit Insurance Corporation	88%	12%
Federal Trade Commission	82%	18%
General Services Administration	80%	20%
Government Printing Office	100%	0%
National Aeronautics & Space Administration	80%	20%
National Archives & Records Administration	100%	0%
National Credit Union Administration	100%	0%
National Labor Relations Board	76%	24%
National Science Foundation	100%	0%
Nuclear Regulatory Commission	85%	15%
Office of Personnel Management	69%	31%
Securities & Exchange Commission	81%	19%
Small Business Administration	76%	24%
Smithsonian Institution	68%	32%
Social Security Administration	77%	23%
TOTAL	**78%**	**22%**

* Data as of June, 2010.

Agency for International Development

Description:
The United States Agency for International Development (USAID) administers U.S. foreign economic and humanitarian assistance programs worldwide in the developing world, Central and Eastern Europe, and Eurasia.

USAID is an independent Federal agency established by 22 U.S.C. 6563. Its principal statutory authority is the Foreign Assistance Act of 1961, as amended (22 U.S.C. 2151 et seq.). USAID serves as the focal point within the Government for economic matters affecting U.S. relations with developing countries. USAID administers international economic and humanitarian assistance programs. The Administrator is under the direct authority and foreign policy guidance of the Secretary of State.

The Office of the General Counsel provides legal advice and guidance for all of the agency's operations worldwide.

Address: U.S. Agency for International Development
1300 Pennsylvania Avenue, NW
Washington, DC 20523-1000

Website: www.usaid.gov

Phone: 202-712-0000   **Fax**:   202-216-3524

► **USAID Foreign Service Attorneys**
www.usaid.gov/careers/gcvacancies.html   lawyers2@usaid.gov

► **USAID General Counsel Legal Internships**
www.usaid.gov/careers/gcintern.html   202-712-5389

USAID Location of Attorneys	Number of Attorneys
District of Columbia	47
Egypt	2
Kenya	1
South Africa	1
Afghanistan	3
El Salvador	2
Jordan	1
Sudan	1
Bolivia	1
Dominican Republic	1
Georgia	1
Ghana	2
Indonesia	1
Iraq	3
Israel	1
Kazakhstan	1
Mozambique	1
Nigeria	1
Pakistan	1
Peru	1
Russia	3
Senegal	2
Thailand	1
Ukraine	1
TOTAL	80

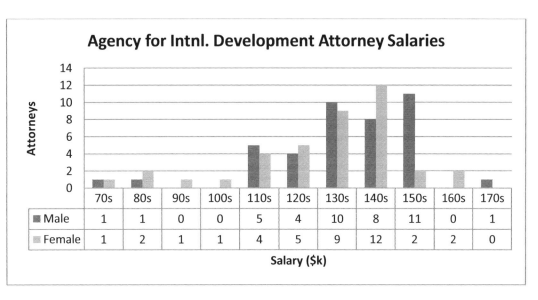

Agency for Intnl. Development Attorney Salaries

	70s	80s	90s	100s	110s	120s	130s	140s	150s	160s	170s
Male	1	1	0	0	5	4	10	8	11	0	1
Female	1	2	1	1	4	5	9	12	2	2	0

Salary ($k)

125

Broadcasting Board of Governors

Description:

The mission of the Broadcasting Board of Governors (BBG) is to promote freedom and democracy and to enhance understanding by broadcasting accurate, objective, and balanced news and information about the U.S. and the world to audiences abroad. The BBG became an independent agency on October 1, 1999, by authority of the Foreign Affairs Reform and Restructuring Act of 1998 (22 U.S.C. 6501 note). It is composed of nine members. Eight members are appointed by the President and confirmed by the Senate; the ninth, an ex-officio member, is the Secretary of State.

The BBG serves as the governing body for all nonmilitary U.S. broadcasting and provides programming in 56 languages via radio, television, and the Internet. The BBG broadcast services include the Voice of America, the Office of Cuba Broadcasting, Radio Free Europe/Radio Liberty, Radio Free Asia, and the Middle East Broadcasting Networks.

The BBG General Counsel's responsibilities include advising senior agency officials on legal matters, providing interpretations as to authority and application of laws, regulations, Executive Orders, contracts, international agreements, and legal decisions, and making determinations on all legal matters affecting Broadcasting operations, drafting legislation, Executive orders, international agreements, and other legal documents involving Broadcasting operations, handling all legal matters referred to Broadcasting by other government departments or agencies; and representing the agency in litigation matters involving employment claims, contract claims, and other matters raised before the agency or administrative tribunals and assisting Department of Justice attorneys in litigation in U.S. Federal courts or litigation in foreign jurisdictions.

Address: Broadcasting Board of Governors
330 Independence Avenue, SW
Washington, DC 20237

Website: www.bbg.gov

Phone: 202-203-4545   **Fax**:   202-203-4585
Human Resources Phone: 202-382-7500   **Fax**:   202-382-7541

BBG Atty Location	Gender	Length of Service	Salary
District of Columbia	Male	Less than 1 year	$154,600
District of Columbia	Female	10 - 14 years	$144,997
District of Columbia	Male	3 - 4 years	$144,997
District of Columbia	Female	15 - 19 years	$140,969
District of Columbia	Female	10 - 14 years	$124,858
Virginia	Female	Less than 1 year	$120,830
District of Columbia	Female	1 - 2 years	$106,145
District of Columbia	Female	1 - 2 years	$102,721
AVERAGE			$130,015

Central Intelligence Agency

Description:
The Central Intelligence Agency (CIA) collects, evaluates, and disseminates vital information on political, military, economic, scientific, and other developments abroad needed to safeguard national security.

The General Counsel is the chief legal officer of the CIA. The General Counsel serves as the legal advisor to the Director of the Central Intelligence Agency and is responsible for the sound and efficient management of the legal affairs of the CIA. The General Counsel is nominated by the President and confirmed by the Senate.

The CIA Office of General Counsel (OGC) is an independent office of the CIA that is headed by the General Counsel and assists the General Counsel in carrying out his/her statutory and other responsibilities. On behalf of the General Counsel, OGC provides legal advice and guidance to the Agency and to the Director of the CIA. OGC is responsible for advising the Director on all legal matters relating to his/her statutory responsibilities and his/her role as head of the CIA. OGC also provides advice and guidance to those officers and employees within the CIA who have specific responsibility for the conduct of US intelligence activities.

[Data on attorney employment is intentionally omitted.]

Address: Central Intelligence Agency
                Office of Public Affairs
                Washington, DC 20505

Website: www.cia.gov

Phone: 703-482-0623   **Fax**:   703-482-1739

▶ **CIA Office of General Counsel Lateral Hires**:
https://www.cia.gov/offices-of-cia/general-counsel/careers/lateral-hires.html

▶ **CIA Honors Attorney Program**:
https://www.cia.gov/offices-of-cia/general-counsel/careers/honors-attorneys-program.html

▶ **CIA Office of General Counsel Summer Law Clerk Program**:
https://www.cia.gov/offices-of-cia/general-counsel/careers/summer-law-clerk-program.html

Court Services & Offender Supervision Agency for the District of Columbia

Description:

The Court Services and Offender Supervision Agency for the District of Columbia (CSOSA) is a Federal, executive branch agency, created by Congress in 1997 to perform the offender supervision function for D.C. Code offenders. It does so in coordination with the Superior Court of the District of Columbia and the U.S. Parole Commission. CSOSA's mission is to increase public safety, prevent crime, reduce recidivism, and support the fair administration of justice in close collaboration with the community. CSOSA provides community supervision to 15,000 individuals on probation, parole or supervised release each day.

The General Counsel deals with legal and ethical advice, legal representation, records management and matters related to the Freedom of Information Act.

Address: Court Services and Offender Supervision Agency
633 Indiana Avenue, NW
Washington, DC 20004-2902

Website: www.csosa.gov

Phone: 202-220-5300   **Fax**:   202-220-5350

CSOSA Office	Attorney Location	Gender	Length of Service	Salary
Office of the Director	District of Columbia	Female	10 - 14 years	$149,025
Office of the Director	District of Columbia	Male	1 - 2 years	$133,543
Pretrial Services Agency	District of Columbia	Female	15 - 19 years	$133,543
Office of the Director	District of Columbia	Female	10 - 14 years	$109,570
Office of the Director	District of Columbia	Male	5 - 9 years	$102,721

Environmental Protection Agency

Description:
The Environmental Protection Agency (EPA) protects human health and safeguards the natural environment. The EPA was established in the executive branch as an independent agency pursuant to Reorganization Plan No. 3 of 1970 (5 U.S.C. app.), effective December 2, 1970. It was created to permit coordinated and effective governmental action on behalf of the environment. The Agency is designed to serve as the public's advocate for a livable environment.

The Office of General Counsel (OGC) is the chief legal adviser to EPA, providing legal support for Agency rules and policies, case-by-case decisions (such as permits and response actions), and legislation. In addition, OGC lawyers, together with attorneys in the U.S. Department of Justice's Environmental and Natural Resources Division, represent the Agency in court challenges to agency actions (such as regulations), appeals of enforcement cases, and Supreme Court litigation. OGC lawyers carry out these functions not only with respect to EPA's environmental programs, but also in connection with EPA's day-to-day operations, including entering into contracts, awarding grants, managing property and money, and working with EPA's employees. The primary role of OGC lawyers is to provide legal advice to EPA and to articulate the Agency's legal positions in the Federal courts and before other tribunals and organizations.

The EPA Offices of Regional Counsel (ORCs) are located within each EPA regional office and provide day-to-day support to each Region and Headquarters for all general legal matters, including defensive litigation and counseling issues. The regional attorneys give legal advice on dozens of Federal laws, numerous Presidential executive orders, EPA regulations, policies, and guidelines, case decisions, international treaties, State laws and local ordinances. Specifically, these responsibilities entail counseling regional program staff and managers on the application of statutes, regulations, case law, and policies, as well as any other legal issues that arise. Counseling is also provided by the ORCs on the National Historic Preservation Act, the Endangered Species Act, the Freedom of Information Act, Indian law, grants, and labor and personnel law issues.

In addition, the ORCs provide ethics counseling to regional staff and management, and most ORCs provide support to the Agency's enforcement program by supplying a Regional Judicial Officer and a Regional Hearing Clerk. Furthermore, regional attorneys draft Federal rules and defend the Agency in litigation. Finally, most of the ORCs also provide legal support for all enforcement matters.

The ORCs support regional and national priorities and commitments. The regional attorneys play a unique role in ensuring that legal requirements and obligations are met -- priorities are often driven by mandates or deadlines imposed by courts, statutes, or regulations.

In addition to the regional program offices and the Office of General Counsel, ORCs also work closely with EPA's Office of Enforcement and Compliance Assurance, other EPA national program managers, U.S. Department of Justice, U.S. Attorneys, State Attorneys General, and other State and Federal agencies such as the U.S. Army Corps of Engineers, U.S. Coast Guard, and U.S. Department of the Interior.

Address: U.S. Environmental Protection Agency
1200 Pennsylvania Avenue, NW
Washington, DC 20460-0001

Website: www.epa.gov   **Phone**:   202-272-0167

▶ **EPA Office of General Counsel Employment Opportunities**
www.epa.gov/ogc/employment.htm

▶ **EPA Office of General Counsel Honors Fellowship Program**
www.epa.gov/ogc/fellowship.htm

Environmental Protection Agency - Office of General Counsel

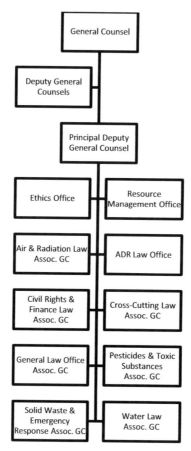

(Table below does not include law clerks or intermittent personnel)

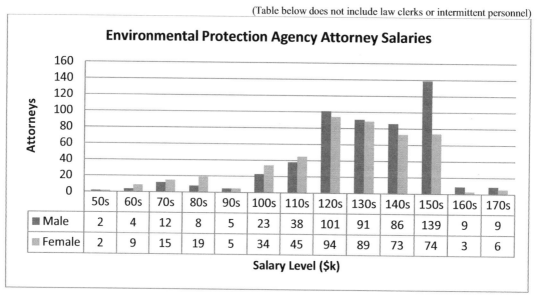

Environmental Protection Agency Attorney Salaries

Salary Level ($k)	50s	60s	70s	80s	90s	100s	110s	120s	130s	140s	150s	160s	170s
Male	2	4	12	8	5	23	38	101	91	86	139	9	9
Female	2	9	15	19	5	34	45	94	89	73	74	3	6

Equal Employment Opportunity Commission

Description:

The Equal Employment Opportunity Commission (EEOC) enforces laws prohibiting employment discrimination based on race, color, gender, religion, national origin, age, and disability in the Federal and private sectors. Through its administrative enforcement process, the Commission receives, investigates, and resolves charges of employment discrimination filed against private sector employers, employment agencies, labor unions, and State and local governments, including charges of systemic discrimination. Where the Commission does not resolve these charges through conciliation or other informal methods, the Commission may also engage in litigation against private sector employers, employment agencies and labor unions (and against State and local governments in cases alleging age discrimination or equal pay violations).The EEOC also leads and coordinates equal employment opportunity efforts across the Federal government and conducts administrative hearings and issues appellate decisions on complaints of discrimination filed by Federal employees and applicants for Federal employment.

The EEOC was created by title VII of the Civil Rights Act of 1964 (42 U.S.C. 2000e–4), and became operational July 2, 1965. Laws under the EEOC's enforcement mission include title VII of the Civil Rights Act of 1964 (42 U.S.C. 2000e et seq.), the Age Discrimination in Employment Act of 1967 (29 U.S.C. 621 et seq.), sections of the Rehabilitation Act of 1973 (29 U.S.C. 791 et seq.), the Equal Pay Act of 1963 (29 U.S.C. 206), title I of the Americans with Disabilities Act of 1990 (42 U.S.C. 12101 et seq.), and sections of the Civil Rights Act of 1991 (105 Stat. 1071). The EEOC is a bipartisan commission composed of five members appointed by the President, with the advice and consent of the Senate, for staggered 5-year terms. The President designates a Chairman and Vice Chairman. In addition to the members of the Commission, the President appoints a General Counsel, with the advice and consent of the Senate, to support the Commission and provide direction, coordination, and supervision of the EEOC's litigation program. The General Counsel serves for a term of 4 years.

Address: U.S. Equal Employment Opportunity Commission
                1801 L Street NW
                Washington, DC 20507

Website: www.eeoc.gov   **Phone**:   202-663-4900

► **EEOC Attorney Honors Program (DC)**
www.eeoc.gov/eeoc/jobs/honorprogram.cfm   202-663-7175

► **Office of Legal Counsel – Legal Intern Program (DC)**
www.eeoc.gov/eeoc/jobs/intern-olc.cfm

► **Office of General Counsel – Summer Intern Program (DC)**
www.eeoc.gov/eeoc/jobs/intern-ogc.cfm   202-663-4729

► **Office of Federal Operations – Federal Sector Intern Program (DC)**
www.eeoc.gov/eeoc/jobs/intern-ofo.cfm   202-663-4542

► **Office of Equal Opportunity – Legal Intern Program (DC)**
www.eeoc.gov/eeoc/jobs/interns-oeo.cfm   202-663-4938

► **Boston Area Office – Legal Internships**
www.eeoc.gov/eeoc/jobs/intern-boston.cfm

► **New York District Office - Judicial Internship Program**
www.eeoc.gov/eeoc/jobs/intern-ny-aj.cfm   212-336-3746

► **New York District Office – Law Student Internships**
www.eeoc.gov/eeoc/jobs/intern-ny-legal.cfm

► **Washington Field Office – Law Student Internships**
www.eeoc.gov/eeoc/jobs/intern-washingtonfo.cfm   202-419-0732

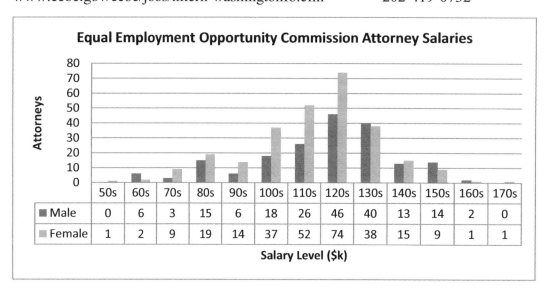

Equal Employment Opportunity Commission Attorney Salaries

	50s	60s	70s	80s	90s	100s	110s	120s	130s	140s	150s	160s	170s
Male	0	6	3	15	6	18	26	46	40	13	14	2	0
Female	1	2	9	19	14	37	52	74	38	15	9	1	1

Salary Level ($k)

Federal Communications Commission

Description:

The Federal Communications Commission (FCC) regulates interstate and foreign communications by radio, television, wire, satellite, and cable. It is responsible for the orderly development and operation of broadcast services and the provision of rapid, efficient nationwide and worldwide telephone and telegraph services at reasonable rates. Its responsibilities also include the use of communications for promoting safety of life and property and for strengthening the national defense.

The FCC was created by the Communications Act of 1934 (47 U.S.C. 151 et seq.) to regulate interstate and foreign communications by wire and radio in the public interest. The scope of FCC regulation includes radio and television broadcasting; telephone, telegraph, and cable television operation; two-way radio and radio operators; and satellite communication. The Commission is composed of five members, who are appointed by the President with the advice and consent of the Senate. One of the members is designated by the President as Chairman.

The Office of General Counsel (OGC) serves as the chief legal advisor to the Commission and to its various bureaus and offices. The General Counsel also represents the Commission in litigation in Federal courts, recommends decisions in adjudicatory matters before the Commission, assists the Commission in its decision making capacity and performs a variety of legal functions.

The attorneys of the Administrative Law Division of the OGC provide the Commissioners, and the agency's Bureaus and Offices, with legal advice on a broad range of communications and general administrative law issues. They also provide the public with legal information on such matters. The Division reviews all draft Commission decisions for legal sufficiency. Division staff provide legal advice to the Commission concerning a wide array of statutes, regulations, and procedures, including, for example, the Communications Act of 1934, as amended by the Telecommunications Act of 1996, the Administrative Procedure Act, the Freedom of Information Act, the Privacy Act, the Regulatory Flexibility Act, the Paperwork Reduction Act of 1995, the Government in the Sunshine Act, the Contract with America Advancement Act of 1996, negotiated rulemaking, and alternative dispute resolution, the Commission's procedural rules, procurement issues, the agency's ex parte and ethics rules (including receipt of gifts by the Commission and its employees, reimbursed travel expenses, and lobbying disclosure). The Division staff

135

is available to answer inquiries from the public concerning these matters. The Division also drafts all Commission decisions involving matters on review from Administrative Law Judges, Freedom of Information Act applications for review, and regulatory and filing fee applications for review.

The Litigation Division of the OGC represents the Commission in Federal courts of appeals when parties challenge Commission actions, and, in conjunction with the U.S. Department of Justice and U.S. Attorneys offices, represents the Commission in litigation in Federal district courts. In addition, Litigation Division attorneys work with the Solicitor General of the United States in representing the Commission in actions in the Supreme Court of the United States.

The OGC Transaction Team coordinates the FCC's review of applications for the transfer of control and assignment of licenses and authorizations involved in major transactions, such as mergers. The Transaction Team helps ensure that the Commission's internal procedures are transparent and uniform across the various Bureaus.

The Office of Administrative Law Judges of the Federal Communications Commission is responsible for conducting the hearings ordered by the Commission. The hearing function includes acting on interlocutory requests filed in the proceedings such as petitions to intervene, petitions to enlarge issues, and contested discovery requests. An Administrative Law Judge, appointed under the Administrative Procedures Act, presides at the hearing during which documents and sworn testimony are received in evidence, and witnesses are cross-examined. At the conclusion of the evidentiary phase of a proceeding, the Presiding Administrative Law Judge issues an Initial Decision which may be appealed to the Commission.

Address: Federal Communications Commission
445 Twelfth Street, SW
Washington, DC 20554

Website: www.fcc.gov   **Phone**:   888-225-5322

▶ **FCC Office of General Counsel Internships**
www.fcc.gov/internships/ogc.html

▶ **FCC Legal Internships**
www.fcc.gov/internships/

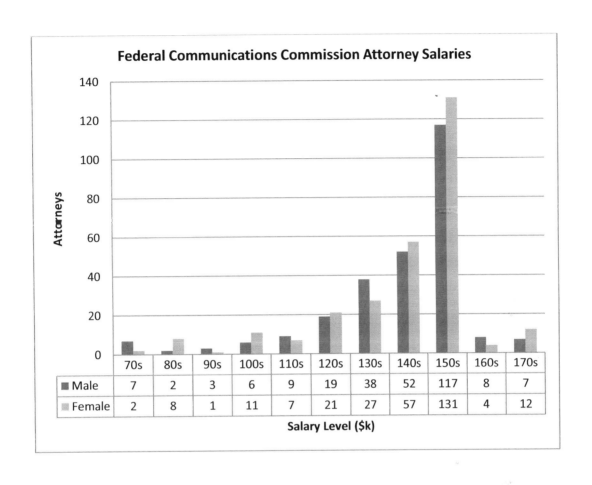

Federal Communications Commission Attorney Salaries

	70s	80s	90s	100s	110s	120s	130s	140s	150s	160s	170s
Male	7	2	3	6	9	19	38	52	117	8	7
Female	2	8	1	11	7	21	27	57	131	4	12

Salary Level ($k)

Federal Deposit Insurance Corporation

Description:

The Federal Deposit Insurance Corporation (FDIC) promotes and preserves public confidence in U.S. financial institutions by insuring bank and thrift deposits up to the legal limit; by periodically examining State-chartered banks that are not members of the Federal Reserve System for safety and soundness as well as compliance with consumer protection laws; and by liquidating assets of failed institutions to reimburse the insurance funds for the cost of failures.

The FDIC was established under the Banking Act of 1933 in response to numerous bank failures during the Great Depression. FDIC began insuring banks on January 1, 1934. Management of the FDIC consists of a Board of Directors that includes the Chairman, Vice Chairman, and Appointive Director. The Comptroller of the Currency, whose office supervises national banks, and the Director of the Office of Thrift Supervision, which supervises federally or State-chartered savings associations, are also members of the Board. All five Board members are appointed by the President and confirmed by the Senate, with no more than three being from the same political party.

Address: Federal Deposit Insurance Corporation
550 Seventeenth Street, NW
Washington, DC 20429

Website: www.fdic.gov   **Phone**: 703-562-2222

► **FDIC Legal Honors Program**
www.fdic.gov/about/legalhonors/

► **FDIC Summer Legal Intern Program**
www.fdic.gov/about/legalinterns/

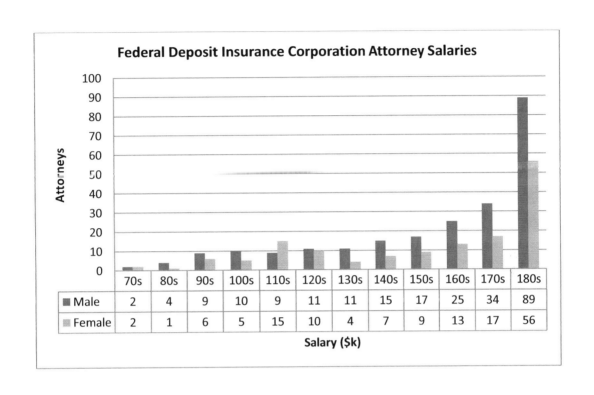

Federal Deposit Insurance Corporation Attorney Salaries

	70s	80s	90s	100s	110s	120s	130s	140s	150s	160s	170s	180s
■ Male	2	4	9	10	9	11	11	15	17	25	34	89
■ Female	2	1	6	5	15	10	4	7	9	13	17	56

Salary ($k)

Federal Trade Commission

Description:
The Federal Trade Commission (FTC) has jurisdiction to enhance consumer welfare and protect competition in broad sectors of the economy. The Commission enforces the laws that prohibit business practices that are anticompetitive, deceptive, or unfair to consumers; promotes informed consumer choice and public understanding of the competitive process; and seeks to accomplish its mission without impeding legitimate business activity.

The FTC was established in 1914 by the Federal Trade Commission Act (15 U.S.C. 41–58). The Commission is composed of five members appointed by the President, with the advice and consent of the Senate, for a term of 7 years. Not more than three of the Commissioners may be members of the same political party. One Commissioner is designated by the President as Chairman of the Commission and is responsible for its administrative management.

The General Counsel is the Commission's chief legal officer and adviser. The Office of General Counsel's (OGC) major functions are representing the Commission in court and providing legal counsel to the Commission, the operating bureaus, and other offices. OGC has developed a summary of the Commission's legal authority, which outlines the statutes enforced by the FTC. The OGC also issues a quarterly Litigation Status Report, which summarizes the current status of pending court actions involving the Commission. OGC also plays an active role in advancing the development of the law, and, when appropriate, files amicus briefs for the Commission.

Address: Federal Trade Commission
600 Pennsylvania Avenue, NW
Washington, DC 20580

Website: www.ftc.gov   **Phone**:   202-326-2222

▶ **FTC Entry Level Attorneys**
www.ftc.gov/ftc/oed/hrmo/jobops.shtm#elap

▶ **FTC Summer Legal Interns**
www.ftc.gov/ftc/oed/hrmo/interns.shtm#sli

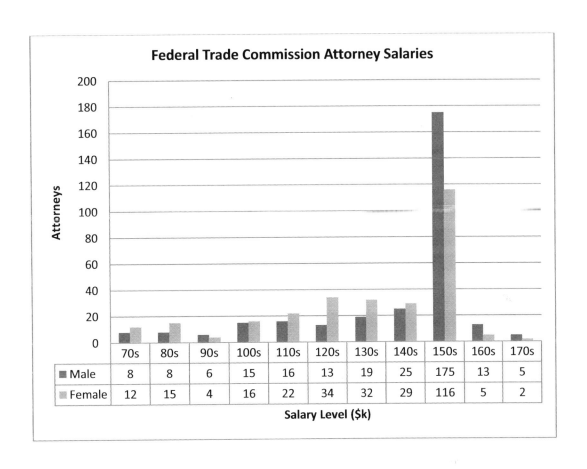

	70s	80s	90s	100s	110s	120s	130s	140s	150s	160s	170s
▪ Male	8	8	6	15	16	13	19	25	175	13	5
▪ Female	12	15	4	16	22	34	32	29	116	5	2

Government Printing Office

Description:

The U.S Government Printing Office (GPO) provides publishing & dissemination services for the official & authentic government publications to Congress, Federal agencies, Federal depository libraries, & the American public. The GPO is part of the legislative branch.

The General Counsel is the chief legal officer for the agency. The Office of the General Counsel provides legal opinions and advice to the Public Printer, and represents the GPO in all legal matters involving government and non-government organizations. In addition to providing legal opinions and advice for the agency, the Office of the General Counsel represents GPO before all Federal administrative forums, including the Merit Systems Protection Board, the Equal Employment Opportunity Commission, and the GAO Board of Contract Appeals.

Address: U.S. Government Printing Office
710 North Capitol Street, NW
Washington, DC 20401

Website: www.gpo.gov   **Phone**:   866-512-1800

Attorney Location	Gender	Length of Service	Salary
District of Columbia	Male	35 years or more	$157,739
District of Columbia	Male	10 - 14 years	$153,200
District of Columbia	Male	25 - 29 years	$152,053
District of Columbia	Male	5 - 9 years	$144,997
District of Columbia	Female	5 - 9 years	$132,914
District of Columbia	Female	10 - 14 years	$119,844
District of Columbia	Male	20 - 24 years	$116,419
District of Columbia	Female	5 - 9 years	$112,995
District of Columbia	Female	1 -2 years	$86,927
AVERAGE			**$130,788**

National Aeronautics and Space Administration

Description:
The National Aeronautics and Space Administration (NASA) was established by the National Aeronautics and Space Act of 1958, as amended (42 U.S.C. 2451 et seq.). NASA's mission is to pioneer the future in space exploration, scientific discovery, and aeronautics research.

The Office of the General Counsel (OGC) provides functional leadership regarding legal services and issues related to all aspects of NASA activities for Center Chief and Patent Counsel and, for Agency-wide issues, the Administrator. These services and issues include establishing and disseminating legal policy and interpreting new statutes and cases. The OGC is also responsible for developing the ethics and patent program requirements, establishing metrics, and developing quality standards. As a functional office Associate Administrator, the General Counsel serves in an advisory capacity to the Administrator, and works with Enterprise Associate Administrators and Center Directors to ensure that Agency activities are conducted in accordance with all statutory and regulatory requirements.

The OGC also serves as litigation counsel, provides litigation expertise to the Agency, and acts as the Agency representative before the U.S. Patent and Trademark Office. The Office also provides expert advice, oversight and overflow support to Centers, and provides legal services to all the offices at Headquarters. The OGC is organized into a front office, one legal program and four legal practice groups:

- Acquisition Integrity Program -- Has primary responsibility for legal issues regarding procurement fraud and other related irregularities, remedies coordination, and suspension and debarment. The Program is responsible for preventing, detecting, and deterring procurement fraud through education and training of the NASA workforce as well as for supporting the investigation and prosecution of fraud and corruption related to the acquisition process.
- Commercial & Intellectual Property -- Has primary responsibility for intellectual property issues in domestic and international agreements, technical data issues, patent and copyright licensing, and the distribution of computer software, as well as non-procurement (Space Act) agreements with commercial and international entities.

143

- Contracts & Procurement -- Has primary responsibility for contracts, grants, and cooperative agreements.

- General Law -- Has primary responsibility for areas such as ethics, personnel, fiscal, environmental, and safety and security law, as well as legislation and other areas not specifically assigned to one of the other divisions.

- International Law -- Has primary responsibility over legal issues regarding export control, Freedom of Information Act appeals, and general matters of international law.

Address: National Aeronautics and Space Administration
300 E Street SW
Washington, DC 20546

Website: www.nasa.gov **Phone**: 202-358-0000

NASA Department	Attorneys	Male	Female	Avg Salary
Ames Research Center	11	7	4	$146,549
Dryden Flight Research	3	3	-	$136,389
George C. Marshal Space Flight Ctr.	11	6	5	$131,103
Goddard Space Flight Center	15	8	7	$144,960
NASA Headquarters	42	28	14	$143,184
John C. Stennis Space Center	4	1	3	$120,719
John F. Kennedy Space Center	13	9	4	$111,485
John Glenn Research Center	7	4	3	$142,177
Langley Research Center	11	7	4	$129,810
Lyndon B. Johnson Space Center	16	9	7	$133,575
TOTAL	133	82	51	$136,421
Percent of Positions		62%	38%	

Ames Research Center

(11 attorneys, www.nasa.gov/centers/ames/)

Ames Research Center is located in the heart of California's Silicon Valley at the core of the research cluster of high-tech companies, universities and laboratories that define the region's character. With over $3 billion in capital equipment, 2,300 research personnel and a $600 million annual budget, Ames' economic impact is significant. Ames plays a role in virtually all NASA missions in support of America's space and aeronautics programs.

As a leader in information technology research with a focus on supercomputing, networking and intelligent systems, Ames conducts research and development enabling technologies that make NASA missions possible. Ames also is a leader in nanotechnology, fundamental space biology, biotechnology, aerospace and thermal protection systems, and human factors research. Ames research in astrobiology focuses on the effects of gravity on living things, and the nature and distribution of stars, planets and life in the universe.

In addition, Ames works collaboratively with the FAA, conducting research in air traffic management to make safer, cheaper and more efficient air travel a reality. Ames engages in information and education outreach, forms collaborative partnerships, and fosters commercial application of NASA technologies. Ames is developing NASA Research Park, an integrated, dynamic research and education community created to cultivate diverse partnerships with academia, industry and non-profit organizations in support of NASA's mission.

Dryden Flight Research
(3 attorneys, www.nasa.gov/centers/dryden/)

The Dryden Flight Research Center is NASA's primary center for atmospheric flight research and operations. NASA Dryden is critical in carrying out the agency's missions of space exploration, space operations, scientific discovery, and aeronautical research and development. Located at Edwards, California, in the western Mojave Desert, Dryden is situated to take advantage of the excellent year-round flying weather, remote area, and visibility to test some of the Nation's most exciting air vehicles.

George C. Marshall Space Flight Center
(11 attorneys, www.nasa.gov/centers/marshall/)

The George C. Marshall Space Flight Center (Marshall) is responsible for space shuttle propulsion elements, hardware and payload operations for the International Space Station and such science missions as the Discovery and New Frontiers programs and the Chandra X-ray Observatory.

As a natural extension of its historical involvement in the Mercury, Apollo and shuttle programs, Marshall is designing and developing America's next generation of launch vehicles. It is also developing specialized scientific spacecraft and participating in NASA's new robotic lunar initiatives.

Goddard Space Flight Center
(15 attorneys, www.nasa.gov/centers/goddard/)

NASA's Goddard Space Flight Center is home to the Nation's largest organization of combined scientists, engineers and technologists that build spacecraft, instruments and new technology to study the Earth, the Sun, our solar system, and the universe.

The center is a major U.S. laboratory for developing and operating unmanned scientific spacecraft. The center manages many of NASA's Earth observation, astronomy, and space physics missions. The center includes several other facilities: the Wallops Flight Facility at Wallops Island, Virginia; The Goddard Institute for Space Studies in New York City; and the Independent Verification and Validation Facility in West Virginia.

NASA Headquarters
(42 attorneys, www.nasa.gov/centers/hq/)

NASA Headquarters, in Washington DC, provides overall guidance and direction to the agency, under the leadership of the Administrator. Ten field centers and a variety of installations around the country conduct the day-to-day work in laboratories, on air fields, in wind tunnels, and in control rooms. Together, this diverse group of scientists, engineers, managers, and support personnel share the Vision, Mission, and Values that are NASA. To implement NASA's Mission, NASA Headquarters is organized into four principal organizations called Mission Directorates:

- Aeronautics: Pioneers and proves new flight technologies that improve NASA's ability to explore and which have practical applications on Earth.
- Exploration Systems: Creates new capabilities and spacecraft for affordable, sustainable human and robotic exploration
- Science: Explores the Earth, moon, Mars, and beyond; charts the best route of discovery; and reaps the benefits of Earth and space exploration.
- Space Operations: Provides critical enabling technologies for much of the rest of NASA through the space shuttle, the International Space Station, and flight support.

John C. Stennis Space Center
(4 attorneys, www.nasa.gov/centers/stennis/)

The John C. Stennis Space Center in South Mississippi is home to America's largest rocket engine test complex where every space shuttle main engine is tested and future engines and stages will be tested for potentially returning astronauts to the moon with possible journeys beyond. Because of its role in engine testing for four decades, Stennis is NASA's program manager for rocket propulsion testing with total responsibility for conducting and/or managing all NASA propulsion test programs.

After the Space Shuttle Program ends a new fleet of launch vehicles will power America's next-generation spacecraft, Orion, which will carry astronauts back to the moon with possible journeys beyond the lunar surface. Stennis is testing core components for the J-2X rocket engine that will power the upper stage of the new crew launch vehicle, Ares I, and the Earth departure stage of Ares V, the new cargo launch vehicle.

John F. Kennedy Space Center
(13 attorneys, www.nasa.gov/centers/kennedy/)

John F. Kennedy Space Center has helped set the stage for America's adventure in space for more than four decades. The spaceport has served as the departure gate for every American manned mission and hundreds of advanced scientific spacecraft. From the early days of Project Mercury to the space shuttle and International Space Station, from the Hubble Space Telescope to the Mars Exploration Rovers, the center enjoys a rich heritage in its role as NASA's processing and launch center.

John Glenn Research Center
(7 attorneys, www.nasa.gov/centers/glenn/)

Glenn Research Center, in partnership with U.S. industry, universities, and other government institutions, is developing critical systems technologies and capabilities that address national priorities. Its world-class research, technology, and capability development efforts are keys to advancing exploration of our solar system and beyond while maintaining global leadership in aeronautics. Its work is focused on technological advancements in spaceflight systems development, aeropropulsion, space propulsion, power systems, nuclear systems, communications and human research.

Langley Research Center

(11 attorneys, www.nasa.gov/centers/langley/)

Researchers at the Langley Research Center are focusing on some of the biggest technical challenges of our time: global climate change, access to space and revolutionizing airplanes and the air transportation system.

Langley scientists study the atmosphere to improve life on Earth and to better understand the conditions planes and spacecraft fly through. Langley engineers work on technologies to make civilian and military planes safer, quieter and more efficient, while designing tomorrow's supersonic and even hypersonic aircraft. Langley researchers analyze materials and structures to help spacecraft withstand unforgiving extraterrestrial environments.

Lyndon B. Johnson Space Center

(16 attorneys, www.nasa.gov/centers/johnson/home/)

Johnson Space Center was established in 1961 as the Manned Spacecraft Center. In 1973, the Center was renamed in honor of the late President, Lyndon B. Johnson. From the early Gemini, Apollo and Skylab projects to the Space Shuttle and International Space Station Programs, the Center continues to lead NASA's efforts in human space exploration.

National Archives and Records Administration

Description:
The National Archives and Records Administration (NARA) safeguards and preserves the records of the Federal government, establishes policies and procedures for managing U.S. Government records, manages the Presidential Libraries system, and publishes the laws, regulations, and Presidential and other public documents. NARA is the successor agency to the National Archives Establishment, which was created in 1934 and subsequently incorporated into the General Services Administration as the National Archives and Records Service in 1949. NARA was established as an independent agency in the executive branch of the Government by act of October 19, 1984 (44 U.S.C. 2101 et seq.).

NARA attorneys provides legal advice, conducts legal research and analysis, and engage in administrative and Federal court litigation in support of all of NARA's programs and activities. These issues arise under NARA's governing statutes and related access and information laws, including the Federal Records Act, Presidential Records Act, Presidential Libraries Act, Presidential Recordings and Materials Preservation Act, Freedom of Information Act, and Privacy Act.

Address: U.S. National Archives and Records Administration
8601 Adelphi Road
College Park, MD 20740-6001

Website: www.archives.gov   **Phone:**   866-272-6272

Attorney Location	Gender	Length of Service	Salary
Maryland	Male	15 - 19 years	$162,900
Maryland	Male	25 - 29 years	$162,900
Maryland	Male	25 - 29 years	$153,200
Maryland	Female	5 - 9 years	$128,886
District of Columbia	Female	5 - 9 years	$124,858
Maryland	Male	10 - 14 years	$119,844
District of Columbia	Female	3 - 4 years	$106,145
Maryland	Male	5 - 9 years	$106,145
Maryland	Female	1 -2 years	$89,825
Maryland	Female	Less than 1 year	$73,100
Maryland	Male	1 – 2 years	$60,989
AVERAGE			**$117,163**

National Credit Union Administration

Description:

The National Credit Union Administration (NCUA) is responsible for chartering, insuring, supervising, and examining Federal credit unions and administering the National Credit Union Share Insurance Fund. The Administration also administers the Community Development Revolving Loan Fund and manages the Central Liquidity Facility, a mixed-ownership Government corporation whose purpose is to supply emergency loans to member credit unions.

NCUA was established by act of March 10, 1970 (12 U.S.C. 1752), and reorganized by act of November 10, 1978 (12 U.S.C. 226), as an independent agency in the executive branch of the Federal Government. It regulates and insures all Federal credit unions and insures State-chartered credit unions that apply and qualify for share insurance.

The Office of General Counsel has responsibility for all legal matters affecting NCUA, including: representing the agency in litigation; bringing enforcement actions against directors, managers and other parties affiliated with credit unions; providing interpretations of the Federal Credit Union Act and NCUA Rules and Regulations to the agency and to outside parties; processing Freedom of Information Act requests and appeals; advising the Board and the agency on general legal matters; and drafting regulations designed to ensure the safety and soundness of credit unions.

Address: National Credit Union Administration
1775 Duke Street
Alexandria, VA 22314-3428

Website: www.ncua.gov   **Phone**:   703-518-6300

NCUA Atty Location	Gender	Length of Service	Salary
Virginia	Male	35 years or more	$265,559
Virginia	Male	20 - 24 years	$216,938
Virginia	Female	20 - 24 years	$202,325
Virginia	Male	25 - 29 years	$196,136
Virginia	Male	10 - 14 years	$171,041
Virginia	Female	25 - 29 years	$170,538
Virginia	Female	20 - 24 years	$170,538
Virginia	Female	25 - 29 years	$170,538
Virginia	Male	20 - 24 years	$170,538
Virginia	Male	25 - 29 years	$170,538
Virginia	Male	25 - 29 years	$170,538
Virginia	Female	20 - 24 years	$168,948
Virginia	Male	15 - 19 years	$157,434
Virginia	Female	10 - 14 years	$153,662
Virginia	Female	15 - 19 years	$147,582
Virginia	Male	20 - 24 years	$147,582
Virginia	Female	15 - 19 years	$145,613
Virginia	Female	3 - 4 years	$141,410
Texas	Male	10 - 14 years	$137,476
Virginia	Female	10 - 14 years	$124,821
Virginia	Female	10 - 14 years	$120,411
Virginia	Female	15 - 19 years	$117,926
Virginia	Female	Less than 1 year	$86,844
Virginia	Male	1 - 2 years	$83,657
Virginia	Male	Less than 1 year	$83,000
AVERAGE			$155,664

National Labor Relations Board

Description:
The National Labor Relations Board (NLRB) is vested with the power to prevent and remedy unfair labor practices committed by private sector employers and unions and to safeguard employees' rights to organize and determine whether to have unions as their bargaining representative.

NLRB is an independent agency created by the National Labor Relations Act of 1935 (Wagner Act; 29 U.S.C. 167). The Board is authorized to designate appropriate units for collective bargaining and to conduct secret ballot elections to determine whether employees desire representation by a labor organization.

The General Counsel, appointed by the President to a 4-year term with Senate consent, is independent from the Board and is responsible for the investigation and prosecution of unfair labor practice cases and for the general supervision of the NLRB field offices in the processing of cases. Each Regional Office is headed by a Regional Director who is responsible for making the initial determination in cases arising within the geographical area served by the region.

Address: National Labor Relations Board
1099 Fourteenth St., NW
Washington, DC 20570-0001

Website: www.nlrb.gov   **Phone**:   202-273-1000

▶ NLRB Attorney Honors Program
www.nlrb.gov/Honors

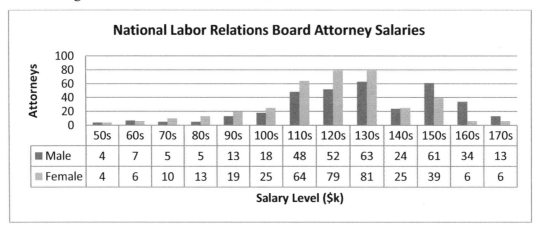

	50s	60s	70s	80s	90s	100s	110s	120s	130s	140s	150s	160s	170s
Male	4	7	5	5	13	18	48	52	63	24	61	34	13
Female	4	6	10	13	19	25	64	79	81	25	39	6	6

National Labor Relations Board Attorney Salaries

National Science Foundation

Description:

The National Science Foundation (NSF) promotes the progress of science and engineering through the support of research and education programs. NSF is an independent agency created by the National Science Foundation Act of 1950, as amended (42 U.S.C. 1861– 1875).

The purposes of the Foundation are to increase the Nation's base of scientific and engineering knowledge and strengthen its ability to conduct research in all areas of science and engineering; to develop and help implement science and engineering education programs that can better prepare the Nation for meeting the challenges of the future; and to promote international cooperation through science and engineering. In its role as a leading Federal supporter of science and engineering, the agency also has an important role in national policy planning.

The Director and the Deputy Director are appointed by the President, with the advice and consent of the Senate, to a 6- year term and an unspecified term, respectively. The Foundation's activities are guided by the National Science Board. The National Science Board is composed of 24 members and the Director ex officio. Members are appointed by the President with the advice and consent of the Senate for 6- year terms, with one-third appointed every 2 years. They are selected because of their records of distinguished service in science, engineering, education, research management, or public affairs to be broadly representative of the views of national science and engineering leadership. The Board also has a broad national policy responsibility to monitor and make recommendations to promote the health of U.S. science and engineering research and education.

The Office of the General Counsel is the legal advisor and advocate for the Foundation, providing legal advice and assistance on all aspects of the Foundation's programs, policies, and operations, as well as areas affecting science and technology more broadly. Advice is provided in a wide variety of areas, such as: grants, contracts and cooperative agreements; intellectual property; conflicts-of-interest; employee and labor relations; civil rights; health, safety and environment; public regulation of research; Federal fiscal and administrative law and procedure; international law and agreements; and national security restrictions of scientific research (including export controls). The Office of the General Counsel also provides litigation expertise to the agency coordinating each phase of complex litigation with various divisions of the U.S. Department of Justice.

Address: The National Science Foundation
4201 Wilson Boulevard
Arlington, VA 22230

Website: www.nsf.gov   **Phone**:   703-292-5111

NSF Atty Location	Gender	Length of Service	Salary
Virginia	Male	30 - 34 years	$177,000
Virginia	Female	10 - 14 years	$173,938
Virginia	Female	25 - 29 years	$162,899
Virginia	Male	20 - 24 years	$162,899
Virginia	Female	15 - 19 years	$160,078
Virginia	Female	10 - 14 years	$160,078
Virginia	Male	10 - 14 years	$160,078
Virginia	Male	25 - 29 years	$160,078
Virginia	Male	15 - 19 years	$158,840
Virginia	Male	5 - 9 years	$155,174
Virginia	Male	5 - 9 years	$153,943
Virginia	Female	5 - 9 years	$136,941
Virginia	Female	25 - 29 years	$136,941
Virginia	Female	10 - 14 years	$134,147
Colorado	Female	10 - 14 years	$122,395
Virginia	Male	3 - 4 years	$121,109
Virginia	Female	5 - 9 years	$121,053
Virginia	Female	10 - 14 years	$119,894
Virginia	Female	5 - 9 years	$114,092
AVERAGE			**$146,925**

Nuclear Regulatory Commission

Description:

The Nuclear Regulatory Commission (NRC) licenses and regulates civilian use of nuclear energy to protect public health and safety and the environment. NRC was established as an independent regulatory agency under the provisions of the Energy Reorganization Act of 1974 (42 U.S.C. 5801 et seq.) and Executive Order 11834 of January 15, 1975. All licensing and related regulatory functions formerly assigned to the Atomic Energy Commission were transferred to the Commission.

The Commission's major program components are the Office of Nuclear Reactor Regulation, the Office of New Reactors, the Office of Nuclear Material Safety and Safeguards, the Office of Federal and State Materials and Environmental Management Programs, and the Office of Nuclear Regulatory Research. Headquarters offices are located in Maryland, and there are four regional offices.

The Commission ensures that the civilian uses of nuclear materials and facilities are conducted in a manner consistent with the public health and safety, environmental quality, national security, and the antitrust laws. Most of the Commission's effort is focused on regulating the use of nuclear energy to generate electric power.

The General Counsel is the chief legal advisor to the NRC and directs all matters of law and legal policy for the agency. The Office of the General Counsel consists of seven divisions that provide advice and assistance to the General Counsel and the NRC staff. The Solicitor, in conjunction with legal counsel, has primary responsibility for supervising litigation in courts of law.

Address: U.S. Nuclear Regulatory Commission
Washington, DC 20555-0001

Website: www.nrc.gov   **Phone**: 301-415-7000

▶ Office of the General Counsel Summer Intern Program
www.nrc.gov/about-nrc/employment/ogc-intern.html

Nuclear Regulatory Commission - Office of the General Counsel

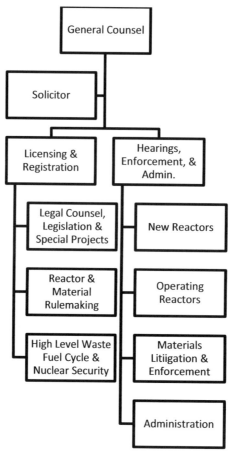

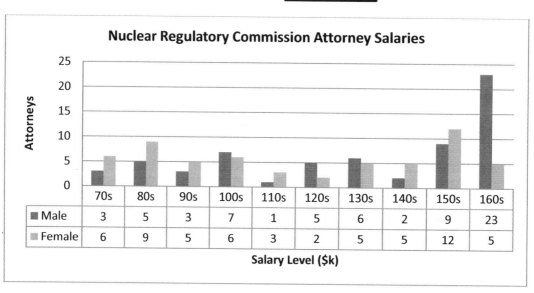

Nuclear Regulatory Commission Attorney Salaries

	70s	80s	90s	100s	110s	120s	130s	140s	150s	160s
Male	3	5	3	7	1	5	6	2	9	23
Female	6	9	5	6	3	2	5	5	12	5

Salary Level ($k)

Office of Personnel Management

Description:

The Office of Personnel Management (OPM) administers a merit system to ensure compliance with personnel laws and regulations and assists agencies in recruiting, examining, and promoting people on the basis of their knowledge and skills, regardless of their race, religion, sex, political influence, or other nonmerit factors.

OPM was created as an independent establishment by Reorganization Plan No. 2 of 1978 (5 U.S.C. app.), pursuant to Executive Order 12107 of December 28, 1978. Many of the functions of the former United States Civil Service Commission were transferred to OPM.

OPM administers the Administrative Law Judge Examination on behalf of Federal agencies.

Address: U.S. Office of Personnel Management
1900 E Street, NW
Washington, DC 20415-0001

Website: www.opm.gov   **Phone**:   202-606-1800

OPM Atty Location	Gender	Length of Service	Salary
District of Columbia	Female	10 - 14 years	$177,000
District of Columbia	Female	10 - 14 years	$169,950
District of Columbia	Male	30 - 34 years	$168,500
District of Columbia	Male	35 years or more	$164,250
District of Columbia	Female	10 - 14 years	$153,200
District of Columbia	Male	30 - 34 years	$153,200
District of Columbia	Male	35 years or more	$153,200
District of Columbia	Female	10 - 14 years	$149,025
District of Columbia	Male	25 - 29 years	$149,025
District of Columbia	Male	Less than 1 year	$144,997
District of Columbia	Male	20 - 24 years	$144,997
District of Columbia	Female	10 - 14 years	$140,969
District of Columbia	Male	15 - 19 years	$136,941
District of Columbia	Female	35 years or more	$133,543
District of Columbia	Male	25 - 29 years	$133,543
District of Columbia	Female	5 - 9 years	$130,118
District of Columbia	Female	5 - 9 years	$128,886
District of Columbia	Female	10 - 14 years	$123,269
District of Columbia	Female	20 - 24 years	$123,269
District of Columbia	Female	Less than 1 year	$120,830
District of Columbia	Male	5 - 9 years	$116,419
District of Columbia	Male	10 - 14 years	$116,419
District of Columbia	Male	5 - 9 years	$113,007
District of Columbia	Female	5 - 9 years	$109,570
District of Columbia	Female	1 - 2 years	$101,416
District of Columbia	Female	Less than 1 year	$92,723
District of Columbia	Female	1 - 2 years	$86,927
District of Columbia	Female	3 - 4 years	$86,927
AVERAGE			$132,933

Securities and Exchange Commission

Description:
The Securities and Exchange Commission (SEC) administers Federal securities laws that seek to provide protection for investors; to ensure that securities markets are fair and honest; and, when necessary, to provide the means to enforce securities laws through sanctions.

The SEC was created under authority of the Securities Exchange Act of 1934 (15 U.S.C. 78a–78jj) and was organized on July 2, 1934. The Commission serves as adviser to United States district courts in connection with reorganization proceedings for debtor corporations in which there is a substantial public interest. The Commission also has certain responsibilities under section 15 of the Bretton Woods Agreements Act of 1945 (22 U.S.C. 286k–1) and section 851(e) of the Internal Revenue Code of 1954 (26 U.S.C. 851(e)).

The Commission is vested with quasijudicial functions. Persons aggrieved by its decisions in the exercise of those functions have a right of review by the United States courts of appeals.

The General Counsel is the chief legal officer of the Commission and heads the Office of the General Counsel (OGC). The office provides a variety of legal services to the Commission and staff, and is divided into five groups: Appellate, General Litigation, Adjudication, Ethics, and Legal Policy. The office prepares all of the Commission's appellate and amicus briefs, litigates all non-enforcement matters on behalf of the agency, assists in preparing Commission opinions on appeal from administrative law judges, stock exchanges, the Financial Industry Regulatory Authority (FINRA) and the Public Company Accounting Oversight Board, and provides legal advice and counseling concerning the Federal securities laws, administrative laws, government ethics rules, and other laws that affect independent agencies.

The OGC Appellate Litigation Group represents the Commission in litigation to which it is a party in the Federal courts of appeals and (in conjunction with the Solicitor General) in the Supreme Court of the United States. For the most part, these cases involve appeals from Commission injunctive actions and petitions seeking review of Commission administrative orders. In addition, the group represents the Commission as amicus curiae in private litigation raising important issues under the Federal securities laws. The Appellate Litigation Group is also responsible for representing the Commission in proceedings under Chapter 11 of the Bankruptcy Code in cases involving companies with a significant number of public security holders and raising issues of significance.

The OGC General Litigation Group represents the Commission, its members, and its employees at the trial and appellate levels, when they are parties to civil or administrative litigation arising from the performance of the Commission's official functions, such as enforcement investigations and rulemaking proceedings. Along with the Federal securities law questions, these cases often involve issues arising under a variety of Federal administrative statutes, such as the Administrative Procedure, Freedom of Information and the Right to Financial Privacy Acts. In addition, the Group litigates administrative disciplinary proceedings against attorneys under Rule 102(e) of the Commission's Rules of Practice. These cases involve allegations that an attorney has violated the Federal securities laws or breached their professional responsibilities in practicing before the Commission.

The OGC Adjudication Group advises and assists the Commission in issuing published opinions in contested appeals. The Commission's opinions guide the securities industry on questions of law. Adjudication attorneys advise the Commission on complex factual and legal issues, study the evidentiary records on appeal, and research the relevant substantive and procedural requirements. The appeals present challenges to decisions by Administrative Law Judges, stock exchanges, the FINRA, and the Public Company Accounting Oversight Board. Many cases involve disciplinary actions against brokerage firms and other securities professionals.

The Office of the Ethics Counsel is responsible for advising and counseling all Commission employees and members on such issues as personal and financial conflicts of interest, post-employment restrictions, securities holdings and transactions of Commission employees and their immediate families, gifts, seeking and negotiating other employment, outside activities, and financial disclosure. The Ethics staff also drafts, comments on, and implements regulations concerning ethical conduct issues. The Ethics Office assists Presidential appointees with various aspects of financial disclosure to the Senate and the U.S. Office of Government Ethics in connection with the confirmation process. Annually, the Ethics Office handles thousands of ethics counseling matters for Commission officials and staff.

The OGC Legal Policy Group provides legal and policy analysis and advice to the Commission, individual Commissioners, and the Commission's divisions and office concerning the Federal securities laws, administrative laws, and other applicable laws. The Group analyzes all enforcement and regulatory recommendations to the Commission from the operating divisions and offices. In addition, the Legal Policy Group provides legal and policy assistance on legislative matters, working on testimony, participating in briefings of Congressional staff, and responding to Congressional correspondence.

The SEC's Division of Enforcement investigations into possible violations of the Federal securities laws, and prosecutes the Commission's civil suits in the Federal courts as well as its administrative proceedings.

Address: SEC Headquarters
100 F Street, NE
Washington, DC 20549

Website: www.sec.gov   **Phone**:   202-551-7500

► **SEC Experienced Attorneys**
www.sec.gov/jobs/jobs_fulllist.shtml#exatty

► **SEC Summer Honors Law Program**
www.sec.gov/jobs/jobs_students.shtml#shlp

► **SEC Law Student Observer Program**
www.sec.gov/jobs/jobs_students.shtml#lsop

► **SEC Advanced Commitment Program**
www.sec.gov/jobs/jobs_students.shtml#acp

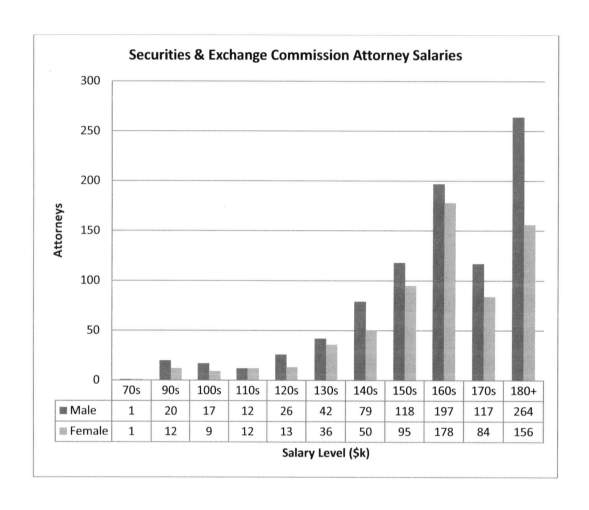

	70s	90s	100s	110s	120s	130s	140s	150s	160s	170s	180+
Male	1	20	17	12	26	42	79	118	197	117	264
Female	1	12	9	12	13	36	50	95	178	84	156

Small Business Administration

Description:
The Small Business Administration (SBA) aids, counsels, assists, and protects the interests of small business; ensures that small business concerns receive a fair portion of Government purchases, contracts, and subcontracts, as well as of the sales of Government property; makes loans to small business concerns, State and local development companies, and the victims of floods or other catastrophes, or of certain types of economic injury; and licenses, regulates, and makes loans to small business investment companies.

The SBA was created by the Small Business Act of 1953 and derives its present existence and authority from the Small Business Act (15 U.S.C. 631 et seq.) and the Small Business Investment Act of 1958 (15 U.S.C. 661).

The Office of General Counsel develops and implements plans, procedures, and standards for providing legal services in support of Agency program operations. The General Counsel is responsible for providing legal assistance and advice to the Administrator and other Agency officials on the development and execution of Agency policies, programs, and activities. The General Counsel also has full responsibility for the technical and professional guidance of all SBA counsel. The Deputy General Counsel and associate general counsels assist the General Counsel by providing professional and technical guidance and supervision over field activities of Agency. District counsel, supervisory attorneys, and attorney/advisors give legal advice to district directors, other field office managers, and field personnel on all aspects of SBA's programs and on administrative and employee relations matters.

Address: U.S. Small Business Administration
409 Third Street, SW
Washington, DC 20416

Website: www.sba.gov   **Phone**:   202-205-6600

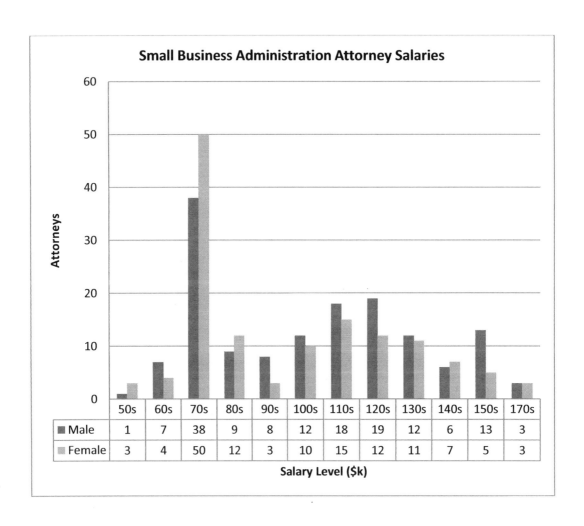

Salary Level ($k)	50s	60s	70s	80s	90s	100s	110s	120s	130s	140s	150s	170s
Male	1	7	38	9	8	12	18	19	12	6	13	3
Female	3	4	50	12	3	10	15	12	11	7	5	3

Smithsonian Institution

Description:

The Smithsonian Institution is an independent trust instrumentality of the United States which comprises the world's largest museum and research complex; includes 19 museums and galleries, the National Zoo, and research facilities in several States and the Republic of Panama; and is dedicated to public education, national service, and scholarship in the arts, sciences, history, and culture.

The Smithsonian Institution was created by an act of Congress on August 10, 1846 (20 U.S.C. 41 et seq.), to carry out the terms of the will of British scientist James Smithson (1765–1829), who in 1826 had bequeathed his entire estate to the United States "to found at Washington, under the name of the Smithsonian Institution, an establishment for the increase and diffusion of knowledge among men." On July 1, 1836, Congress accepted the legacy and pledged the faith of the United States to the charitable trust.

In September 1838, Smithson's legacy, which amounted to more than 100,000 gold sovereigns, was delivered to the mint at Philadelphia. Congress vested responsibility for administering the trust in the Secretary of the Smithsonian and the Smithsonian Board of Regents, composed of the Chief Justice, the Vice President, three Members of the Senate, three Members of the House of Representatives, and nine citizen members appointed by joint resolution of Congress. To carry out Smithson's mandate, the Institution executes the following functions:

- conducts scientific and scholarly research;
- publishes the results of studies, explorations, and investigations;
- preserves for study and reference more than 136 million artifacts, works of art, and scientific specimens;
- organizes exhibits representative of the arts, sciences, and American history;
- shares Smithsonian resources with communities throughout the Nation; and
- engages in educational programming and national and international cooperative research.

The Office of the General Counsel (OGC) protects the legal interests of the Smithsonian Institution. The OGC has several attorneys who provide legal advice and counsel to the Board of Regents, Secretary, and other Smithsonian staff on various issues including: the legal nature and administration of the Institution, intellectual property, employment, collections management, contracts, ethics, tax, tort claims, Freedom of Information Act, etc.

The OGC represents the Smithsonian in litigation and other adversarial proceedings to which the Institution is a party and before Federal, State, and local government entities on administrative matters; issues final determinations on administrative tort and personal property claims against the Smithsonian; and generally monitors developments in the law for application to Smithsonian programs. The Smithsonian Institution is represented in litigation by the Department of Justice and the Offices of the United States Attorney.

Address: Smithsonian Institution
1000 Jefferson Drive SW
Washington, DC 20560

Website: www.smithsonian.org   **Phone**:   202-633-1000

SMITHSONIAN:			
Attorney Location	**Gender**	**Length of Service**	**Salary**
District of Columbia	Female	5 - 9 years	$162,900
District of Columbia	Female	30 - 34 years	$162,900
District of Columbia	Female	15 - 19 years	$162,900
District of Columbia	Male	35 years or more	$153,200
District of Columbia	Male	15 - 19 years	$144,997
District of Columbia	Female	10 - 14 years	$132,914
District of Columbia	Male	5 - 9 years	$132,914
District of Columbia	Female	5 - 9 years	$128,886
District of Columbia	Male	5 - 9 years	$120,830
District of Columbia	Female	3 - 4 years	$113,007
Virginia	Female	5 - 9 years	$109,570
Virginia	Female	3 - 4 years	$102,721
Virginia	Male	1 - 2 years	$102,721
Virginia	Female	3 - 4 years	$95,620
Virginia	Female	1 - 2 years	$89,825
Virginia	Female	3 - 4 years	$86,927
Virginia	Male	1 - 2 years	$82,845

NATIONAL GALLERY OF ART:			
Attorney Location	**Gender**	**Length of Service**	**Salary**
District of Columbia	Female	20 - 24 years	$162,900
District of Columbia	Female	10 - 14 years	$153,200
District of Columbia	Male	15 - 19 years	$144,997
District of Columbia	Male	5 - 9 years	$144,997
District of Columbia	Female	10 - 14 years	$140,969
District of Columbia	Female	15 - 19 years	$140,969
District of Columbia	Male	20 - 24 years	$126,693
District of Columbia	Female	Less than 1 year	$50,408

Social Security Administration

Description:
The Social Security Administration (SSA) manages the Nation's social insurance program— consisting of retirement, survivors, and disability insurance programs— commonly known as Social Security; administers the Supplemental Security Income program for the aged, blind, and disabled; assigns Social Security numbers to U.S. citizens; and maintains earnings records for workers under their Social Security numbers.

The SSA was established by Reorganization Plan No. 2 of 1946 (5 U.S.C. app.), effective July 16, 1946. It became an independent agency in the executive branch by the Social Security Independence and Program Improvements Act of 1994 (42 U.S.C. 901), effective March 31, 1995. The Administration is headed by a Commissioner, appointed by the President with the advice and consent of the Senate.

In administering the programs necessary to carry out the Administration's mission, the Commissioner is assisted by a Deputy Commissioner who performs duties assigned or delegated by the Commissioner, a Chief Financial Officer, a Chief Information Officer, a General Counsel, a Chief Actuary, and an Inspector General.

The Office of the General Counsel advises the Commissioner on legal matters, is responsible for providing all legal advice to the Commissioner, Deputy Commissioner, and all subordinate organizational components (except OIG) of SSA in connection with the operation and administration of SSA. Responsible for the policy formulation and decision making related to the collection, access, and disclosure of such information in the records of the Social Security Administration; and processing of Freedom of Information requests and appeals.
For a detailed description of the office see: www.socialsecurity.gov/org/orgogc.htm

Address: Social Security Administration
              6401 Security Blvd.
              Baltimore, MD 21235

Website: www.socialsecurity.gov   **Phone**:   410-965-1234

► **SSA Legal Careers**
www.socialsecurity.gov/careers/legalcareers.htm

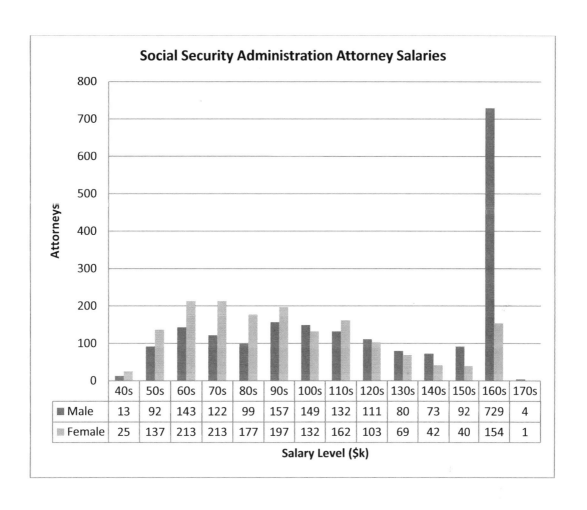

Social Security Administration Attorney Salaries

Salary Level ($k)	40s	50s	60s	70s	80s	90s	100s	110s	120s	130s	140s	150s	160s	170s
■ Male	13	92	143	122	99	157	149	132	111	80	73	92	729	4
■ Female	25	137	213	213	177	197	132	162	103	69	42	40	154	1

Medium Independent Agencies

(100 to 999 employees)

Agency	Attorneys	Admin. Law Judges	Law Clerks	Avg. Salary
Commodity Futures Trading Commission	195	2	4	$158,839
Consumer Product Safety Commission	30	-	-	$139,627
Corp. for National & Community Svc	9	-	-	$139,225
Defense Nuclear Facilities Safety Board	5	-	-	$148,936
Export-Import Bank of the United States	20	-	-	$145,171
Farm Credit Administration	12	-	-	$170,163
Federal Election Commission	91	-	2	$124,044
Federal Housing Finance Agency	29	-	-	$175,961[1]
Federal Labor Relations Authority	62	3	1	$121,081
Federal Maritime Commission	22	1	-	$122,947
Federal Mediation & Conciliation Service	3	-	-	$136,671
International Boundary and Water Commission: United States and Mexico	2	-	-	$62,952
Merit Systems Protection Board	114	-	-	$141,350
Millennium Challenge Corporation	13	-	-	$151,014
National Found. on the Arts & Humanities	8	-	-	$119,573
National Transportation Safety Board	10	4	-	$146,655
Office of Administration	3	-	1	$116,343
Office of Management and Budget	11	-	-	$155,048
Office of Special Counsel	56	-	-	$113,543
Office of the U.S. Trade Representative	41	-	-	$137,722
Overseas Private Investment Corporation	20	-	-	$140,712
Peace Corps	6	-	-	$148,188
Pension Benefit Guaranty Corporation	98	-	5	$126,739
Presidio Trust	5	-	-	$170,993
Railroad Retirement Board	14	-	-	$143,997
Selective Service System	1	-	-	$136,941
U.S. Holocaust Memorial Museum	2	-	-	$147,907
U.S. International Trade Commission	72	6	3	$134,605
U.S. Tax Court	61	-	17	$100,265
TOTAL	**1,015**	**16**	**33**	**$135,244**

[1] FHFA Data as of June, 2010.

Medium Independent Agency – General Attorney Minority Status

Agency	Non-Minority	Minority
Commodity Futures Trading Commission	85%	15%
Consumer Product Safety Commission	86%	14%
Corp. for National & Community Svc	100%	0%
Defense Nuclear Facilities Safety Board	100%	0%
Export-Import Bank of the United States	69%	31%
Farm Credit Administration	100%	0%
Federal Election Commission	78%	22%
Federal Housing Finance Agency	73%	27%
Federal Labor Relations Authority	81%	19%
Federal Maritime Commission	72%	28%
Federal Mediation & Conciliation Service	NA	NA
International Boundary and Water Commission: United States and Mexico	NA	NA
Merit Systems Protection Board	81%	19%
Millennium Challenge Corporation	100%	0%
National Foundation on the Arts & Humanities	100%	0%
National Transportation Safety Board	100%	0%
Office of Administration	NA	NA
Office of Management and Budget	100%	0%
Office of Special Counsel	71%	29%
Office of the U.S. Trade Representative	80%	20%
Overseas Private Investment Corporation	81%	19%
Peace Corps	100%	0%
Pension Benefit Guaranty Corporation	85%	15%
Presidio Trust	100%	0%
Railroad Retirement Board	100%	0%
Selective Service System	NA	NA
U.S. Holocaust Memorial Museum	NA	NA
U.S. International Trade Commission	75%	25%
U.S. Tax Court	87%	13%
TOTAL	82%	18%

* Data as of June, 2010.

Commodity Futures Trading Commission

Description:

The mission of the Commodity Futures Trading Commission (CFTC) is to protect market users and the public from fraud, manipulation, and abusive practices related to the sale of commodity futures and options, and to foster open, competitive, and financially sound commodity futures and option markets.

The CFTF, the Federal regulatory agency for futures trading, was established by the Commodity Futures Trading Commission Act of 1974 (7 U.S.C. 4a). The Commission began operation in April 1975, and its authority to regulate futures trading was renewed by Congress in 1978, 1982, 1986, 1992, 1995, and 2000.

The Commission consists of five Commissioners who are appointed by the President, with the advice and consent of the Senate. One Commissioner is designated by the President to serve as Chairman. The Commissioners serve staggered 5-year terms, and by law no more than three Commissioners can belong to the same political party.

The Commission has six major operating components: the Divisions of Market Oversight, Clearing and Intermediary Oversight, and Enforcement and the Offices of the Executive Director, General Counsel, and Chief Economist.

The Office of the General Counsel is the Commission's legal advisor, represents the Commission in appellate litigation and certain trial-level cases, including bankruptcy proceedings involving futures industry professionals, and advises the Commission on the application and interpretation of the Commodity Exchange Act and other administrative statutes.

Address: Commodity Futures Trading Commission
1155 Twenty-first Street, NW
Washington, DC 20581

Website: www.cftc.gov   **Phone**:   202-418-5000

Employment: Call 202-418-5003, or fax resume to 202-418-5530

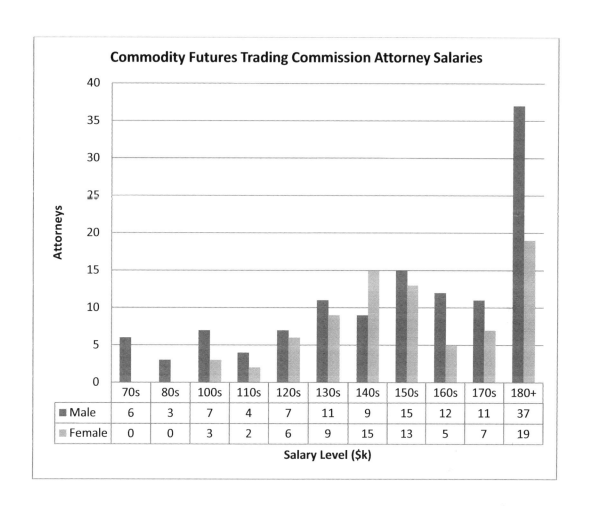

	70s	80s	100s	110s	120s	130s	140s	150s	160s	170s	180+
▓ Male	6	3	7	4	7	11	9	15	12	11	37
▓ Female	0	0	3	2	6	9	15	13	5	7	19

Salary Level ($k)

Consumer Product Safety Commission

Description:
The Consumer Product Safety Commission protects the public against unreasonable risks of injury from consumer products; assists consumers in evaluating the comparative safety of consumer products; develops uniform safety standards for consumer products and minimizes conflicting State and local regulations; and promotes research and investigation into the causes and prevention of product-related deaths, illnesses, and injuries.

The Consumer Product Safety Commission was established as an independent regulatory agency by the Consumer Product Safety Act (15 U.S.C. 2051 et seq.) in 1973 and reauthorized by the Consumer Product Safety Improvement Act of 2008. The Commission consists of up to five members, who are appointed by the President with the advice and consent of the Senate, for 7-year terms.

The Commission implements provisions of the Flammable Fabrics Act (15 U.S.C. 1191); Poison Prevention Packaging Act of 1970 (15 U.S.C. 1471); Federal Hazardous Substances Act (15 U.S.C. 1261); act of August 2, 1956 (15 U.S.C. 1211), prohibiting the transportation of refrigerators without door safety devices; Children's Gasoline Burn Prevention Act (15 U.S.C. 2056 note); and Virginia Graeme Baker Pool and Spa Safety Act (15 U.S.C. 8001 et seq.).

The Legal Division within the Office of Compliance participates in hazard team investigations and voluntary remedial action negotiations and represents the agency in administrative litigation if negotiations are unsuccessful. The Division also negotiates the voluntary payment of civil penalties to address knowing violations.

Address: U.S. Consumer Product Safety Commission
4330 East West Highway
Bethesda, MD 20814

Website: www.cpsc.gov   **Phone**:   301-504-7923

▶ **Commission Employment Opportunities**
www.cpsc.gov/about/hr.html

CPSC Atty Location	Gender	Length of Service	Salary
Maryland	Male	10 - 14 years	$176,531
Maryland	Female	1 - 2 years	$176,436
Maryland	Male	15 - 19 years	$159,232
Maryland	Female	5 - 9 years	$153,200
Maryland	Female	Less than 1 year	$153,200
Maryland	Female	20 - 24 years	$153,200
Maryland	Female	15 - 19 years	$153,200
Maryland	Female	20 - 24 years	$153,200
Maryland	Male	5 - 9 years	$153,200
Maryland	Male	30 - 34 years	$153,200
Maryland	Male	35 years or more	$153,200
Maryland	Male	25 - 29 years	$153,200
Maryland	Female	20 - 24 years	$153,053
Maryland	Male	30 - 34 years	$153,053
Maryland	Female	10 - 14 years	$149,025
Maryland	Male	20 - 24 years	$144,997
Maryland	Male	30 - 34 years	$140,969
Maryland	Female	10 - 14 years	$136,941
Maryland	Female	10 - 14 years	$136,941
Maryland	Male	15 - 19 years	$136,941
Maryland	Female	5 - 9 years	$132,914
Maryland	Male	10 - 14 years	$132,914
Maryland	Male	10 - 14 years	$132,914
Maryland	Male	10 - 14 years	$130,118
Maryland	Female	5 - 9 years	$119,844
Maryland	Male	5 - 9 years	$119,844
Maryland	Female	15 - 19 years	$116,419
Maryland	Male	5 - 9 years	$112,995
Maryland	Male	Less than 1 year	$86,927
Maryland	Female	Less than 1 year	$60,989
AVERAGE			**$139,627**

Corporation for National and Community Service

Description:

The Corporation for National and Community Service engages Americans of all ages and backgrounds in community-based service that addresses the Nation's educational, public safety, environmental, and other human needs to achieve direct and demonstrable results. In so doing, the Corporation fosters civic responsibility, strengthens the ties that bind us together as a people, and provides educational opportunity for those who make a substantial commitment to service. The Corporation was established on October 1, 1993, by the National and Community Service Trust Act of 1993 (42 U.S.C. 12651 et seq.). In addition to creating several new service programs, the Act consolidated the functions and activities of the former Commission on National and Community Service and the Federal agency ACTION (Federal Domestic Volunteer Agency).

For more than a decade, the Corporation for National Community Service, through its Senior Corps, AmeriCorps, and Learn and Serve America programs, has mobilized a new generation of engaged citizens. Annually, more than 2 million individuals of all ages and backgrounds will serve through those programs to help thousands of national and community nonprofit organizations, faith-based groups, schools, and local agencies meet local needs in education, the environment, public safety, homeland security, and other critical areas. National and community service programs work closely with traditional volunteer organizations to broaden, deepen, and strengthen the ability of America's volunteers to contribute not only to their community, but also to the Nation.

The Corporation is a Federal corporation governed by a 15-member bipartisan Board of Directors, appointed by the President with the advice and consent of the Senate. The Board has responsibility for overall policy direction of the Corporation's activities and has the power to make all final grant decisions, approve the strategic plan and annual budget, and advise and make recommendations to the President and the Congress regarding changes in the national service laws.

Address: Corporation for National and Community Service
1201 New York Avenue, NW
Washington, DC 20525

Website: www.nationalservice.gov   **Phone**:   202-606-5000

CNCS Atty Location	Gender	Length of Service	Salary
District of Columbia	Male	15 - 19 years	$162,900
District of Columbia	Female	25 - 29 years	$153,200
District of Columbia	Male	10 - 14 years	$153,200
District of Columbia	Male	15 - 19 years	$153,200
District of Columbia	Male	30 - 34 years	$153,200
District of Columbia	Male	15 - 19 years	$139,997
District of Columbia	Female	15 - 19 years	$138,943
District of Columbia	Female	1 - 2 years	$113,106
District of Columbia	Female	3 - 4 years	$85,282
AVERAGE			**$139,225**

Defense Nuclear Facilities Safety Board

Description:
The Defense Nuclear Facilities Safety Board reviews and evaluates the content and implementation of standards relating to the design, construction, operation, and decommissioning of defense nuclear facilities of the Department of Energy.

The Defense Nuclear Facilities Safety Board was established as an independent agency on September 29, 1988, by the Atomic Energy Act of 1954, as amended (42 U.S.C. 2286–2286i).

The Board is composed of five members appointed by the President with the advice and consent of the Senate. Members of the Board are appointed from among United States citizens who are respected experts in the field of nuclear safety.

Address: Defense Nuclear Facilities Safety Board
625 Indiana Avenue NW, Suite 700
Washington, DC 20004

Website: www.dnfsb.gov   **Phone**:   202-694-7000

Attorney Location	Gender	Length of Service	Salary
District of Columbia	Male	35 years or more	$162,900
District of Columbia	Male	35 years or more	$162,900
District of Columbia	Female	25 - 29 years	$140,969
District of Columbia	Male	10 - 14 years	$140,969
District of Columbia	Female	5 - 9 years	$136,941
AVERAGE			$148,936

Export-Import Bank of the United States

Description:

The Export-Import Bank of the United States (Ex-Im Bank) helps the private sector to create and maintain U.S. jobs by financing exports of the Nation's goods and services. To accomplish this mission, the Bank offers a variety of loan, guarantee, and insurance programs to support transactions that would not be awarded to U.S. companies without the Bank's assistance.

The Ex-Im Bank, established in 1934, operates as an independent agency of the U.S. Government under the authority of the Export-Import Bank Act of 1945, as amended (12 U.S.C. 635 et seq.). Its Board of Directors consists of a President and Chairman, a First Vice President and Vice Chair, and three other Directors, all are appointed by the President with the advice and consent of the Senate.

Ex-Im Bank's mission is to help American exporters meet government supported financing competition from other countries, so that U.S. exports can compete for overseas business on the basis of price, performance, and service, and in doing so help create and sustain U.S. jobs. The Bank also fills gaps in the availability of commercial financing for creditworthy export transactions.

Ex-Im Bank is required to find a reasonable assurance of repayment for each transaction it supports. Its legislation requires it to meet the financing terms of competitor export credit agencies, but not to compete with commercial lenders. Legislation restricts the Bank's operation in some countries and its support for military goods and services.

The General Counsel serves as the Bank's chief legal officer and corporate Secretary. The General Counsel manages the Bank's attorneys, oversees diverse transactions and litigation portfolios, and represents Ex-Im Bank in negotiations with key external stakeholders.

Address: Export-Import Bank of the United States
811 Vermont Avenue, N.W.
Washington, DC 20571

Website: www.exim.gov   **Phone**:   202-565-3946

Ex-Im Atty Location	Gender	Length of Service	Salary
District of Columbia	Female	5 - 9 years	$162,900
District of Columbia	Female	5 - 9 years	$162,900
District of Columbia	Male	1 - 2 years	$162,900
District of Columbia	Male	3 - 4 years	$162,900
District of Columbia	Male	5 - 9 years	$162,900
District of Columbia	Male	10 - 14 years	$162,900
District of Columbia	Male	5 - 9 years	$154,519
District of Columbia	Female	20 - 24 years	$153,200
District of Columbia	Male	5 - 9 years	$153,200
District of Columbia	Male	15 - 19 years	$153,200
District of Columbia	Male	5 - 9 years	$144,997
District of Columbia	Male	5 - 9 years	$140,969
District of Columbia	Female	15 - 19 years	$133,543
District of Columbia	Female	10 - 14 years	$133,543
District of Columbia	Female	10 - 14 years	$133,543
District of Columbia	Male	Less than 1 year	$133,543
District of Columbia	Male	5 - 9 years	$133,543
District of Columbia	Female	10 - 14 years	$130,118
District of Columbia	Female	10 - 14 years	$126,693
District of Columbia	Female	5 - 9 years	$101,416
AVERAGE			**$145,171**

Farm Credit Administration

Description:
The Farm Credit Administration (FCA) is responsible for ensuring the safe and sound operation of the banks, associations, affiliated service organizations, and other entities that collectively comprise what is known as the Farm Credit System, and for protecting the interests of the public and those who borrow from Farm Credit institutions or invest in Farm Credit securities. The FCA was established as an independent financial regulatory agency in the executive branch of the Federal Government by Executive Order 6084 on March 27, 1933. FCA carries out its responsibilities by conducting examinations of the various Farm Credit lending institutions, which are Farm Credit Banks, the Agricultural Credit Bank, Agricultural Credit Associations, and Federal Land Credit Associations. FCA also examines the service organizations owned by the Farm Credit lending institutions, as well as the National Cooperative Bank.

The Office of General Counsel provides the FCA Board and staff with legal counsel, as well as guidance on general corporate, personnel, ethics, and administrative matters. The office supports the Agency's development and promulgation of regulations, civil litigation, enforcement of applicable laws and regulations, and implementation of conservatorships and receiverships. The office serves as the liaison to the Federal Register, creates and maintains the Agency's public rulemaking files, and handles the Agency's submission of the Unified Agenda of Federal Regulatory and Deregulatory Actions. The office also handles Freedom of Information Act requests and matters pertaining to the Privacy Act.

Address: Farm Credit Administration
1501 Farm Credit Drive
McLean, VA 22102-5090

Website: www.fca.gov   **Phone**:   703-883-4000

FCA Atty Location	Gender	Length of Service	Salary
Virginia	Male	25 - 29 years	$240,970
Virginia	Female	25 - 29 years	$215,783
Virginia	Female	20 - 24 years	$200,966
Virginia	Female	20 - 24 years	$182,318
Virginia	Female	10 - 14 years	$158,945
Virginia	Male	10 - 14 years	$156,660
Virginia	Female	15 - 19 years	$156,280
Virginia	Female	20 - 24 years	$154,669
Virginia	Male	20 - 24 years	$151,949
Virginia	Female	15 - 19 years	$147,478
Virginia	Female	5 - 9 years	$142,519
Virginia	Female	15 - 19 years	$133,423
AVERAGE			**$170,163**

Federal Election Commission

Description:

The Federal Election Commission has exclusive jurisdiction in the administration and civil enforcement of laws regulating the acquisition and expenditure of campaign funds to ensure compliance by participants in the Federal election campaign process. Its chief mission is to provide public disclosure of campaign finance activities and effect voluntary compliance by providing the public with information on the laws and regulations concerning campaign finance.

The Federal Election Commission is an independent agency established by section 309 of the Federal Election Campaign Act of 1971, as amended (2 U.S.C. 437c). It is composed of six Commissioners appointed by the President with the advice and consent of the Senate. The act also provides for three statutory officers—the Staff Director, the General Counsel, and the Inspector General—who are appointed by the Commission.

The Office of General Counsel consists of five organizational units: the Policy Division; the Enforcement Division; the Litigation Division; the General Law and Advice Division; and the Office of Complaints Examination and Legal Administration.

Address: Federal Elections Commission
999 E Street, NW
Washington, DC 20463

Website: www.fec.gov   **Phone**:   800-424-9530

▶ **FEC Office of General Counsel, Summer Law Clerk Program**
www.fec.gov/pages/jobs/SummerInternshipOpportunities.shtml

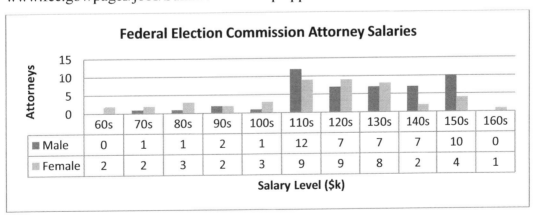

Salary Level ($k)	60s	70s	80s	90s	100s	110s	120s	130s	140s	150s	160s
Male	0	1	1	2	1	12	7	7	7	10	0
Female	2	2	3	2	3	9	9	8	2	4	1

Federal Housing Finance Agency

Description:

The Federal Housing and Finance Agency (FHFA) works to promote a stable and liquid mortgage market, affordable housing, and community investment through safety and soundness oversight of Fannie Mae, Freddie Mac, and the Federal Home Loan Banks.

The FHFA was established by the Federal Housing Finance Regulatory Reform Act of 2008 (12 U.S.C. 4501 et seq.) as an independent agency in the executive branch. The FHFA is the result from the merger of the Federal Housing Finance Board and the Office of Federal Housing Enterprise Oversight, as well as the transfer of the Department of Housing and Urban Development's government-sponsored enterprise mission team into the agency.

FHFA is managed by a Director who is appointed by the President and confirmed by the Senate. The FHFA Director also serves as the Chairman of the Federal Housing Oversight Board, an advisory board that testifies before Congress on the status of the Federal housing market enterprises. The Secretary of the Treasury, the Secretary of Housing and Urban Development, and the Securities and Exchange Commission Chairman are also members of the Board.

FHFA was created to ensure the security and supervision of Fannie Mae, Freddie Mac, the 12 Federal Home Loan Banks, and the Office of Finance. The agency's increased regulatory powers and affordable housing goals were designed to restore confidence in the 14 government-sponsored loan enterprises, enabling these entities to provide more effective assistance to troubled mortgage markets.

Address: Federal Housing Finance Agency
1700 G Street, NW
Washington, DC 20552

Website: www.fhfa.gov   **Phone**:   866-796-5595

FHFA	Male	Female	TOTAL
Number of Attorneys	16	13	29
Average Salary	$183,394	$166,812	$175,961
Average Length of Service (years)	14.3	16.0	15.1

* Data as of June, 2010.

Federal Labor Relations Authority

Description:
The Federal Labor Relations Authority (FLRA) oversees the Federal service labor management relations program. It administers the law that protects the right of employees of the Federal Government to organize, bargain collectively, and participate through labor organizations of their own choosing in decisions affecting them. The Authority also ensures compliance with the statutory rights and obligations of Federal employees and the labor organizations that represent them in their dealings with Federal agencies.

The FLRA was created as an independent establishment by Reorganization Plan No. 2 of 1978 (5 U.S.C. app.), effective January 1, 1979, pursuant to Executive Order 12107 of December 28, 1978, to consolidate the central policymaking functions in Federal labor-management relations. Its duties and authority are specified in title VII (Federal Service Labor-Management Relations) of the Civil Service Reform Act of 1978 (5 U.S.C. 7101–7135).

General Counsel
Pursuant to section 7104(f) of the Statute, the General Counsel has direct authority over, and responsibility for, all employees in the Office of the General Counsel, including employees of the General Counsel in the Regional Offices. The Regional staff perform the following tasks on behalf of the General Counsel:
- investigate alleged unfair labor practices
- file and prosecute unfair labor practice complaints
- process and determine representation matters
- provide training and alternative dispute resolution services

To accomplish this task, the General Counsel has a management staff in the Authority's Headquarters, located in Washington, D.C., and seven Regional Offices. Headquarters management staff provide administrative oversight, and develop policies, guidances, procedures, and manuals that provide programmatic direction for the OGC's seven Regions. Each Regional Office has a Regional Director who provides leadership and management expertise for their respective Region. The Dallas and Washington Regions also have a Regional Attorney and the San Francisco Region has a Deputy Regional Director to assist the Regional Director in the operations of the Region.

185

Solicitor

The Office of the Solicitor represents the FLRA in court proceedings before all United States courts, including the Supreme Court of the United States, U.S. Courts of Appeals, and Federal District Courts. The Office also serves as the FLRA's in-house counsel, providing legal advice to all FLRA components. In addition, the Office performs various functions under the FOIA and Privacy Acts. The Solicitor serves as the designated agency ethics officer.

Administrative Law Judges

Administrative Law Judges for the FLRA perform a variety of functions related primarily to conducting hearings and rendering recommended decisions in cases involving alleged unfair labor practices. In addition, FLRA Regulations require that judges render decisions involving applications for attorney fees filed under the Back Pay Act and the Equal Access to Justice Act.

Address: Federal Labor Relations Authority
1400 K Street, NW
Washington, DC 20005

Website: www.flra.gov   **Phone**:   202-218-7770

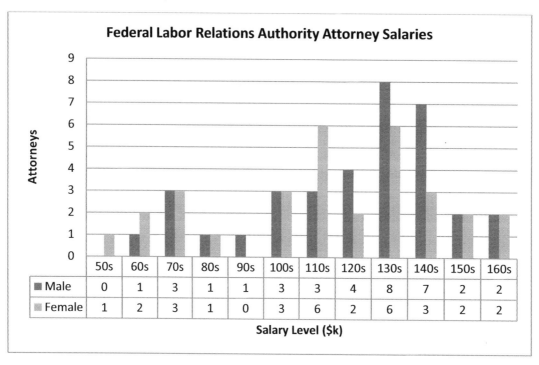

Federal Labor Relations Authority Attorney Salaries

	50s	60s	70s	80s	90s	100s	110s	120s	130s	140s	150s	160s
Male	0	1	3	1	1	3	3	4	8	7	2	2
Female	1	2	3	1	0	3	6	2	6	3	2	2

Salary Level ($k)

Federal Maritime Commission

Description:
The Federal Maritime Commission regulates the waterborne foreign commerce of the United States. It ensures that U.S. oceanborne trades are open to all on fair and equitable terms and protects against concerted activities and unlawful practices.

The Commission was established by Reorganization Plan No. 7 of 1961 (46 U.S.C. 301–307), effective August 12, 1961. It is an independent agency that regulates shipping under the following statutes: the Shipping Act of 1984, as amended (46 U.S.C. 40101– 41309); Section 19 of the Merchant Marine Act, 1920 (46 U.S.C. 42101– 42109); the Foreign Shipping Practices Act of 1988 (46 U.S.C. 42301– 42307); and the act of November 6, 1966 (46 U.S.C. 44101–44106).

The General Counsel provides legal services to the Commission. This includes reviewing for legal sufficiency staff recommendations for Commission action; drafting proposed rules to implement Commission policies; drafting memoranda evaluating adjudicatory and investigatory proceedings; and preparing final decisions, orders and regulations for Commission ratification. The General Counsel also provides written and oral legal opinions to the Commission, its staff, and the general public in appropriate instances.

The General Counsel represents the Commission's interests in matters before Congress. This includes commenting on proposed legislation, preparing testimony for Commission officials, proposing legislation, and responding to congressional requests for information or assistance.

The General Counsel represents the Commission in trial and appellate litigation in the Federal courts and other fora. This includes representing the Commission in appeals of its orders and rulemakings; seeking injunctions and other forms of relief against statutory violations in the Federal District Courts; and representing the Commission's interests before other Federal agencies.

The General Counsel is also responsible for the Commission's International Affairs Program. The Commission has the statutory authority to take actions to correct or counterbalance adverse, unfair or unfavorable foreign practices which affect U.S. shipping or U.S. carriers in international commerce. The General Counsel monitors and investigates restrictive foreign practices, and makes recommendations for appropriate Commission action. In addition, the General Counsel maintains a list of ocean common carriers that are owned or controlled by the governments of the foreign countries in which they are registered. These "controlled carriers" are subject to strict rate review standards to ensure that they do not unjustly take advantage of their government-supported position in the marketplace.

Address: Federal Maritime Commission
800 North Capitol Street NW
Washington, DC 20573-0001

Website: www.fmc.gov   **Phone**:   202-523-5707

FMC Atty Location	Gender	Length of Service	Salary
District of Columbia	Male	25 - 29 years	$162,900[1]
District of Columbia	Male	20 - 24 years	$162,900
District of Columbia	Male	20 - 24 years	$162,900
District of Columbia	Male	35 years or more	$153,200
District of Columbia	Female	10 - 14 years	$140,969
District of Columbia	Male	5 - 9 years	$140,969
District of Columbia	Male	5 - 9 years	$140,969
District of Columbia	Female	10 - 14 years	$136,941
District of Columbia	Female	10 - 14 years	$136,941
District of Columbia	Female	10 - 14 years	$132,914
District of Columbia	Female	15 - 19 years	$124,858
District of Columbia	Female	5 - 9 years	$123,269
District of Columbia	Male	1 - 2 years	$120,830
District of Columbia	Female	5 - 9 years	$116,419
District of Columbia	Female	5 - 9 years	$112,995
District of Columbia	Male	5 - 9 years	$106,145
District of Columbia	Female	3 - 4 years	$102,721
District of Columbia	Female	5 - 9 years	$102,721
District of Columbia	Male	1 - 2 years	$95,620
District of Columbia	Female	1 - 2 years	$89,825
District of Columbia	Female	1 - 2 years	$86,927
District of Columbia	Male	1 - 2 years	$86,927
District of Columbia	Male	1 - 2 years	$86,927
AVERAGE			**$122,947**

[1] Administrative Law Judge.

Federal Mediation and Conciliation Service

Description:

The Federal Mediation and Conciliation Service (FMCS) assists labor and management in resolving disputes in collective bargaining contract negotiation through voluntary mediation and arbitration services. The FMCS was created by the Labor Management Relations Act, 1947 (29 U.S.C. 172). The Director is appointed by the President with the advice and consent of the Senate.

The Office of General Counsel (OGC) carries out all legal activities of the FMCS; ensures full and proper implementation of the Agency's statutory responsibilities; provides legal counsel to the Director, the Deputy Director, and other officials of FMCS. In addition to legal aspects of general administrative matters such as contracts, personnel, and regulatory compliance, the OGC is actively concerned with the evolving law of dispute resolution. Issues including mediation confidentiality, ethical standards for third party neutrals, and the relationship between alternative dispute resolution and the courts are becoming increasingly important.

At the same time, as mediation and dispute resolution takes place, the OGC provides advice and analysis to FMCS regarding developments in labor and employment law and interpretation of legislation impacting the Service and the substantive issues that FMCS mediators are called upon to handle.

Address: Federal Mediation and Conciliation Service
2100 K Street, NW
Washington, DC 20427

Website: www.fmcs.gov   **Phone**:   202-606-8100

FMCS Atty Location	Gender	Length of Service	Salary
District of Columbia	Female	5 - 9 years	$153,200
District of Columbia	Male	5 - 9 years	$133,543
District of Columbia	Female	20 - 24 years	$123,269
AVERAGE			**$136,671**

International Boundary & Water Comm.: United States & Mexico

Description:

The mission of the International Boundary and Water Commission (IBWC) is to apply the rights and obligations which the Governments of the United States and Mexico assume under the numerous boundary and water treaties and related agreements, and to do so in a way that benefits the social and economic welfare of the peoples on the two sides of the boundary and improves relations between the two countries.

The Office of Legal Advisor performs the traditional house counsel role for the Agency. It provides, to the staff and management, representational services in litigation, including administrative hearings management and representation in matters before the Equal Employment Opportunity, Merit Systems Protection Board and FLRA related arbitrations. It anticipates and advises on matters of authorization and appropriations, acquisitions/contract, environmental assessment planning, report review, and the issuance of FONSI and other environmental assessment determinations. In the area of personnel management it consults on discipline, awards, grievances, hiring, promotion, and reorganization. Externally, the Office advises and represents the Agency in matters raised by other international organizations, the Congress, Federal agencies, State and local governments, and non-governmental organizations. The Office also has assigned Internal Audit, claims management, Governmental Ethics, Privacy Act and FOIA. Under the Treaty of 1944 between the United State and Mexico the General Counsel is a treaty officer holding diplomatic status. The office thus provides guidance in the formulation of the United States Sections position on bi-national issues and interprets international law as part of the implementation of the Agency's Foreign Policy Program.

Address:　　International Boundary and Water Commission
　　　　　　　　U.S. Section
　　　　　　　　4171 North Mesa, Suite C-100
　　　　　　　　El Paso, TX 79902-1441

Website:　　www.ibwc.gov　　　　　　**Phone**:　　800-262-8857

Attorney Location	Gender	Length of Service	Salary
Texas	Female	Less than 1 year	$67,613
Texas	Male	3 - 4 years	$58,291
AVERAGE			$62,952

Merit Systems Protection Board

Description:
The Merit Systems Protection Board is a successor agency to the United States Civil Service Commission, established by act of January 16, 1883 (22 Stat. 403). Reorganization Plan No. 2 of 1978 (5 U.S.C. app.) redesignated part of the Commission as the Merit Systems Protection Board.

The Merit Systems Protection Board protects the integrity of the Federal personnel merit systems and the rights of Federal employees. In overseeing the personnel practices of the Federal Government, the Board conducts special studies of the merit systems, hears and decides charges of wrongdoing and employee appeals of adverse agency actions, and orders corrective and disciplinary actions when appropriate.

In appellate cases, the Board's final decision, whether it is an initial decision or Board decision, may be appealed to the United States Court of Appeals for the Federal Circuit or, in cases involving allegations of discrimination, to a U.S. District Court. The Director of OPM may petition the Board for reconsideration of a final decision, and may also seek judicial review of Board decisions that have substantial impact on a civil service law, rule, regulation or policy.

The Board's decisions in cases brought by the Special Counsel may be appealed to the U.S. Court of Appeals for the Federal Circuit, except in Hatch Act cases involving State or local government employees. State or local government employees affected by the Board's Hatch Act decisions may file appeals in the U.S. district courts.

The Board's decisions in other original jurisdiction cases may be appealed to the U.S. Court of Appeals for the Federal Circuit.

Address: U.S. Merit Systems Protection Board
1615 M Street, NW
Washington, DC 20419

Website: www.mspb.gov   **Phone**:   202-653-7200

► MSPB Office of General Counsel and Other Internships
www.mspb.gov/contact/internships.htm

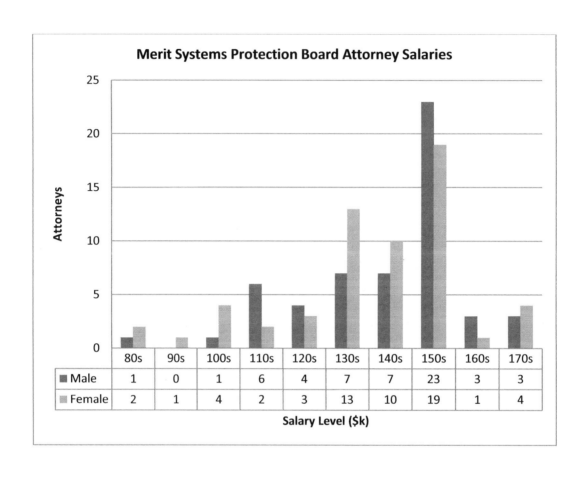

	80s	90s	100s	110s	120s	130s	140s	150s	160s	170s
Male	1	0	1	6	4	7	7	23	3	3
Female	2	1	4	2	3	13	10	19	1	4

Millennium Challenge Corporation

Description:

The Millennium Challenge Corporation (MCC) is an independent U.S. foreign aid agency that is helping lead the fight against global poverty. MCC provides countries with large-scale grants to fund country-led solutions for reducing poverty through sustainable economic growth. MCC grants complement other U.S. and international development programs. MCC is managed by a chief executive officer, who is part of the nine-member Board of Directors. The Secretary of State, the Secretary of the Treasury, the U.S. Trade Representative, and the USAID Administrator serve on the board along with four private sector representatives.

The Office of the General Counsel:

- Provides advice to MCC's Board of Directors and MCC staff on all legal issues affecting MCC, its programs, policies and procedures.
- Advises the department of Policy and International Relations on all aspects of country eligibility, the threshold country program and other initiatives.
- Provides legal advice to transaction teams developing compact programs; addresses and resolves legal issues associated with compact program development; conducts and evaluates due diligence on country proposals; conducts compact negotiation, and assists with legal aspects of compact implementation.
- Provides advice to the Department of Administration & Finance on all issues affecting the internal operation of MCC, including personnel law, government contracts, fiscal law, information technology, and corporate records management.
- Advises the Department of Congressional and Public Affairs on matters of statutory interpretation, interagency agreements and communications, and other public initiatives.
- Performs the function of Secretary to the MCC Board of Directors.
- Manages MCC's ethics program, providing related training and guidance.

Address: Millennium Challenge Corporation
875 Fifteenth Street NW
Washington, DC 20005-2221

Website: www.mcc.gov   **Phone**:   202-521-3600

MCC Atty Location	Gender	Length of Service	Salary
District of Columbia	Male	5 - 9 years	$170,200
District of Columbia	Male	15 - 19 years	$170,200
District of Columbia	Male	10 - 14 years	$164,688
District of Columbia	Male	25 - 29 years	$163,051
District of Columbia	Male	3 - 4 years	$161,561
District of Columbia	Female	5 - 9 years	$160,000
District of Columbia	Female	3 - 4 years	$160,000
District of Columbia	Male	1 - 2 years	$137,940
District of Columbia	Female	1 - 2 years	$136,320
District of Columbia	Female	1 - 2 years	$135,850
District of Columbia	Male	3 - 4 years	$135,850
District of Columbia	Male	1 - 2 years	$133,760
District of Columbia	Male	1 - 2 years	$133,760
AVERAGE			$151,014

National Foundation on the Arts and the Humanities

Description:

The purpose of the National Foundation on the Arts and the Humanities is to develop and promote a broadly conceived national policy of support for the humanities and the arts in the United States, and for institutions which preserve the cultural heritage of the United States.

The National Foundation on the Arts and the Humanities was created as an independent agency by the National Foundation on the Arts and the Humanities Act of 1965 (20 U.S.C. 951). The Foundation consists of the National Endowment for the Arts, the National Endowment for the Humanities, the Federal Council on the Arts and the Humanities, and the Institute of Museum and Library Services. The Federal Council on the Arts and the Humanities assists the Endowments in coordinating their programs and other activities with those of Federal agencies. Each Endowment is advised on its respective grantmaking and related policies, programs, and procedures by its own National Council, composed of the Endowment Chairman and other members appointed by the President and confirmed by the Senate. Members of Congress, appointed by the leadership of the House and the Senate, serve in an ex officio, non-voting capacity on the National Council on the Arts. The Federal Council's membership comprises the Chairmen of the two Endowments, the Director of Museum and Library Services, and other key Federal cultural officials.

Address: National Foundation on the Arts and the Humanities
1100 Pennsylvania Avenue NW
Washington, DC 20506

Website: www.arts.gov   **Phone**: 202-682-5400

Attorney Location	Gender	Length of Service	Salary
District of Columbia	Male	10 - 14 years	$162,068
District of Columbia	Female	10 - 14 years	$155,000
District of Columbia	Female	25 - 29 years	$140,969
District of Columbia	Female	5 - 9 years	$132,914
District of Columbia	Male	15 - 19 years	$126,693
District of Columbia	Female	5 - 9 years	$112,995
District of Columbia	Female	1 - 2 years	$75,537
District of Columbia	Female	1 - 2 years	$50,408
AVERAGE			$119,573

National Transportation Safety Board

Description:

The National Transportation Safety Board (NTSB) seeks to ensure that all types of transportation in the United States are conducted safely. The Board investigates accidents, conducts studies, and makes recommendations to Government agencies, the transportation industry, and others on safety measures and practices.

The NTSB was established in 1967 and became totally independent on April 1, 1975, by the Independent Safety Board Act of 1974 (49 U.S.C. 1111). NTSB consists of five Members appointed for 5-year terms by the President with the advice and consent of the Senate. The President designates two of these Members as Chairman and Vice Chairman of the Board for 2-year terms. The designation of the Chairman is made with the advice and consent of the Senate.

The General Counsel, as the legal advisor to the NTSB, has responsibility for determining legal policy for the agency. The Office of General Counsel advises, assists and represents the Board as it fulfills its statutory duty by investigating and determining the probable cause of accidents in a variety of transportation modes, and studying a range of issues related to transportation safety. Additionally, the Office of General Counsel serves as legal advisor to the Board in its capacity as the appellate authority for particular disciplinary actions taken with regard to the certificates of airmen, mechanics, and mariners.

The NTSB's Administrative Law Judges conduct formal hearings and issue initial decisions on appeals from all FAA certificate actions and civil penalty actions involving pilots, engineers, mechanics, and repairmen. Also covered are petitions for certification that have been denied by the FAA.

Address: National Transportation Safety Board
490 L'Enfant Plaza SW
Washington, DC 20594

Website: www.ntsb.gov   **Phone**:   202-314-6000

NTSB Atty Location	Gender	Length of Service	Salary
District of Columbia	Male	3 - 4 years	$176,024
Colorado	Male	35 years or more	$162,900[1]
District of Columbia	Male	35 years or more	$162,900[1]
District of Columbia	Male	35 years or more	$162,900[1]
Texas	Male	25 - 29 years	$162,900[1]
District of Columbia	Female	25 - 29 years	$153,200
District of Columbia	Female	20 - 24 years	$153,200
District of Columbia	Male	10 - 14 years	$153,200
District of Columbia	Female	10 - 14 years	$144,997
District of Columbia	Female	15 - 19 years	$144,997
District of Columbia	Male	25 - 29 years	$126,693
District of Columbia	Male	10 - 14 years	$123,269
District of Columbia	Male	1 - 2 years	$123,269
District of Columbia	Female	3 - 4 years	$102,721
AVERAGE			$146,655

[1] Administrative Law Judges.

Office of Administration

Description:
The Office of Administration (OA) was formally established within the Executive Office of the President (EOP) by Executive Order 12028 of December 12, 1977. The Office provides administrative support services to all units within the Executive Office of the President. The services provided include information, personnel, technology, and financial management; data processing; library and research services; security; legislative liaisons; and general office operations such as mail, messenger, printing, procurement, and supply services.

The Office of General Counsel provides legal support, services, and advice to the OA Director and OA departments, as well as to other components of the EOP as it relates to functions managed on behalf of the EOP by OA.

Address: Eisenhower Executive Office Building
1650 Pennsylvania Avenue, NW
Washington, DC 20503

Website: www.whitehouse.gov/oa   **Phone:**   202-456-2861

Attorney Location	Gender	Length of Service	Salary
District of Columbia	Female	20 - 24 years	$144,997
District of Columbia	Female	Less than 1 year	$130,500
District of Columbia	Female	1 - 2 years	$128,886
District of Columbia	Female	Less than 1 year	$60,989[1]
AVERAGE			$116,343

[1] Law Clerk.

Office of Management and Budget

Description:
The Office of Management and Budget (OMB) evaluates, formulates, and coordinates management procedures and program objectives among Federal agencies. It also controls the administration of the Federal budget, while routinely providing the President with recommendations regarding budget proposals and relevant legislative enactments. OMB, formerly the Bureau of the Budget, was established in the Executive Office of the President pursuant to Reorganization Plan No. 1 of 1939 (5 U.S.C. app.).

OMB's Office of General Counsel provides legal advice to the Director and the OMB components and staff. In addition, the General Counsel's Office manages the Executive Order and Presidential Memoranda process for OMB and the Administration; reviews and clears all legal and constitutional comments by the Department of Justice and other agencies on proposed legislation before comments are conveyed to Congress; participates in the drafting of bill signing statements for the President; reviews all proposed legislative text comprising the President's Budget and for all budget-related legislative proposals; evaluates legal issues in proposed regulations; convenes meetings of agency general counsels and coordinates legal issues across agencies.

Address: Office of Management and Budget
                 Executive Office Building
                 Washington, DC 20503

Website: www.whitehouse.gov/omb   **Phone**:   202-395-3080

Attorney Location	Gender	Length of Service	Salary
District of Columbia	Male	20 - 24 years	$177,000
District of Columbia	Female	3 - 4 years	$175,000
District of Columbia	Male	20 - 24 years	$162,767
District of Columbia	Female	30 - 34 years	$153,200
District of Columbia	Male	1 - 2 years	$153,200
District of Columbia	Male	20 - 24 years	$153,200
District of Columbia	Male	35 years or more	$153,200
District of Columbia	Male	25 - 29 years	$149,025
District of Columbia	Female	10 - 14 years	$140,969
District of Columbia	Female	5 - 9 years	$132,914
AVERAGE			$155,048

Office of Special Counsel

Description:
The Office of Special Counsel (OSC) investigates allegations of certain activities prohibited by civil service laws, rules, or regulations and litigates before the Merit Systems Protection Board.

OSC was established on January 1, 1979, by Reorganization Plan No. 2 of 1978 (5 U.S.C. app.). The Civil Service Reform Act of 1978 (5 U.S.C. 1101 note), which became effective on January 11, 1979, enlarged its functions and powers. Pursuant to provisions of the Whistleblower Protection Act of 1989 (5 U.S.C. 1211 et seq.), OSC functions as an independent investigative and prosecutorial agency within the executive branch which litigates before the Merit Systems Protection Board.

The primary role of OSC is to protect employees, former employees, and applicants for employment from prohibited personnel practices, especially reprisal for whistleblowing. Its basic areas of statutory responsibility are to:

- receive and investigate allegations of prohibited personnel practices and other activities prohibited by civil service law, rule, or regulation and, if warranted, initiating corrective or disciplinary action;
- provide a secure channel through which information evidencing a violation of any law, rule, or regulation, gross mismanagement, gross waste of funds, abuse of authority, or substantial and specific danger to public health or safety may be disclosed without fear of retaliation and without disclosure of identity, except with the employee's consent; and
- enforce the provisions of the Hatch Act and the Uniformed Services Employment and Reemployment Rights Act.

Address: Office of Special Counsel
                  1730 M Street NW
                  Washington, DC 20036-4505

Website: www.osc.gov   **Phone**:   202-254-3600

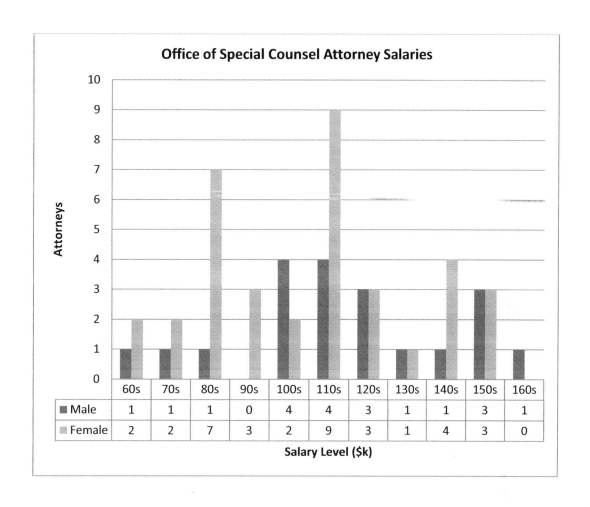

Office of Special Counsel Attorney Salaries

	60s	70s	80s	90s	100s	110s	120s	130s	140s	150s	160s
Male	1	1	1	0	4	4	3	1	1	3	1
Female	2	2	7	3	2	9	3	1	4	3	0

Salary Level ($k)

Office of the U.S. Trade Representative

Description:
The United States Trade Representative (USTR) is responsible for directing all trade negotiations of and formulating trade policy for the United States. The Office of the United States Trade Representative was created as the Office of the Special Representative for Trade Negotiations by Executive Order 11075 of January 15, 1963. The Trade Act of 1974 (19 U.S.C. 2171) established the Office as an agency of the Executive Office of the President charged with administering the trade agreements program.

The Office is responsible for setting and administering overall trade policy. It also provides that the USTR shall be chief representative of the United States for the following:

- all activities concerning the General Agreement on Tariffs and Trade;
- discussions, meetings, and negotiations in the Organization for Economic Cooperation and Development when such activities deal primarily with trade and commodity issues;
- negotiations in the U.N. Conference on Trade and Development and other multilateral institutions when such negotiations deal primarily with trade and commodity issues;
- other bilateral and multilateral negotiations when trade, including East- West trade, or commodities is the primary issue;
- negotiations under sections 704 and 734 of the Tariff Act of 1930 (19 U.S.C. 1671c and 1673c); and
- negotiations concerning direct investment incentives and disincentives and bilateral investment issues concerning barriers to investment.

The Office is headed by the USTR, a Cabinet level official with the rank of Ambassador, who is directly responsible to the President. There are three Deputy USTRs, who also hold the rank of Ambassador—two located in Washington and one in Geneva. The Chief Agricultural Negotiator also holds the rank of Ambassador.

The USTR serves as an ex officio member of the Boards of Directors of the Export-Import Bank and the Overseas Private Investment Corporation, and serves on the National Advisory Council for International Monetary and Financial Policy.

The Office of the General Counsel provides legal advice to the USTR, Deputy U.S. Trade Representatives, and regional and other USTR offices on negotiations, agreements, trade legislation, certain trade remedies, administrative law, and government ethics. In addition, the office monitors compliance by foreign governments with their obligations under trade agreements with the United States. The office also prosecutes and defends cases in WTO and U.S. free trade agreement dispute settlement proceedings.

Address: Office of the U.S. Trade Representative
600 Seventeenth Street NW
Washington, DC 20508

Website: www.ustr.gov   **Phone**:   202-395-3230

▶ **USTR Student Internship Program**
www.ustr.gov/about-us/human-resources/employment/student-internship-program

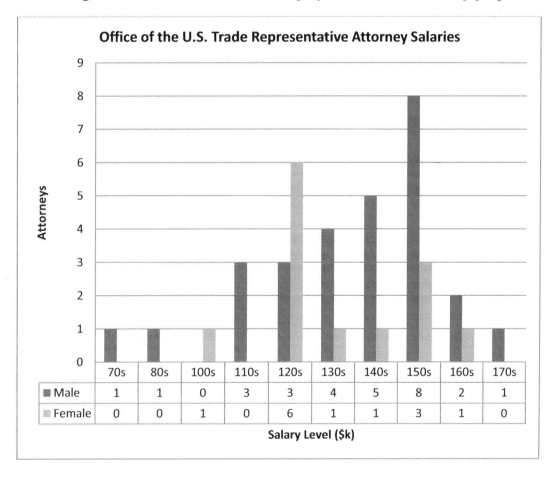

Overseas Private Investment Corporation

Description:

The Overseas Private Investment Corporation (OPIC) is a self-sustaining Federal agency whose purpose is to promote economic growth in developing countries and emerging markets by encouraging U.S. private investment in those nations.

OPIC was established in 1971 as an independent agency by the Foreign Affairs Reform and Restructuring Act (112 Stat. 2681–790). OPIC helps U.S. businesses invest overseas, fosters economic development in new and emerging markets, complements the private sector in managing risks associated with foreign direct investment, and supports U.S. foreign policy. OPIC charges market-based fees for its products, and it operates on a self-sustaining basis at no net cost to taxpayers.

OPIC helps U.S. businesses compete in emerging markets when private sector support is not available. OPIC offers up to $250 million in long-term financing and/or political risk insurance to U.S. companies investing in over 150 emerging markets and developing countries. Backed by the full faith and credit of the U.S. Government, OPIC advocates for U.S. investment, offers experience in risk management, and draws on an outstanding record of success.

OPIC mobilizes America's private sector to advance U.S. foreign policy and development initiatives. Projects supported by OPIC expand economic development, which encourages political stability and free market reforms. Over the agency's 35 year history, OPIC has supported $177 billion worth of investments that have helped developing countries to generate over $13 billion in host government revenues and create over 800,000 host country jobs. OPIC projects have also generated $71 billion in U.S. exports and supported more than 271,000 American jobs. OPIC promotes U.S. best practices by requiring projects to adhere to international standards on the environment, worker rights, and human rights.

Address: Overseas Private Investment Corporation
1100 New York Avenue, NW
Washington, DC 20527

Website: www.opic.gov   **Phone**:   202-336-8400

▶ **OPIC Legal Internships**
www.opic.gov/about/jobs/internship/legal

OPIC Atty Location	Gender	Length of Service	Salary
District of Columbia	Male	10 - 14 years	$162,900
District of Columbia	Female	5 - 9 years	$153,200
District of Columbia	Female	5 - 9 years	$153,200
District of Columbia	Female	5 - 9 years	$153,200
District of Columbia	Female	15 - 19 years	$153,200
District of Columbia	Male	15 - 19 years	$153,200
District of Columbia	Male	5 - 9 years	$153,200
District of Columbia	Male	30 - 34 years	$153,200
District of Columbia	Male	10 - 14 years	$153,200
District of Columbia	Male	15 - 19 years	$153,053
District of Columbia	Female	5 - 9 years	$149,025
District of Columbia	Male	5 - 9 years	$149,025
District of Columbia	Female	5 - 9 years	$144,997
District of Columbia	Male	1 - 2 years	$144,997
District of Columbia	Male	1 - 2 years	$144,997
District of Columbia	Male	1 - 2 years	$140,969
District of Columbia	Female	1 - 2 years	$119,844
District of Columbia	Female	3 - 4 years	$116,419
District of Columbia	Female	Less than 1 year	$101,416
District of Columbia	Female	Less than 1 year	$60,989
AVERAGE			$140,712

Peace Corps

Description:

The mission of the Peace Corps is to help the people of interested countries in meeting their need for trained men and women, and to help promote better mutual understanding between Americans and citizens of other countries.

The Peace Corps was established by the Peace Corps Act of 1961, as amended (22 U.S.C. 2501), and was made an independent agency by title VI of the International Security and Development Cooperation Act of 1981 (22 U.S.C. 2501–1). Since that time, nearly 200,000 Peace Corps Volunteers have served in 139 host countries to work on issues ranging from AIDS education to information technology and environmental preservation.

The Peace Corps currently consists of a Washington, DC, headquarters; 9 area offices; and overseas operations in 76 countries, utilizing nearly 8,000 volunteers.

Address: Peace Corps
               1111 Twentieth Street NW
               Washington, DC 20526

Website: www.peacecorps.gov   **Phone**:   202-692-2000

Attorney Location	Gender	Length of Service	Salary
District of Columbia	Male	25 - 29 years	$162,380
District of Columbia	Female	5 - 9 years	$153,200
District of Columbia	Female	25 - 29 years	$153,200
District of Columbia	Female	10 - 14 years	$144,277
District of Columbia	Female	15 - 19 years	$140,075
District of Columbia	Female	10 - 14 years	$135,995
AVERAGE			**$148,188**

Pension Benefit Guaranty Corporation

Description:

The Pension Benefit Guaranty Corporation (PBGC) protects the pension benefits of nearly 44 million Americans who participate in defined-benefit pension plans sponsored by private-sector employees. The PBGC is a self-financing, wholly owned Government corporation subject to the Government Corporation Control Act (31 U.S.C. 9101–9109). The Corporation, established by title IV of the Employee Retirement Income Security Act of 1974 (29 U.S.C. 1301–1461), operates in accordance with policies established by its Board of Directors, which consists of the Secretaries of Labor, Commerce, and the Treasury. The Secretary of Labor is Chairman of the Board. A seven-member Advisory Committee, composed of two labor, two business, and three public members appointed by the President, advises the agency on investment issues.

The Office of the Chief Counsel provides comprehensive legal services relating to PBGC's Employee Retirement Income Security Act (ERISA) programs involving ongoing and terminated pension plans. The office represents PBGC in litigation in all courts relating to ERISA functions, represents PBGC in bankruptcy or insolvency proceedings, provides legal advice and services to support negotiations and settlements, and makes recommendations concerning the initiation of litigation.

Address: Pension Benefit Guaranty Corporation
1200 K Street NW
Washington, DC 20005

Website: www.pbgc.gov   **Phone**:   202-326-4400

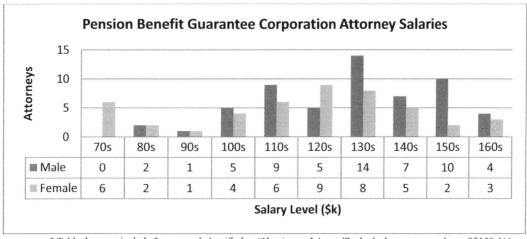

Salary Level ($k)	70s	80s	90s	100s	110s	120s	130s	140s	150s	160s
Male	0	2	1	5	9	5	14	7	10	4
Female	6	2	1	4	6	9	8	5	2	3

* Table does not include 3 personnel classified as "Hearing and Appeal" who had an average salary of $150,466.

* Table includes 5 Law Clerks who all had salaries of $79,280.

Presidio Trust

Description:
The Presidio Trust was established by Congress in 1996 to administer the Presidio of San Francisco, an urban national park that is part of the Golden Gate National Recreation Area and is located at the base of the Golden Gate Bridge. The areas overseen by the Trust include expansive open space and spectacular views, a 300-acre historic forest, and rare and endangered plants and wildlife. The National Park Service oversees the coastal areas of the Presidio. The park comprises nearly 6 million square feet of buildings, including 469 historic structures that contribute to the Presidio's status as a National Historic Landmark District.

The Presidio Trust's mission is to preserve and enhance the Presidio as an enduring resource for the American public. The Trust receives Federal appropriations that diminish each year, and cease at the end of fiscal year 2012. The Trust uses these funds and lease revenues to rehabilitate the park's buildings, restore its open spaces and historic resources, provide programs for visitors, maintain utilities and infrastructure, and fund the Presidio's long-term care. The Presidio Trust is governed by a seven-member board of directors. Six members are appointed by the President of the United States. The seventh is the U.S. Secretary of the Interior or his/her designee.

Address: Presidio Trust
P.O. Box 29052
34 Graham Street
San Francisco, CA 94129

Website: www.presidio.gov   **Email**: presidio@presidiotrust.gov

Phone: 415-561-5300   **Fax**: 415-561-5315

Attorney Location	Gender	Length of Service	Salary
California	Female	10 - 14 years	$208,111
California	Male	25 - 29 years	$172,031
California	Male	5 - 9 years	$166,595
California	Female	3 - 4 years	$156,922
California	Female	1 - 2 years	$151,308
AVERAGE			**$170,993**

Railroad Retirement Board

Description:
The Railroad Retirement Board (RRB) administers comprehensive retirement-survivor and unemployment-sickness benefit programs for the Nation's railroad workers and their families. The RRB was originally established by the Railroad Retirement Act of 1934, as amended (45 U.S.C. 201—228z–1).

The Board derives statutory authority from the Railroad Retirement Act of 1974 (45 U.S.C. 231–231u) and the Railroad Unemployment Insurance Act (45 U.S.C. 351–369). It administers these acts and participates in the administration of the Social Security Act and the Health Insurance for the Aged Act insofar as they affect railroad retirement beneficiaries.

The Board is composed of three members appointed by the President with the advice and consent of the Senate—one upon recommendations of representatives of employees; one upon recommendations of carriers; and one, the Chairman, as a public member.

The Office of General Counsel is organized into four units:
- Office of Legislative Affairs: Provides liaison services to the Administration, members of Congress and other Federal agencies.
- Bureau of Law: Provides legal, legislative and library services for the agency.
- Bureau of Hearings and Appeals: Reviews appeals and conducts hearings for individuals who disagree with the decisions reached in their case.
- Secretary to the Board: Maintains the official record of proceedings and actions by the three-member Board, also issuing correspondence, notices and reports in its behalf.

Address: Railroad Retirement Board
844 North Rush Street
Chicago, IL 60611-2092

Website: www.rrb.gov   **Phone**:   312-751-4777

RRB Atty Location	Gender	Length of Service	Salary
Illinois	Male	35 years or more	$177,000
Illinois	Female	10 - 14 years	$153,200
Illinois	Female	15 - 19 years	$153,200
Illinois	Female	25 - 29 years	$153,200
Illinois	Female	25 - 29 years	$153,200
Illinois	Male	15 - 19 years	$153,200
Illinois	Male	35 years or more	$153,200
Illinois	Male	3 - 4 years	$153,200
Illinois	Male	35 years or more	$142,538
Illinois	Female	25 - 29 years	$135,029
Illinois	Male	15 - 19 years	$135,029
Illinois	Male	35 years or more	$135,029
Illinois	Female	15 - 19 years	$128,103
Illinois	Male	5 - 9 years	$90,825
AVERAGE			$143,997

* Table does not include 8 personnel classified as "Hearing and Appeal" who had an average salary of $126,375.

Selective Service System

Description:
The Selective Service System provides manpower to the Armed Forces in an emergency and operates an Alternative Service Program during a draft for men classified as conscientious objectors.

The Selective Service System was established by the Military Selective Service Act (50 U.S.C. app. 451–471a). The act requires the registration of male citizens of the United States and all other male persons who are in the United States and who are ages 18 to 25. The act exempts members of the active Armed Forces and nonimmigrant aliens. Proclamation 4771 of July 20, 1980, requires male persons born on or after January 1, 1960, and who have attained age 18 but have not attained age 26 to register.

The act imposes liability for training and service in the Armed Forces upon registrants who are ages 18 to 26, except those who are exempt or deferred. Persons who have been deferred remain liable for training and service until age 35. Aliens are not liable for training and service until they have remained in the United States for more than 1 year. Conscientious objectors who are found to be opposed to all service in the Armed Forces are required to perform civilian work in lieu of induction into the Armed Forces. The authority to induct registrants, including doctors and allied medical specialists, expired July 1, 1973.

Address: Selective Service System
National Headquarters
Arlington, VA 22209-2425

Website: www.sss.gov   **Phone**:   703-605-4000

Attorney Location	Gender	Length of Service	Salary
Virginia	Male	15 - 19 years	$136,941

U.S. Holocaust Memorial Museum

Description:

The United States Holocaust Memorial Museum inspires citizens and leaders worldwide to confront hatred, promote human dignity, and prevent genocide. A public-private partnership, Federal support guarantees the Museum's permanence, and its far-reaching educational programs and global impact are made possible by donors nationwide.

The Museum teaches about the dangers of unchecked hatred and the need to prevent genocide. The Museum works closely with many key segments of society who will affect the future of our Nation. Professionals from the fields of law enforcement, the judiciary and the military, as well as diplomacy, medicine, education and religion study the Holocaust, with emphasis on the role of their particular professions and the implications for their own responsibilities. These programs intensify their sense of commitment to the core values of their fields and their roles in the protection of individuals and society.

In addition to its leadership training programs, the Museum sponsors on-site and traveling exhibitions, educational outreach, Web site, campus outreach and Holocaust commemorations, including the Nation's annual observance in the U.S. Capitol. The Center for Advanced Holocaust Studies works to ensure the continued growth and vitality of the field of Holocaust studies. The Museum works to prevent genocide in the future through its Academy for Genocide Prevention which trains foreign policy professionals.

Address: U.S. Holocaust Memorial Museum
100 Raoul Wallenberg Place, SW
Washington, DC 20024-2126

Website: www.ushmm.org   **Phone**:   202-488-0400

Attorney Location	Gender	Length of Service	Salary
District of Columbia	Male	20 - 24 years	$162,900
District of Columbia	Female	5 - 9 years	$132,914
AVERAGE			$147,907

U.S. International Trade Commission

Description:

The United States International Trade Commission (USITC) furnishes studies, reports, and recommendations involving international trade and tariffs to the President, the U.S. Trade Representative, and Congressional committees. The Commission also conducts a variety of investigations pertaining to international trade relief.

The USITC is an independent agency created by the Revenue Act (39 Stat, 795) and originally named the United States Tariff Commission. The name was changed to the United States International Trade Commission by section 171 of the Trade Act of 1974 (19 U.S.C. 2231). Six Commissioners are appointed by the President with the advice and consent of the Senate for 9-year terms, unless appointed to fill an unexpired term. The Chairman and Vice Chairman are designated by the President for 2- year terms, and succeeding Chairmen may not be of the same political party. The Chairman generally is responsible for the administration of the Commission. Not more than three Commissioners may be members of the same political party (19 U.S.C. 1330).

The General Counsel's office serves as USITC's chief legal advisor. The General Counsel provides: legal advice and support to the Commissioners and USITC staff on investigations and research studies; prepares briefs and represents the USITC in court and before dispute resolution panels and administrative tribunals; and provides assistance and advice on general administrative matters, including personnel, labor relations, and contract issues.

Address: United States International Trade Commission
500 E Street SW
Washington, DC 20436

Website: www.usitc.gov   **Phone**:   202-205-2000

Employment Inquiries: Director of Human Resources. Phone: 202-205-2651

▶ **USITC Attorney-Adviser and Internship Opportunities**
www.usitc.gov/employment/positions.htm

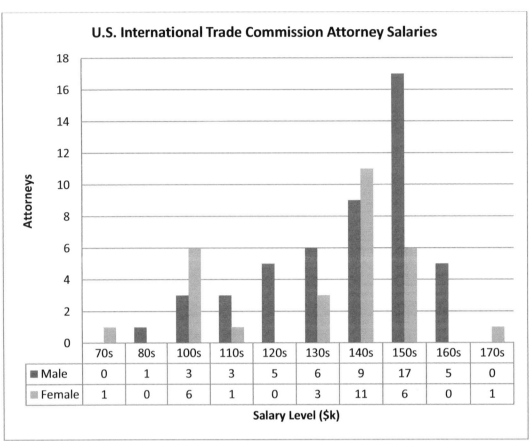

U.S. International Trade Commission Attorney Salaries

	70s	80s	100s	110s	120s	130s	140s	150s	160s	170s
Male	0	1	3	3	5	6	9	17	5	0
Female	1	0	6	1	0	3	11	6	0	1

Salary Level ($k)

* Includes 8 Administrative Law Judges with an average salary of $158,661.
* Does not include 3 Law Clerks with an average salary of $39,835

U.S. Tax Court

U.S. Tax Court Building. Photo: Carol M. Highsmith Photography, Inc.

Description:

The United States Tax Court was established by Congress under Article I of the U.S. Constitution. When the Commissioner of Internal Revenue has determined a tax deficiency, the taxpayer may dispute the deficiency in the Tax Court before paying any disputed amount. The Tax Court's jurisdiction also includes the authority to redetermine transferee liability, make certain types of declaratory judgments, adjust partnership items, order abatement of interest, award administrative and litigation costs, redetermine worker classification, determine relief from joint and several liability on a joint return, and review certain collection actions. The U.S. Tax Court is part of the legislative branch.

Address: U.S. Tax Court
400 Second Street, N.W.
Washington, DC 20217

Website: www.ustaxcourt.gov   **Phone**:   202-521-0700

► **Law Clerk Program**
www.ustaxcourt.gov/lc_program.htm

► **Trial Clerk Recruitment**
www.ustaxcourt.gov/employment/Trial_Clerk.pdf

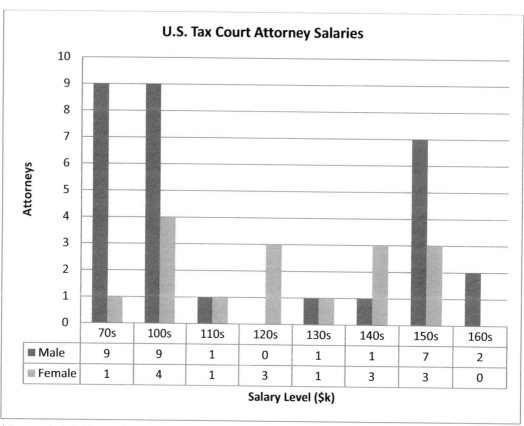

U.S. Tax Court Attorney Salaries

Salary Level ($k)	70s	100s	110s	120s	130s	140s	150s	160s
Male	9	9	1	0	1	1	7	2
Female	1	4	1	3	1	3	3	0

* Does not include 11 Law Clerks with an average salary of $58,683.

Small Independent Agencies

(less than 100 employees)

Agency	Attorneys	Avg Salary
Advisory Council on Historic Preservation	1	$119,844
African Development Foundation	3	$144,315
Architectural & Transportation Barriers Compliance Board	2	$158,050
Chemical Safety & Hazard Investigation Board	3	$140,405
Commission on Civil Rights	6	$127,232
Committee for Purchase from People Who Are Blind or Severely Disabled	1	$153,200
Council on Env. Quality/Office of Environmental Quality	1	$153,200
Election Assistance Commission	5	$97,556
Farm Credit System Insurance Corporation	1	$210,267
Federal Financial Institutions Exam. Council	1	$124,858
Federal Mine Safety and Health Review Commission	24	$131,996
Federal Retirement Thrift Investment Board	3	$105,537
Inter-American Foundation	2	$113,948
International Joint Commission: United States and Canada	1	$120,830
Marine Mammal Commission	1	$153,200
Morris K. Udall Scholarship and Excellence in National Environmental Policy Foundation	1	$109,731
National Capital Planning Commission	1	$153,200
National Council on Disability	2	$130,118
National Mediation Board	9	$131,814
Occupational Safety and Health Review Commission	29	$139,660
Office of Government Ethics	15	$140,855
Office of National Drug Control Policy	3	$140,969
Office of Navajo and Hopi Indian Relocation	1	$122,937
Office of Science and Technology Policy	1	$136,941
Office of the Federal Coordinator for Alaska Natural Gas Transportation Projects	1	$144,997
Recovery Act Accountability & Transparency Board	1	$86,927
Trade and Development Agency	5	$128,075
U.S. Commission on International Religious Freedom	1	$125,000
TOTAL	**125**	**$133,774**

* Attorneys includes ALJ's and Law Clerks. 11 ALJ's for the FMSHRC and 12 for the OSHRC had average salaries of $161,307 and $162,900, respectively. 2 Law Clerks for the FAC and 1 for the FRTIB had salaries of $58,436 and $60,989, respectively.

Advisory Council on Historic Preservation

Description:

The Advisory Council on Historic Preservation (ACHP) is an independent Federal agency that promotes the preservation, enhancement, and productive use of our Nation's historic resources, and advises the President and Congress on national historic preservation policy.

The goal of the National Historic Preservation Act, which established the ACHP in 1966, is to have Federal agencies act as responsible stewards of our Nation's resources when their actions affect historic properties. The ACHP is the only entity with the legal responsibility to encourage Federal agencies to factor historic preservation into Federal project requirements.

Address: Advisory Council on Historic Preservation
1100 Pennsylvania Avenue NW, Suite 803
Old Post Office Building
Washington, DC 20004

Website: www.achp.gov   **Phone**:   202-606-8503

Attorney Location	Gender	Length of Service	Salary
District of Columbia	Male	10 - 14 years	$119,844

African Development Foundation

Description:
The African Development Foundation's goals are to alleviate poverty and promote broad-based sustainable development and empowerment in Africa; to expand local capacity to promote and support grassroots, participatory development; and to enhance and strengthen U.S. relations with Africa through effective development assistance.

The African Development Foundation was established by the African Development Foundation Act (22 U.S.C. 290h) as a Government corporation to support the self-help efforts of the poor in Africa.

The Foundation invests in private and nongovernmental organizations in Africa to promote and support innovative enterprise development, create jobs, and increase incomes of the poor. It seeks to expand local institutional and financial capacities to foster entrepreneurship, ownership, and community-based economic development.

The Foundation also works within the United States, in African countries, and with other nation states to gather and expand resources for grassroots development. It achieves this through strategic partnerships with U.S. and international private sector corporations, African host governments, U.S. and other government agencies, and philanthropic organizations.

Address: African Development Foundation
1400 I Street NW, Suite 1000
Washington, DC 20005

Website: www.usadf.gov   **Phone**: 202-673-3916

Attorney Location	Gender	Length of Service	Salary
District of Columbia	Female	20 - 24 years	$153,200
District of Columbia	Female	10 - 14 years	$153,053
District of Columbia	Female	1 - 2 years	$126,693
AVERAGE			**$144,315**

Architectural and Transportation Barriers Compliance Board

Description:

The Architectural and Transportation Barriers Compliance Board (Access Board) is responsible for developing accessibility guidelines to ensure that new construction and alterations of facilities subject to the Americans with Disabilities Act of 1990 and the Architectural Barriers Act of 1968 are readily accessible to and usable by individuals with disabilities. The Americans with Disabilities Act applies to State and local government facilities, places of public accommodation, and commercial facilities. The Architectural Barriers Act applies to federally financed facilities.

Address: United States Access Board
1331 F Street, NW, Suite 1000
Washington, DC 20004-1111

Website: www.access-board.gov   **Phone**:   202-272-0080

Attorney Location	Gender	Length of Service	Salary
District of Columbia	Male	20 - 24 years	$162,900
District of Columbia	Female	20 - 24 years	$153,200
AVERAGE			$158,050

Chemical Safety and Hazard Investigation Board

Description:
The Chemical Safety and Hazardous Investigation Board (CSB) is an independent Federal agency charged with investigating industrial chemical accidents. The agency's board members are appointed by the President and confirmed by the Senate.

The CSB conducts root cause investigations of chemical accidents at fixed industrial facilities. Root causes are usually deficiencies in safety management systems, but can be any factor that would have prevented the accident if that factor had not occurred. Other accident causes often involve equipment failures, human errors, unforeseen chemical reactions or other hazards. The agency does not issue fines or citations, but does make recommendations to plants, regulatory agencies such as the Occupational Safety and Health Administration and the Environmental Protection Agency, industry organizations, and labor groups. Congress designed the CSB to be non-regulatory and independent of other agencies so that its investigations might, where appropriate, review the effectiveness of regulations and regulatory enforcement.

Address: U.S. Chemical Safety and Hazard Investigation Board
2175 K Street NW, Suite 400
Washington, DC 20037-1809

Website: www.csb.gov   **Phone**:   202-261-7600

Attorney Location	Gender	Length of Service	Salary
District of Columbia	Male	30 - 34 years	$159,798
District of Columbia	Male	10 - 14 years	$144,997
District of Columbia	Male	5 - 9 years	$116,419
AVERAGE			$140,405

Commission on Civil Rights

Description:
The Commission on Civil Rights collects and studies information on discrimination or denials of equal protection of the laws because of race, color, religion, sex, age, disability, national origin, or in the administration of justice in such areas as voting rights, enforcement of Federal civil rights laws, and equal opportunity in education, employment, and housing.

The Commission on Civil Rights was first created by the Civil Rights Act of 1957, as amended, and reestablished by the United States Commission on Civil Rights Act of 1994, as amended (42 U.S.C. 1975).

The Office of General Counsel provides the legal expertise and activity required to conduct hearings and to ensure the legal integrity of Commission products.

Address: United States Commission on Civil Rights
624 Ninth Street NW
Washington, DC 20425

Website: www.usccr.gov   **Phone**:   202-376-8177

Employment:
United States Commission on Civil Rights
Human Resources Office, Room 510
624 Ninth Street NW
Washington, DC 20425.
Phone: 202–376–8364

Attorney Location	Gender	Length of Service	Salary
District of Columbia	Female	25 - 29 years	$153,200
District of Columbia	Male	5 - 9 years	$153,200
District of Columbia	Male	5 - 9 years	$124,858
District of Columbia	Female	5 - 9 years	$112,995
District of Columbia	Female	3 - 4 years	$109,570
District of Columbia	Female	1 - 2 years	$109,570
AVERAGE			$127,232

Committee for Purchase from People Who Are Blind or Severely Disabled

Description:
Providing employment opportunities to more than 40,000 Americans who are blind or have other severe disabilities, the AbilityOne Program is the single largest source of jobs for such individuals in the United States. The AbilityOne Program uses the purchasing power of the Federal government to buy products and services from participating, community-based nonprofit agencies nationwide dedicated to training and employing individuals with disabilities.

Address: Committee for Purchase from
People Who Are Blind or Severely Disabled
1421 Jefferson Davis Highway
Jefferson Plaza 2, Suite 10800
Arlington, VA 22202-3259

Website: www.abilityone.gov   **Phone**: 703-603-7740

Attorney Location	Gender	Length of Service	Salary
Virginia	Male	5 - 9 years	$153,200

Council on Environmental Quality/Office of Environmental Quality

Description:

The Council on Environmental Quality (CEQ) formulates and recommends national policies and initiatives to improve the environment.

The CEQ was established within the Executive Office of the President by the National Environmental Policy Act of 1969 (NEPA) (42 U.S.C. 4321 et seq.). The Environmental Quality Improvement Act of 1970 (42 U.S.C. 4371 et seq.) established the Office of Environmental Quality (OEQ) to provide professional and administrative support for the Council. The Council and OEQ are collectively referred to as the Council on Environmental Quality, and the CEQ Chair, who is appointed by the President and confirmed by the Senate, serves as the Director of OEQ.

The Council develops policies which bring together the Nation's social, economic, and environmental priorities, with the goal of improving Federal decision-making. As required by NEPA, CEQ evaluates, coordinates, and mediates Federal activities. It advises and assists the President on both national and international environmental policy matters. CEQ also oversees Federal agency and department implementation of NEPA.

Address: Council on Environmental Quality
722 Jackson Place NW
Washington, DC 20503

Website: www.whitehouse.gov/ceq

Phone: 202-395-5750   **Fax:** 703-603-0655

Attorney Location	Gender	Length of Service	Salary
District of Columbia	Male	15 - 19 years	$153,200

Election Assistance Commission

Description:
The U.S. Election Assistance Commission (EAC) was established by the Help America Vote Act of 2002 (HAVA). EAC is an independent, bipartisan commission charged with developing guidance to meet HAVA requirements, adopting voluntary voting system guidelines, and serving as a national clearinghouse of information about election administration. EAC also accredits testing laboratories and certifies voting systems, as well as audits the use of HAVA funds.

Other responsibilities include maintaining the national mail voter registration form developed in accordance with the National Voter Registration Act of 1993.

Address: U.S. Election Assistance Commission
1201 New York Avenue, NW, Suite 300
Washington, DC 20005

Website: www.eac.gov   **Phone**:   202-566-3100

Attorney Location	Gender	Length of Service	Salary
District of Columbia	Female	5 - 9 years	$143,034
District of Columbia	Male	10 - 14 years	$124,525
District of Columbia	Female	3 - 4 years	$103,350
District of Columbia	Male	1 - 2 years	$58,436[1]
District of Columbia	Male	Less than 1 year	$58,436[1]
AVERAGE			**$97,556**

[1] Law Clerk.

Farm Credit System Insurance Corporation

Description:

The Farm Credit System Insurance Corporation was established by the Agricultural Credit Act of 1987 as an independent U.S. Government controlled corporation. The Corporation's primary purpose is to ensure the timely payment of principal and interest on insured notes, bonds, and other obligations issued on behalf of Farm Credit System banks.

The General Counsel oversees all the Corporation's legal matters.

Address: Farm Credit System Insurance Corporation
1501 Farm Credit Drive
McLean, VA 22102

Website: www.fcsic.gov   **Phone**:   703-883-4380

Attorney Location	Gender	Length of Service	Salary
Virginia	Male	20 - 24 years	$210,267

Federal Financial Institutions Examination Council

Description:
The Federal Financial Institutions Examination Council was established on March 10, 1979, pursuant to title X of the Financial Institutions Regulatory and Interest Rate Control Act of 1978 (FIRA), 95. In 1989, title XI of the Financial Institutions Reform, Recovery and Enforcement Act of 1989 established The Appraisal Subcommittee within the Examination Council.

The Council is a formal interagency body empowered to prescribe uniform principles, standards, and report forms for the Federal examination of financial institutions by the Board of Governors of the Federal Reserve System, the Federal Deposit Insurance Corporation, the National Credit Union Administration, the Office of the Comptroller of the Currency, and the Office of Thrift Supervision and to make recommendations to promote uniformity in the supervision of financial institutions.

The Council was given additional statutory responsibilities by section 340 of the Housing and Community Development Act of 1980 to facilitate public access to data that depository institutions must disclose under the Home Mortgage Disclosure Act of 1975 (HMDA) and the aggregation of annual HMDA data, by census tract, for each metropolitan statistical area. The Council has established, in accordance with the requirement of the statute, an advisory State Liaison Committee composed of five representatives of State supervisory agencies.

Address: Federal Financial Institutions Examination Council
3501 Fairfax Drive, Mailstop D-8073a
Arlington, VA 22226-3550

Website: www.ffiec.gov   **Phone**:   703-516-5590

Attorney Location	Gender	Length of Service	Salary
District of Columbia	Female	5 - 9 years	$124,858

Federal Mine Safety and Health Review Commission

Description:
The Federal Mine Safety and Health Review Commission ensures compliance with occupational safety and health standards in the Nation's surface and underground coal, metal, and nonmetal mines.

The Commission is an independent, adjudicative agency established by the Federal Mine Safety and Health Act of 1977 (30 U.S.C. 801 et seq.), as amended. It provides administrative trial and appellate review of legal disputes arising from enforcement actions taken by the Department of Labor. The Commission consists of five members who are appointed by the President with the advice and consent of the Senate and who serve staggered 6- year terms. The Chairman is appointed from among the Commissioners by the President.

The Commission and its Office of Administrative Law Judges are charged with deciding cases brought before it by the Mine Safety and Health Administration, mine operators, and miners or their representatives. These cases generally involve review of the Administration's enforcement actions, including citations, mine-closure orders, and proposals for civil penalties issued for violations of the act or the mandatory safety and health standards promulgated by the Secretary of Labor. The Commission also has jurisdiction over discrimination complaints filed by miners or their representatives in connection with their safety and health, complaints for compensation filed on behalf of miners idled as a result of mine closure orders issued by the Administration, and disputes over mine emergency response plans.

Address: Federal Mine Safety and Health Review Commission
601 New Jersey Avenue NW, Suite 9500
Washington, DC 20001-2021

Website: www.fmshrc.gov **Phone**: 202-434-9900

FMSHRC Atty Location	Gender	Length of Service	Salary
District of Columbia	Female	30 - 34 years	$162,900[1]
Colorado	Female	15 - 19 years	$162,900[1]
District of Columbia	Male	30 - 34 years	$162,900[1]
District of Columbia	Male	35 years or more	$162,900[1]
Colorado	Male	25 - 29 years	$162,900[1]
District of Columbia	Male	35 years or more	$162,900[1]
District of Columbia	Male	35 years or more	$162,900[1]
District of Columbia	Male	35 years or more	$162,900[1]
District of Columbia	Male	35 years or more	$162,900[1]
District of Columbia	Male	35 years or more	$162,900[1]
District of Columbia	Male	25 - 29 years	$156,673
District of Columbia	Male	15 - 19 years	$145,381[1]
District of Columbia	Female	15 - 19 years	$144,997
District of Columbia	Female	10 - 14 years	$144,997
District of Columbia	Male	10 - 14 years	$140,969
District of Columbia	Female	10 - 14 years	$133,543
District of Columbia	Female	15 - 19 years	$133,543
District of Columbia	Male	10 - 14 years	$133,543
District of Columbia	Female	5 - 9 years	$92,723
District of Columbia	Female	1 - 2 years	$63,021
District of Columbia	Female	1 - 2 years	$63,021
District of Columbia	Female	1 - 2 years	$63,021
District of Columbia	Male	1 - 2 years	$63,021
Colorado	Male	Less than 1 year	$60,459
AVERAGE			$131,996

[1] Administrative Law Judges.

Federal Retirement Thrift Investment Board

Description:
The Federal Retirement Thrift Investment Board administers the Thrift Savings Plan, which provides Federal employees the opportunity to save for additional retirement security.

The Federal Retirement Thrift Investment Board was established as an independent agency by the Federal Employees' Retirement System Act of 1986 (5 U.S.C. 8351 and 8401–79). The act vests responsibility for the agency in six named fiduciaries: the five Board members and the Executive Director. The five members of the Board, one of whom is designated as Chairman, are appointed by the President with the advice and consent of the Senate and serve on the Board on a part-time basis. The members appoint the Executive Director, who is responsible for the management of the agency and the Plan.

Address: Federal Retirement Thrift Investment Board
1250 H Street NW
Washington, DC 20005

Website: www.tsp.gov   **Phone:**   202-942-1600

Attorney Location	Gender	Length of Service	Salary
District of Columbia	Male	5 - 9 years	$162,900
District of Columbia	Female	1 - 2 years	$92,723
District of Columbia	Male	Less than 1 year	$60,989[1]
AVERAGE			**$105,537**

[1] Law Clerk.

Inter-American Foundation

Description:

The Inter-American Foundation (IAF) is an independent Federal agency that supports social and economic development in Latin America and the Caribbean. It makes grants primarily to private, local, and community organizations that carry out self-help projects.

The IAF was created in 1969 (22 U.S.C. 290f) as an experimental U.S. foreign assistance program. IAF is governed by a nine person Board of Directors appointed by the President with the advice and consent of the Senate. Six members are drawn from the private sector and three from the Federal Government. The Board of Directors appoints the President of IAF.

IAF works in Latin America and the Caribbean to promote equitable, participatory, and sustainable self-help development by awarding grants directly to local organizations throughout the region. It also enters into partnerships with public and private sector entities to build support and mobilize local, national, and international resources for grassroots development.

Address: Inter-American Foundation
901 North Stuart Street, Tenth Floor
Arlington, VA 22203

Website: www.iaf.gov   **Phone**:   703-306-4301

Attorney Location	Gender	Length of Service	Salary
Virginia	Female	10 - 14 years	$140,969
Virginia	Female	3 - 4 years	$86,927
AVERAGE			**$113,948**

International Joint Commission: United States and Canada

Description:
The International Joint Commission is an independent binational organization established by the Boundary Waters Treaty of 1909. Its purpose is to help prevent and resolve disputes relating to the use and quality of boundary waters and to advise the United States and Canada on related questions.

Address: International Joint Commission
United States Section
2401 Pennsylvania Avenue, 4th Floor
Washington, DC 20037

Website: www.ijc.org

Phone: 202-736-9000   **Fax:**   202-254-4564

Attorney Location	Gender	Length of Service	Salary
District of Columbia	Female	5 - 9 years	$120,830

Marine Mammal Commission

Description:
The Marine Mammal Commission is an independent agency of the U.S. Government, established under Title II of the Act to provide independent oversight of the marine mammal conservation policies and programs being carried out by Federal regulatory agencies.

The Commission consists of three members who are nominated by the President and confirmed by the Senate. The Marine Mammal Protection Act requires that those serving as commissioners be knowledgeable in marine ecology and resource management.

The Commission is assisted in its work by a nine-member Committee of Scientific Advisors on Marine Mammals. Members are appointed by the Chairman of the Commission after consultation with the Chairman of the Council on Environmental Quality, the Secretary of the Smithsonian Institution, the Director of the National Science Foundation, and the Chairman of the National Academy of Sciences. The Act requires that committee members be knowledgeable in marine ecology and marine mammal affairs.

The Commission also has an Executive Director, who is appointed by the Chairman with the approval of the Commission.

Address:	Marine Mammal Commission 4340 East-West Highway, Suite 700 Bethesda, MD 20814

Website: www.mmc.gov   **Email**: mmc@mmc.gov

Phone: 301-504-0087   **Fax:** 301-504-0099

Attorney Location	Gender	Length of Service	Salary
Maryland	Male	25 - 29 years	$153,200

Morris K. Udall Scholarship & Excellence in National Env. Policy Foundation

Description:

Established by the U.S. Congress in 1992, the Udall Foundation honors Congressman Morris King Udall's thirty-year legacy of public service. As set forth in the founding legislation, the purposes of the Foundation are to:

- Increase the awareness of the importance of, and promote the benefit and enjoyment of, the Nation's natural resources;
- Foster a greater recognition and understanding of the role of the environment, public lands and resources in the development of the United States;
- Identify critical environmental issues;
- Develop resources to train professionals properly in environmental and related fields;
- Provide educational outreach regarding environmental policy;
- Develop resources to train Native American and Alaska Native professionals in health care and public policy;
- Through the U.S. Institute for Environmental Conflict Resolution, provide assessment, mediation, and other related services to resolve environmental disputes involving Federal agencies

In 2011, the Foundation expects to award 80 scholarships of up to $5,000 and 50 honorable mentions of $350 to sophomore and junior level college students committed to careers related to the environment, tribal public policy, or Native American health care.

Address: Morris K. Udall and Stewart L. Udall Foundation
130 South Scott Avenue
Tucson, AZ 85701-1922

Website: www.udall.gov   **Email**: info@udall.gov

Phone: 520-901-8500   **Fax**:   520-670-5530

Attorney Location	Gender	Length of Service	Salary
Arizona	Male	1 - 2 years	$109,731

234

National Capital Planning Commission

Description:
The National Capital Planning Commission is the central agency for conducting planning and development activities for Federal lands and facilities in the National Capital Region. The region includes the District of Columbia and all land areas within the boundaries of Montgomery and Prince George's Counties in Maryland and Fairfax, Loudoun, Prince William, and Arlington Counties and the city of Alexandria in Virginia.

The National Capital Planning Commission was established as a park planning agency by act of June 6, 1924, as amended (40 U.S.C. 71 et seq.). Two years later its role was expanded to include comprehensive planning. In 1952, under the National Capital Planning Act, the Commission was designated the central planning agency for the Federal and District of Columbia governments.

In 1973, the National Capital Planning Act was amended by the District of Columbia Home Rule Act, which made the Mayor of the District of Columbia the chief planner for the District and gave the Commission specific authority for reviewing certain District decisions. The Commission continues to serve as the central planning agency for the Federal Government in the National Capital Region.

The Commission is composed of five appointed and seven ex-officio members. Three citizen members, including the Chairman, are appointed by the President and two by the mayor of the District of Columbia. Presidential appointees include one resident each from Maryland and Virginia and one from anywhere in the United States. The two mayoral appointees must be District of Columbia residents.

Address: National Capital Planning Commission
401 Ninth Street NW, Suite 500
Washington, DC 20004

Website: www.ncpc.gov   **Phone**:   202-482-7200

Attorney Location	Gender	Length of Service	Salary
District of Columbia	Female	20 - 24 years	$153,200

National Council on Disability

Description:

The National Council on Disability (NCD) is an independent Federal agency and is composed of 15 members appointed by the President, by and with the advice and consent of the Senate. The President selects members of NCD after soliciting recommendations from representatives of organizations representing a broad range of individuals with disabilities; and organizations interested in individuals with disabilities.

NDC provides advice to the President, Congress, and executive branch agencies to promote policies, programs, practices, and procedures that guarantee equal opportunity for all individuals with disabilities, regardless of the nature or severity of the disability and to empower individuals with disabilities to achieve economic self-sufficiency, independent living, and inclusion and integration into all aspects of society. As a policy agency, NCD does not have any services or programs.

Address: National Council on Disability
1331 F Street, NW, Suite 850
Washington, DC 20004

Website: www.ncd.gov   **Email**: ncd@ncd.gov

Phone: 202-272-2004   **Fax**:   202-272-2022

Attorney Location	Gender	Length of Service	Salary
District of Columbia	Female	5 - 9 years	$133,543
District of Columbia	Female	10 - 14 years	$126,693
AVERAGE			**$130,118**

National Mediation Board

Description:

The National Mediation Board (NMB) facilitates harmonious labor-management relations within two of the Nation's key transportation sectors: the railroads and the airlines. The Board handles mediation and employee representation disputes and provides administrative and financial support in adjusting grievances in the railroad industry. The NMB is an independent agency established by the 1934 amendments to the Railway Labor Act of 1926 (45 U.S.C. 151–158, 160–162, 1181–1188). The Board is composed of three members, appointed by the President and confirmed by the Senate. The board designates a Chairman on a yearly basis.

The Agency's dispute-resolution processes are designed to resolve disputes over the negotiation of new or revised collective bargaining agreements and the interpretation or application of existing agreements. It also effectuates employee rights of self-organization where a representation dispute exists.

The General Counsel serves as the Chief Legal Officer and manages the Board's representation program and litigation. The General Counsel provides legal advice to the Board Members and agency staff and ensures compliance with the Freedom of Information Act, Government in the Sunshine Act, and other statutes.

Address: National Mediation Board
1301 K Street NW
Suite 250 East
Washington, DC 20005

Website: www.nmb.gov   **Phone**:   202-692-5000

Attorney Location	Gender	Length of Service	Salary
District of Columbia	Female	25 - 29 years	$157,297
District of Columbia	Female	15 - 19 years	$153,200
District of Columbia	Male	30 - 34 years	$153,200
District of Columbia	Male	25 - 29 years	$144,997
District of Columbia	Male	15 - 19 years	$144,997
District of Columbia	Female	5 - 9 years	$123,269
District of Columbia	Female	10 - 14 years	$119,844
District of Columbia	Female	5 - 9 years	$116,419
District of Columbia	Female	Less than 1 year	$73,100
AVERAGE			**$131,814**

Occupational Safety and Health Review Commission

Description:
The Occupational Safety and Health Review Commission ensures the timely and fair resolution of cases involving the alleged exposure of American workers to unsafe or unhealthy working conditions.

The Occupational Safety and Health Review Commission is an independent, quasi-judicial agency established by the Occupational Safety and Health Act of 1970 (29 U.S.C. 651–678).

The Commission rules on cases when disagreements arise over the results of safety and health inspections performed by the Department of Labor's Occupational Safety and Health Administration (OSHA). Employers have the right to dispute any alleged job safety or health violation found during the inspection by OSHA, the penalties it proposes, and the time given to correct any hazardous situation.

The Occupational Safety and Health Act covers virtually every employer in the country. Its purpose is to reduce the incidence of personal injuries, illness, and deaths among working men and women in the United States that result from their employment. It requires employers to provide a working environment free from recognized hazards that are causing or likely to cause death or serious physical harm to the employees and to comply with occupational safety and health standards promulgated under the act.

Address: Occupational Safety and Health Review Commission
1120 Twentieth Street NW
Washington, DC 20036-3457

Website: www.oshrc.gov   **Phone**:   202-606-5050

OSHRC Atty Location	Gender	Length of Service	Salary
District of Columbia	Female	25 - 29 years	$162,900[1]
Georgia	Female	35 years or more	$162,900[1]
Colorado	Male	10 - 14 years	$162,900[1]
District of Columbia	Male	15 - 19 years	$162,900[1]
District of Columbia	Male	25 - 29 years	$162,900[1]
Georgia	Male	35 years or more	$162,900[1]
District of Columbia	Male	35 years or more	$162,900[1]
District of Columbia	Male	35 years or more	$162,900[1]
Georgia	Male	35 years or more	$162,900[1]
Colorado	Male	35 years or more	$162,900[1]
Colorado	Male	30 - 34 years	$162,900[1]
Colorado	Male	30 - 34 years	$162,900[1]
District of Columbia	Male	25 - 29 years	$158,050
District of Columbia	Male	30 - 34 years	$153,200
District of Columbia	Male	35 years or more	$153,200
District of Columbia	Female	15 - 19 years	$145,124
District of Columbia	Female	20 - 24 years	$140,969
District of Columbia	Female	1 - 2 years	$136,941
District of Columbia	Male	20 - 24 years	$133,543
Colorado	Male	5 - 9 years	$132,382
District of Columbia	Female	20 - 24 years	$130,118
Georgia	Female	20 - 24 years	$125,309
District of Columbia	Female	15 - 19 years	$119,844
District of Columbia	Female	20 - 24 years	$113,007
District of Columbia	Male	5 - 9 years	$106,145
District of Columbia	Male	5 - 9 years	$101,416
District of Columbia	Female	10 - 14 years	$85,281
District of Columbia	Female	3 - 4 years	$80,409
District of Columbia	Male	3 - 4 years	$80,409
AVERAGE			$139,660

[1] Administrative Law Judges.

Office of Government Ethics

Description:

The Office of Government Ethics (OGE) directs executive branch policies related to preventing conflicts of interest on the part of Government employees and resolving those conflicts of interest that do occur. OGE is an executive branch agency established under the Ethics in Government Act of 1978, as amended (5 U.S.C. app. 401). The Director of OGE is appointed by the President with the advice and consent of the Senate for a 5-year term.

The Office of General Counsel and Legal Policy is responsible for establishing and maintaining a uniform legal framework of Government ethics for executive branch employees. This Office develops executive branch ethics program policies and regulations, interprets laws and regulations, assists agencies in legal and policy implementations, and recommends changes in conflicts of interest and ethics statutes.

Address:　　Office of Government Ethics
　　　　　　　　　1201 New York Avenue NW, Suite 500
　　　　　　　　　Washington, DC 20005-3917

Website:　　www.usoge.gov　　　　**Phone**:　　202-482-9300

Attorney Location	Gender	Length of Service	Salary
District of Columbia	Male	25 - 29 years	$177,000
District of Columbia	Male	10 - 14 years	$164,320
District of Columbia	Male	3 - 4 years	$162,900
District of Columbia	Female	25 - 29 years	$153,200
District of Columbia	Male	30 - 34 years	$153,200
District of Columbia	Male	15 - 19 years	$149,025
District of Columbia	Male	20 - 24 years	$144,997
District of Columbia	Female	5 - 9 years	$140,969
District of Columbia	Female	5 - 9 years	$140,969
District of Columbia	Male	5 - 9 years	$136,941
District of Columbia	Female	10 - 14 years	$128,886
District of Columbia	Male	3 - 4 years	$124,858
District of Columbia	Female	25 - 29 years	$112,995
District of Columbia	Female	15 - 19 years	$112,995
District of Columbia	Female	5 - 9 years	$109,570
AVERAGE			$140,855

Office of National Drug Control Policy

Description:
The Office of National Drug Control Policy assists the President in establishing policies, priorities, and objectives in the National Drug Control Strategy. It also provides budget, program, and policy recommendations on the efforts of National Drug Control Program agencies. The Office of National Drug Control Policy was established by the National Narcotics Leadership Act of 1988 (21 U.S.C. 1501 et seq.), effective January 29, 1989, reauthorized through the Office of National Drug Control Policy Reauthorization Act of 1988 (21 U.S.C. 1701 et seq.), and again reauthorized through the Office of National Drug Control Policy Reauthorization Act of 2006 (21 U.S.C. 1701 et seq.).

The Director of National Drug Control Policy is appointed by the President with the advice and consent of the Senate. The Director is assisted by a Deputy Director, a Deputy Director for Demand Reduction, a Deputy Director for Supply Reduction, and a Deputy Director for State, Local, and Tribal Affairs. The Director is responsible for establishing policies, objectives, priorities, and performance measurements for the national drug control program, as well as for annually promulgating drug control strategies and supporting reports and a program budget, which the President submits to Congress. The Director also notifies Federal agencies if their policies do not comply with their responsibilities under the National Drug Control Strategy. Additionally, the Office has direct programmatic responsibility for the Drug-Free Communities Program, the National Youth Anti-Drug Media Campaign, the various programs under the Counter-Drug Technology Assessment Center, and the High Intensity Drug Trafficking Areas Program.

Address: Office of National Drug Control Policy
Executive Office of the President
Washington, DC 20503

Website: www.ondcp.gov   **Phone**:   202-395-6700

Attorney Location	Gender	Length of Service	Salary
District of Columbia	Female	10 - 14 years	$144,997
District of Columbia	Male	10 - 14 years	$140,969
District of Columbia	Male	15 - 19 years	$136,941
AVERAGE			$140,969

Office of Navajo and Hopi Indian Relocation

Description:

The Office of Navajo and Hopi Indian Relocation is an independent agency responsible for assisting Hopi and Navajo Indians impacted by the relocation that Congress mandated in 1974 for members of the tribes who were living on each other's land.

Address: Office of Navajo and Hopi Indian Relocation
201 E. Birch Street
Flagstaff, AZ 86001

Website: www.onhir.gov

Phone: 928-779-2721   **Fax**: 928-774-1977

Attorney Location	Gender	Length of Service	Salary
Arizona	Male	1 - 2 years	$122,937

Office of Science and Technology Policy

Description:

The Office of Science and Technology Policy was established within the Executive Office of the President by the National Science and Technology Policy, Organization, and Priorities Act of 1976 (42 U.S.C. 6611).

The Office serves as a source of scientific, engineering, and technological analysis and judgment for the President with respect to major policies, plans, and programs of the Federal Government. In carrying out this mission, the Office advises the President of scientific and technological considerations involved in areas of national concern, including the economy, national security, health, foreign relations, and the environment; evaluates the scale, quality, and effectiveness of the Federal effort in science and technology; provides advice and assistance to the President, the Office of Management and Budget, and Federal agencies throughout the Federal budget development process; and assists the President in providing leadership and coordination for the research and development programs of the Federal Government.

The General Counsel oversees all the Office's legal matters.

Address: Office of Science and Technology Policy
New Executive Office Building
725 17th Street NW
Washington, DC 20502

Website: www.ostp.gov   **Phone**:   202-456-7116

Attorney Location	Gender	Length of Service	Salary
District of Columbia	Female	5 - 9 years	$136,941

Office of the Federal Coordinator for Alaska Natural Gas Transportation Projects

Description:

The Office of the Federal Coordinator for Alaska Natural Gas Transportation Projects (OFC) was established by Congress in 2004 to expedite and coordinate Federal permitting and construction of a pipeline and enhance transparency and predictability of the Federal regulatory system to deliver natural gas from the Arctic to American markets. The OFC coordinates with over 20 Federal agencies, the Canadian federal government, the State of Alaska (which leases all the known natural gas reserves and owns portions of the right of way), tribal governments and other stakeholders.

OFC's mission is to advance the Nation's energy, environmental and economic security by expediting the delivery of clean natural gas from the North Slope of Alaska to North American markets.

The General Counsel is responsible for drafting and implementing Memorandums of Understanding, agreements, policies and regulations that may be required to enable the OFC to carry out its statutorily mandated mission.

Address: Office of the Federal Coordinator
             Alaska Natural Gas Transportation Projects
             1717 H Street, NW, Suite 801
             Washington, DC 20006

Website: www.arcticgas.gov   Email: info@arcticgas.gov

Phone: 202-478-9750   Fax: 202-254-0692

Attorney Location	Gender	Length of Service	Salary
District of Columbia	Male	20 - 24 years	$144,997

Recovery Act Accountability and Transparency Board

Description:
The Recovery Accountability and Transparency Board was created by the American Recovery and Reinvestment Act of 2009. The Board had two goals:
(1) To provide transparency in relation to the use of Recovery-related funds
(2) To prevent and detect fraud, waste, and mismanagement

The mission of the Board is to promote accountability by coordinating and conducting oversight of Recovery funds to prevent fraud, waste, and abuse and to foster transparency on Recovery spending by providing the public with accurate, user-friendly information.

The Board issues quarterly and annual reports to the President and Congress and, if necessary, "flash reports" on matters that require immediate attention. In addition, the Board maintains the Recovery.gov website so the American people can see how Recovery money is being distributed by Federal agencies and how the funds are being used by the recipients.

Address: Recovery Accountability and Transparency Board
P.O. Box 27545
Washington, DC 20038-7958

Website: www.recovery.gov   **Phone**:   877-392-3375

Attorney Location	Gender	Length of Service	Salary
District of Columbia	Male	Less than 1 year	$86,927

Trade and Development Agency

Description:
The U.S. Trade and Development Agency (USTDA) advances economic development and U.S. commercial interest in developing and middle-income countries in the following regions of the world: East Asia, Europe and Eurasia, Latin America and the Caribbean, Middle East and North Africa, South and Southeast Asia, and Sub-Saharan Africa.

The USTDA was established on July 1, 1980, as a component organization of the International Development Cooperation Agency. Section 2204 of the Omnibus Trade and Competitiveness Act of 1988 (22 U.S.C. 2421) made it a separate component agency. The organization was renamed the Trade and Development Agency (USTDA) and made an independent agency within the executive branch of the Federal Government on October 28, 1992, by the Jobs Through Exports Act of 1992 (22 U.S.C. 2421).

USTDA is a foreign assistance agency that delivers its program commitments through overseas grants, contracts with U.S. firms, and the use of trust funds at several multilateral development bank groups. The projects supported by USTDA activities represent strong and measurable development priorities in host countries and offer opportunities for commercial participation by U.S. firms. Public and private sector project sponsors, in developing and middle-income countries, request USTDA support to assist them in implementing their development priorities.

USTDA helps countries establish a favorable trading environment and a modern infrastructure that promotes sustainable economic development. To this end, USTDA funds overseas projects and sponsors access to U.S. private sector expertise in the areas of project definition and investment analysis and trade capacity building and sector development. Project definition and investment analysis involves activities that support large capital investments that contribute to overseas infrastructure development. Trade capacity building and sector development supports the establishment of industry standards, rules and regulations, trade agreements, market liberalization, and other policy reform.

USTDA works with other U.S. Government agencies to bring their particular expertise and resources to a development objective. These agencies include the Departments of State, the Treasury, Commerce, Transportation, Energy,

Agriculture, and Homeland Security; the Office of the U.S. Trade Representative; the Export-Import Bank of the United States; and the Overseas Private Investment Corporation.

The General Counsel oversees all the USTDA's legal matters.

Address: Trade and Development Agency
1000 Wilson Boulevard, Suite 1600
Arlington, VA 22209-3901

Website: www.ustda.gov   **Phone**: 703-875-4357

▶ **USTDA Legal Internships**
www.ustda.gov/about/internships.asp

Attorney Location	Gender	Length of Service	Salary
Virginia	Male	10 - 14 years	$161,000
Virginia	Female	5 - 9 years	$133,543
Virginia	Male	5 - 9 years	$119,844
Virginia	Male	5 - 9 years	$116,419
Virginia	Female	3 - 4 years	$109,570
AVERAGE			**$128,075**

U.S. Commission on International Religious Freedom

Description:
The U.S. Commission on International Religious Freedom (USCIRF) is an independent, bipartisan U.S. Federal Government commission. USCIRF Commissioners are appointed by the President and the leadership of both political parties in the Senate and the House of Representatives. USCIRF's principal responsibilities are to review the facts and circumstances of violations of religious freedom internationally and to make policy recommendations to the President, the Secretary of State and Congress.

Address: U.S. Commission on International Religious Freedom
800 North Capital Street, NW, Suite 790
Washington, DC 20002

Website: www.uscirf.gov   **Email**: communications@uscirf.gov

Phone: 202-523-3240   Fax: 202-523-5020

Attorney Location	Gender	Length of Service	Salary
District of Columbia	Male	Less than 1 year	$125,000

The following is a list of national legal organizations that may be of interest.

Associations

American Bar Association (ABA)
ABA Section of Administrative Law
www.abanet.org/adminlaw/
ABA Judicial Division
http://new.abanet.org/divisions/judicial/
ABA Government & Public Sector
http://new.abanet.org/divisions/govpub/

National Association of Administrative Law Judiciary
www.naalj.org

Association of Administrative Law Judges
www.aalj.org

Federal Bar Association
www.fedbar.org

National Association of Women Judges
www.nawj.org

National Association of Hearing Officials
www.naho.org

Attorneys interested in Federal practice should also consider:

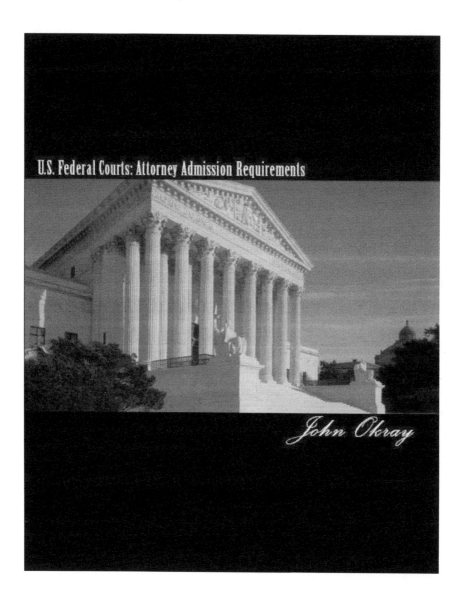

U.S. Federal Courts: Attorney Admission Requirements
by John Okray
ISBN: 978-0-9829658-0-1
www.lawyeruppress.com

16408736R00139

Made in the USA
Lexington, KY
21 July 2012